"James Rosen has a knack for asking probing, unusual, and sometimes uncomfortable questions that knock an interviewee off predictable talking points. His skill as an interviewer is vividly on display in the hours he spent interrogating Dick Cheney. Rosen spent ten years pursuing these interviews. It was worth the wait. *Cheney One on One* offers unique insight into one of the most interesting, influential, and inscrutable public figures of our time and will be an indispensable resource for any student of the Bush presidency for years to come."

> —**JONATHAN KARL**, chief White House correspondent for ABC News

"James Rosen skillfully lets Cheney be Cheney, bringing to life a third of a century on the front lines of history. Here is our country's preeminent conservative statesman, speaking out insightfully and courageously—as he has always done—on his life, his times, and America's challenging future."

> —**I. LEWIS LIBBY**, chief of staff and national security advisor to Vice President Cheney, 2001–2005

"With the depth of a historian and the instincts of an investigative reporter, James Rosen adds considerably to our understanding of Vice President Dick Cheney and the administrations in which he served. *Cheney One on One* offers crucial context and fresh reporting on many of the most controversial and important decisions of the Bush-Cheney years, as well as a long and candid look at the vice president himself. Cheney explains his thinking in expansive detail and even offers a blunt assessment of his own power over the course of George W. Bush's two terms. Rosen has given us an essential document of modern America: a must-read for anyone interested in the Bush administration, the war on terror, and twenty-first century government."

> —**STEPHEN F. HAYES**, senior writer for the *Weekly Standard* and author of *Cheney: The Untold Story of America's Most Powerful and Controversial Vice President*

CHENEY ONE ON ONE

ALSO BY JAMES ROSEN

The Strong Man: John Mitchell and the Secrets of Watergate (2008)

CHENEY
ONE ON ONE

A CANDID CONVERSATION WITH AMERICA'S MOST CONTROVERSIAL STATESMAN

JAMES ROSEN

REGNERY
PUBLISHING
A Division of Salem Media Group

Regnery® is a registered trademark of Salem Communications Holding Corporation

Portions of the material herein previously appeared in *Playboy* magazine and on www.FoxNews.com, and appear here with the kind permission of *Playboy* and Fox News.

Cataloging-in-Publication data on file with the Library of Congress

ISBN 978-1-62157-462-0

Published in the United States by
Regnery Publishing
A Division of Salem Media Group
300 New Jersey Ave NW
Washington, DC 20001
www.Regnery.com

Manufactured in the United States of America

10 9 8 7 6 5 4 3 2 1

Books are available in quantity for promotional or premium use. For information on discounts and terms, please visit our website: www.Regnery.com.

Distributed to the trade by
Perseus Distribution
250 West 57th Street
New York, NY 10107

To Sara,
love of my life

CONTENTS

Introduction   1

    Day One   25

    Day Two   109

    Day Three   195

Acknowledgments   291

Notes   297

Bibliography   309

Index of Major People and Topics   315

About the Author   324

Courtesy U.S. National Archives

Either we're serious about fighting the war on terror or we're not. Either we believe that there are individuals out there doing everything they can to try to launch more attacks, to try to get ever-deadlier weapons to use against [us], or we don't. The president and I believe very deeply that there's a hell of a threat—that it's there for anybody who wants to look at it—and that our obligation and responsibility, given our job, is to do everything in our power to defeat the terrorists. And that's exactly what we're doing.

—Remarks by the vice president to the traveling press aboard Air Force Two en route to Muscat, Oman, December 20, 2005

I think we did a good job. I think we did the right thing. And I don't have any problem defending it.

—Former vice president Dick Cheney to James Rosen, McLean, Virginia, December 3, 2014

INTRODUCTION

On April 24, 2007, a warm spring day in Washington, Vice President Dick Cheney lowered his large frame into one of the two blue wing chairs in the West Wing office of Stephen Hadley, the White House national security advisor, and braced for a meeting that the vice president already knew was going to prove anything but routine.

Seated on a sofa to Cheney's right were Yoram Turbowicz and Shalom Turgeman, aides to the Israeli prime minister, and Meir Dagan, director of the Mossad, the vaunted spy service of the Jewish state. After a quick glance at Hadley, who occupied the chair to Cheney's left, Dagan solemnly opened his briefcase, pulled out a pile of photographs and documents, and spread them out carefully atop the coffee table at his knees. For Dagan, the session, even before it began, was something of a disappointment. The Israeli spy chief had "wanted to see the president," Cheney recalled. "He had to settle for Hadley and Cheney."

Over the next hour, the men pored over a set of images the Mossad had extracted the month before from a computer belonging to Syria's top atomic energy official. In a clandestine mission worthy of a suspense thriller, Israeli spies had—in under an hour—stolen into the Syrian official's secured residence in Vienna, Austria, located the files they were looking for, and downloaded onto their own hardware roughly three dozen color photographs taken inside a nuclear reactor then under construction in the deserts of northeastern Syria, an area known as Al Kibar. Israeli analysts had concluded that the Al Kibar facility, in its design and equipment, bore a striking resemblance to the aging plutonium-based reactor in Yongbyon, North Korea, an installation that had formed the centerpiece of that country's illicit nuclear weapons program for more than two decades.

Another detail captured in the spy photos especially caught Cheney's eye: the presence of North Korean workers inside the Syrian complex. Suddenly, pieces started to fit. "Questions had been raised" about a possible North Korean–Syrian nuclear nexus before, Cheney remembered. "I had raised questions myself."

He was well positioned to do so. In the George W. Bush White House, the vice president exercised considerable influence over national security policy. This was a dividend of the many years Cheney had spent at or near the top echelons of official power in Washington—including a successful tour as a wartime defense secretary under the first President Bush—and of the incumbent president's corresponding faith in Cheney's acumen. This confidence had established the vice president, from the outset, as one of only a handful of officials entrusted to receive the President's Daily Brief (PDB), the highly classified compendium of intelligence and threat reporting that the intelligence community produced each morning. In Cheney's case, he typically reviewed the PDB before the president himself saw it and not infrequently tailored the product so that it more closely reflected Cheney's vision of what intelligence briefers should be presenting to the commander in chief. Asked if Bush had ever explicitly requested this unusual arrangement, Cheney explained how it had come about:

Well, he obviously [wanted it this way]. I can't remember a
discussion about it. What we did was, I would get the brief
at home in the morning and then it always had a tab.
And...whereas the PDB was coming up from the community—from the [Central Intelligence] Agency, primarily—and
might well have stuff in it that the president had asked about,
behind the tab were things that I had asked about, or things
they knew I had a continued interest in. I had more time to
spend on that subject than [President Bush] did. You know,
he's having to pardon a turkey at Thanksgiving and a lot of
ceremonial duties [chuckles] and responsibilities. I don't
mean to [chuckles] diminish the post at all, but I was able to
spend as much time as I wanted on, especially on intelligence,
and it was a special area for me. And so we developed this
habit of "in front of the tab" and "behind the tab," and
occasionally I would see a piece that had been done for me
or that I had asked about, that would come in and have
something I thought especially significant in it that I thought
the president ought to see. And then I would recommend that
that ought to go into the president's brief or it ought to be
presented to him. I don't recall I ever recommended taking
something *out*.

Not long before the session in Hadley's office, Cheney had pressed
the CIA briefers about something disturbing in their presentations:
evidence of regular travel to Damascus by a North Korean nuclear official. "On more than one occasion I questioned that," the former vice
president recalled, "and what would come back was: 'There's no evidence
of any cooperation between the North Koreans and the Syrians on
nuclear matters.' That was sort of the standard pat response that came
back." That answer struck Cheney as unsatisfactory, even dubious. There
had to be a practical reason behind the North Korean's travels to Syria,

nearly ten thousand miles round-trip. "I can remember asking if he had a girlfriend in Damascus; I mean, why the hell is he *doin'* it?"

As a veteran consumer of intelligence—his exposure to the nation's classified secrets dated back to the mid-1970s, when he had served as White House chief of staff under President Ford—the vice president immediately recognized the value and rarity of the photographs Dagan had shown him: "I mean, it was about as solid, guaranteed, valid intelligence as you're ever going to see." Now, at last, he understood the North Korean presence inside Bashar al-Assad's Syria—and it had nothing to do with romance. "And that led, of course, to discussions about...how we were going to deal with it."

To Cheney's mind, the prism through which to view Al Kibar was still the global war on terror that the United States had launched, with allied nations, after the terrorist attacks of September 11, 2001. In such a context, Cheney believed the clandestine construction of a nuclear reactor by one designated state sponsor of terrorism for another could not go unpunished. Just six months earlier, North Korea had tested its first nuclear device and President Bush had publicly vowed to "hold North Korea fully accountable" for any transfers of nuclear weapons or materiel, particularly to Syria—a country Bush had mentioned by name in remarks delivered at the White House Diplomatic Reception Room. The discovery of Al Kibar put America's credibility on the line. Would we forcibly deter the spread of weapons of mass destruction?

When American intelligence independently verified the substance of the Israeli presentation, Cheney saw only one course of action: destroy the Syrian reactor with precision air strikes, and soon. Dagan advocated exactly that. Jerusalem balked at conducting the operation itself, concerned that Israeli air strikes on Syrian soil could ignite a larger regional conflict—possibly drawing in Iran, the most powerful patron of the Assad government. "[The Israelis] obviously didn't want [the reactor] to go hot," Cheney recalled. Luckily, "[t]he fuel hadn't been loaded into it yet."

"I felt strongly that we should take [the reactor] out," Cheney told me. "So we had the debate internally." By then, however, America's armed forces, intelligence services, and diplomatic corps were consumed—*exhausted*—by the twin wars in Afghanistan and Iraq.

> Hadley basically ran the debate [within] the NSC. We had a couple of opportunities [where] I made my case to the president. We ended up in a meeting in the—upstairs in the upstairs oval office—not the Oval Office, but it's a big living room on the second floor [the Yellow Oval Room]. And basically, the National Security Council and staff were there. And I made my pitch that this was something that had to be done, that proliferation of nuclear weapons was one of our biggest concerns, especially [by] the terror-sponsoring states. The president had made a statement when the North Koreans first tested [a nuclear device], back in [October] '06, that a red line was proliferation to any terrorist-sponsoring state, and this was exactly a case of that.... And [I argued] that we could send a very strong signal if we'd take it out, that it was a very straightforward operation from a military standpoint.... When I got through, the president asked if anybody else agreed with the vice president. And nobody did; I was the only one who was advocating this course of action. And that's when he opted to go to the United Nations, which is what the State Department was recommending. I was confident there was no way the Israelis were going to turn the matter over to the United Nations. When they called [Israeli prime minister Ehud] Olmert...the Israelis said, "Thanks, but no thanks," and took it out themselves—which was the right answer.

Near midnight on September 5, 2007, in a mission code-named Operation Orchard, eight Israeli fighter jets flew to Al Kibar and dropped seventeen tons of explosives on the target, flawlessly executing what the Middle East scholar David Makovsky[1] would call "the silent strike." And the Israelis' fears about sparking a regional conflagration—beyond the hot conflicts already roiling the region at the time—proved unfounded. Shortly after the strike, President Assad falsely claimed to have repelled the Israeli jets, while quietly ordering that the remaining rubble of the destroyed complex be cleared. Photographs taken by surveillance satellites showed that after Assad's cleanup operation, the target area—formerly dominated by a symmetrical, rectangular structure—was now virtually blank, as if the physical plant had been painted over with white-out. All trace of Al Kibar had been eradicated.

The episode illustrated not just the threat of the proliferation of weapons of mass destruction in the Middle East, but American hesitation to act in the wake of the Iraq War and to enforce its most critical and firmly stated national security objectives.

Al Kibar also illustrated something else: the gradual yet palpable decline of Dick Cheney's influence in the Bush White House. Instead of sharing Cheney's view that Al Kibar was a challenge that had to be met immediately and forcibly by the United States, Secretary of State Condoleezza Rice took a different view—and she prevailed.

A longtime advisor and intimate of the Bush family, Rice wanted to preserve the Six-Party Talks: the multilateral negotiations in which, two years earlier, North Korea had pledged to dismantle its nuclear program in exchange for badly needed economic aid. And instead of wanting to punish the Syrians for their collusion with Pyongyang, Rice hoped to secure Syria's participation in a conference she was soon to host in Annapolis, Maryland, aimed at reviving the moribund Israeli-Palestinian peace process.

While Rice was—and rightfully remains—widely admired in foreign policy circles for her intellect and savvy, her diplomatic efforts on these interrelated areas did not pay off. Syria's attendance did not prevent Annapolis from becoming another Middle East peace conference that produced no change on the ground, swiftly fading from memory, and the North Korean situation went from bad to worse. Eight months after the Yellow Room debate, North Korea, as required by the Six-Party framework, produced a written declaration of all of its nuclear-related programs and infrastructure. As part of that process, the North turned over to the United States a set of aluminum tubes, a gesture designed to prove the truthfulness of Pyongyang's insistence that it had not, in tandem with its reprocessing of plutonium, also been engaged in producing highly enriched uranium (HEU). As it happened, U.S. technicians discovered traces of HEU on the tubes themselves, and North Korea's declaration was woefully incomplete in other ways, omitting key components of the regime's nuclear apparatus. In due time—but only *after* the Bush administration, once again over Cheney's objections, removed Pyongyang from the State Department's list of state sponsors of terrorism—the Six-Party Talks collapsed completely. The regime of Kim Jong Il resumed its nuclear work in earnest, pursuing both plutonium and uranium pathways to a nuclear weapon and detonating more devices.

Cheney lamented that the United States had held neither the North Koreans nor the Syrians to account.

> That was partly because State was trying to do what State *always* does: leave a legacy of peace in the Middle East, to try to have a conference [at] which the Israelis and the Arabs and the Palestinians come together and solve the age-old conflict.... I thought it was badly handled, still do today.... We made a mistake as an administration when we didn't take [Al Kibar] out. I think we were lucky that the Israelis did, because

later on, obviously, ISIS controls the territory where the nuclear reactor was.

   In the first Bush-Cheney term, the vice president's views on Al Kibar would almost certainly have held sway with the president. Legion were the stories told by Cheney's peers—Rice herself, first-term Secretary of State Colin Powell, other cabinet officials—of how the vice president would, in the early days, use his undisputed *gravitas* and direct access to the Oval Office to shape the decision making of the commander in chief, often before Cheney's rivals knew a particular issue was being decided or that a contest for power was even under way. Now, with the war effort in Iraq bogged down and the administration still reeling from charges that it had manipulated prewar intelligence to justify the march into Baghdad, it seemed as though Bush was following Cheney's advice less and less frequently. This subtle yet significant shift produced ripple effects across the Executive Branch, and carried profound consequences for U.S. foreign policy around the world. I asked the former vice president whether it was true, as the *New York Times* reporter Peter Baker wrote in his book *Days of Fire*, that by fall 2006 the relationship between Cheney and Bush "had grown strained."

> No, I wouldn't consider it strained at all. Um—[pauses]—when it got strained, obviously, was towards the very end, with respect to [Bush's refusal, in early 2007, to issue a full pardon for Cheney's convicted former aide] Scooter Libby. No, in '06, no, we were pretty much—we were in sync, for example, on the surge.

. . .

Is it fair to say, as the consensus in the literature records, that your influence on Bush's decision making waned in the second term?

"Waned in the second term." Well, the second—it *changed*, obviously. The second term, by then he's a much more experienced hand. In the first term, 9/11 and the early months of the administration, he's still feeling his way, in terms of getting comfortable with what we are dealing with and so forth. By the second term, you know, he's a much more experienced hand. He's got all of those years behind him of dealing with problems. He's got relationships that he's developed not only within the government but with respect to other governments. And the way I think of it is, he was more confident of what he wanted to do and how he wanted to do it. I didn't win all the arguments. I didn't win all the arguments on things like, oh, bombing the North Korean–built Syrian reactor. I had strong feelings about that. I still think it was the right thing to do. I lost that argument. The president made the decision but, you know, I don't find that surprising. That's exactly what I would have expected.

. . .

The question is why greater experience and confidence on the part of George W. Bush, rather than *cementing* his faith in your counsel, should have led him to *reject* your counsel more frequently. Why do you suppose that was?

I didn't see it as rejecting my counsel.

Well, if he chooses the option advocated by this advisor and not the option advocated by you, that is in some sense a rejection of [your] counsel.

Well, I didn't think of it in those terms. I mean, he never
guaranteed me that he was going to always do what I wanted
him to do.

———————————————

I interviewed Dick Cheney over the course of three days at his home
in Northern Virginia in December 2014, shortly before his seventy-fourth
birthday. We had originally agreed on six hours, but he willingly
extended the sessions as our conversation kept rolling. No subject was
off-limits. Even religion, the one subject Cheney had warned me in
advance he would not discuss in any depth, we wound up plumbing more
deeply than he had ever before allowed in any interview.

Indeed, on all of the important subjects related to Cheney's extraordinary life and times, it is fair to say that *Cheney One on One* represents
the most detailed and penetrating interrogation of the man yet available
to the public. Proceeding in rough chronological order, while allowing
for the organic spontaneity essential to lively conversation, we covered
Cheney's childhood and family, his unruly college years, his political
coming-of-age amid the catastrophe of Watergate, his ten years in Congress, his direction of three wars under the two Presidents Bush, his epic
cardiac history, and his deeply personal views on life, death, and God.

The nearly ten hours of recorded interviews yielded eighty thousand
words of transcript. Less than one-tenth of that material, culled and
published out of sequential order, appeared as "The *Playboy* Interview
with Dick Cheney" in the magazine's April 2015 issue. In part because
of Cheney's blunt pronouncement to me that Barack Obama is "the worst
president in my lifetime" and his declaration that Obama and Attorney
General Eric Holder were guilty of "playing the race card," the *Playboy*
interview was reported and remarked upon—with the intensity of feeling,
both adulatory and vitriolic, that has long attended mere mention of

Cheney's name—by every major news outlet (print, broadcast, electronic) in America and the Western world and became fodder for daytime talk shows and late-night comedians. The former vice president's candid remarks even drew public comment from Obama, who quipped to the insider Beltway audience at the annual White House Correspondents' Association dinner, "Dick Cheney says he thinks I'm the worst president of his lifetime—which is interesting, because I think Dick Cheney is the worst president of *my* lifetime."

Now the public has access to the complete conversation, as it was recorded (with only minimal edits for the sake of clarity). Much of what I consider the most sensitive and probing parts of the sessions did not appear in *Playboy*. Case in point: We spent several hours dissecting 9/11 and the Iraq War, reconstructing Cheney's thoughts and actions and assessing, with the benefit of a decade's distance, both their practical effects and their moral dimensions.

Cheney opened up more in these interviews than he has anywhere else. That was because of the unspoken recognition we shared, as the sessions were unfolding, that they were historically significant, covering new ground; and that, in turn, was why I was granted more time. Cheney, as if standing before the bar of history, made his case in response to the many questions that still haunt us today about the monstrous attacks on the Twin Towers and the Pentagon: Why did the administration not respond to pre-9/11 warnings about Osama bin Laden and al Qaeda with action that might have prevented the attacks? After the towers had collapsed, did the vice president really order the military to shoot down the plane that ultimately crashed in Pennsylvania? Did President Bush give him the authority to do that, as Cheney always claimed? Why was there no official log of the telephone call in which Cheney claimed Bush conferred that authority? In the tense hours before the president returned to the White House, why was Cheney calling the shots and effectively running the federal government?

Of course, for Dick Cheney the great controversies of his career were only beginning on 9/11, and he didn't shy away from my questions about what became known as the "war on terror." Did he twist the law with respect to detention, rendition, and surveillance? Did he shut out his rivals from access to the president? Does he regret the "torture" of detainees at Guantanamo? What did the president know about it, and when? Did Bush and Cheney allow 9/11 to take on an outsized role in American foreign policy?

Questions linger, too, about the Bush administration's other major legacy, the Iraq War, and Cheney was no less steadfast in confronting them. What were the gravest mistakes Bush and Cheney made in Iraq? What went on behind the scenes as they planned the troop surge? How did Cheney feel when he found himself on the opposite end of the argument from his friend and mentor Don Rumsfeld and the Joint Chiefs of Staff? How does Cheney react to the scathing criticism of former colleagues, such as Condoleezza Rice, who accused him of distorting intelligence about WMD in the run-up to the war?

Cheney One on One, in short, is the personal account of one of the most turbulent periods in American history by a man who stood at the center of its historic events. I covered the Bush-Cheney White House for Fox News, traveled the world with both men for years, and knew, met, or interviewed all of the cabinet players. I prepared for the interviews by carefully reviewing the vast literature of the Bush-Cheney era, from books by renowned journalists like James Risen of the *New York Times* and Bob Woodward of the *Washington Post* to memoirs of key participants like Bush, Rice, Rumsfeld, and Cheney himself. When necessary, I challenged Cheney's account, drawing out and sometimes cornering an elusive and proudly enigmatic subject, eliciting the insider stories that have been told nowhere else.

———————

As always, there's a backstory.

The origins of *Cheney One on One* stretch back a decade. In December 2005, then as now a reporter for Fox News, I accompanied the vice president on an official trip to some exotic—and important—destinations: Iraq, Afghanistan, and Pakistan. Each country was critical to the global war on terror then still in its early years. Traveling on one of the familiar blue and white airplanes that make up the Air Force One fleet, I was occasionally treated, along with the other reporters on the trip—colleagues like Bill Sammon of the *Washington Times* (later managing editor at Fox News), Steve Hayes of the *Weekly Standard* (then at work on the first biography of Cheney), and Dana Bash of CNN (a gracious TV competitor)—to impromptu visits inside the vice president's private cabin. Seated with Mrs. Cheney beneath the vice presidential seal, the man whom aides referred to reverentially as "the Boss" would discourse on the day's events, usually on background as "a senior administration official."

Overshadowing the vice president's trip was James Risen's disclosure on December 16 of the Bush administration's Terrorist Surveillance Program, in which the National Security Agency was secretly monitoring the communications of suspected terrorists, including calls involving American citizens, with warrantless wiretaps. Far from embarrassed by the revelation, Cheney seemed eager to promote a full public vetting of it. As Hayes told me at the time, "He *wants* this fight!" For the vice president, a national discussion about the appropriate limits of surveillance powers to be exercised by the commander in chief in wartime represented a cherished opportunity, not a political minefield, one more front on which to press his decades-long campaign to restore the powers of the executive he saw eroded after Vietnam and Watergate.

My relationship with Cheney at the time of the 2005 trip was cordial but not deep. Having covered the White House for Fox News as the junior member of our team there since the last year of the Clinton presidency, I had been around the block a bit. In late 2000, *TALK* magazine—now long defunct but headed at the time by the legendary Tina

Brown—had asked me, on a crash basis, to compile an oral history of Cheney's life culminating in his assumption of the vice presidency. The article, containing no narrative, would consist entirely of recollections of his friends, family, colleagues, and opponents, strung together in rough chronological order. I also interviewed former President Ford and Lynne Cheney, who delivered the sharpest one-liner. "It's been said," I observed, "that of the two of you, you're the brains of the operation." "Well," Mrs. Cheney shot back, "I am the more assiduous academic." She also informed me that the proper pronunciation of the family surname is "*chee*-nee," but that they had given up on policing that long ago. (Years later, during the discussions that produced *Cheney One on One*, I provided the former vice president a copy of the *TALK* article, and he expressed admiration for it, telling me in an e-mail, "You got to the right sources from my past.")

I had also covered Cheney's first foreign travels as vice president, in early 2002. Then he had visited twelve European and Middle Eastern countries in ten days, hoping to secure Arab support for the Iraq War and instead receiving, at each stop, an earful about the Israeli-Palestinian conflict. Cheney and the members of his team on that odyssey, including his national security advisor, Scooter Libby, had been generous with their insights in background and off-the-record discussions, held invariably in bland conference rooms and smoky hotel bars. Suffice it to say, Cheney and his people knew me and I knew them.

Following the protocol for such trips, each of the TV news correspondents was to receive his or her own sit-down with "the principal," or VIP official—in this case, the man who was understood, even then, to be the most powerful vice president in American history. Given Cheney's unique stature, everyone recognized that an interview with him was not like an interview with any other vice president; it was coveted almost as much as an interview with the president himself.

Except I never got one. Dana Bash conducted hers on the side of a snowy mountain in Pakistan, where the Cheneys, led around by the U.S.

ambassador, Ryan Crocker, toured a makeshift MASH unit tending to victims of a recent earthquake. Bash returned from the session visibly distraught at having allowed Cheney's staff to convince her that the side of a snowy mountain could *possibly* be a suitable setting in which for her to do her job—make news with her interview. While I felt for Dana, I resolved to learn from her experience. Looking at the itinerary ahead of us, I tried to think of the best setting for my own interview with the vice president.

Soon after the MASH tour, though, the trip was abruptly cut short so that the vice president could return to Washington to cast a tie-breaking vote in the U.S. Senate (a vote he wound up never casting). Steve Schmidt, the Republican strategist who was running communications for Cheney, assured me that I would get my interview sometime after we were safely back in Washington. "It'll be you who does it, Rosen, we won't let anyone Big-Foot you," he said. "We promise."

Back in Washington, however, my appeals to arrange that interview fell on deaf ears. Two months went by, and then Cheney accidentally shot his friend Harry Whittington during a hunting trip in south Texas. The vice president's next interview with Fox News—his first interview anywhere after the hunting accident—turned out to be a dramatic sit-down with our managing editor and chief anchor at the time, Brit Hume, in which the vice president explained what had happened and why he had initially kept mum about the incident. I knew then it would be a long time, if ever, before I would get my chance to interview this singular figure.

Many years passed. Cheney conducted a series of high-profile exit interviews when he left the White House, and promotional interviews when he published each of his first two books: *In My Time: A Personal and Political Memoir* (2011) and *Heart: An American Medical Odyssey* (2013). Throughout each of these cycles, I was never one of the chosen.

Finally, in April 2014, I ran into the vice president and his wife at the annual party that my colleague George Will, who had recently joined Fox News after many years at ABC News, throws at his home to celebrate the opening of baseball season. After enduring some good-natured ribbing by Cheney about my recent notoriety as the subject of a criminal investigation by Attorney General Holder and the FBI, I switched topics. "You know, I've got a bone to pick with you, Mr. Vice President." Cheney's face lit up with surprise. I reminded him of the Pakistan trip and The Interview That Never Was. "If we were to amortize the seven and a half to ten minutes I'd have received in 2005," I half-joked, "I think we'd be up to something like twenty-eight hours of Nixon-Frost-style interviews today, sir." Cheney laughed and asked me to set up a meeting by contacting his daughter Liz, who has long played an integral role in her father's activities and who had recently served as a commentator for Fox News.

The meeting turned out to be a two-hour lunch, just the two of us, at a steakhouse near the Cheney residence in Northern Virginia. I was startled when the former vice president strode in and tapped me on my shoulder as I sat in a booth, doffing his cowboy hat and greeting me with that sly grin. "Jim!" he said courteously. Fully aware of Cheney's long history of cardiac problems, I needled him before our waiter arrived: "Sir, I'm *going* to order a big, fat steak. I'm *going* to have it cooked in butter. It's *going* to be a *scene* over on this side of the table." Cheney smiled, told me to eat whatever I wanted, and ordered himself a demure salad with salmon on top of it.

Over that lunch, as we sketched out what an extended interview with him might look like, I discovered something surprising about Dick Cheney. Contrary to his stern image, he enjoys a good joke, and while his taciturnity has imbued him, to some, with an air of menace, he is actually quite garrulous. One stray mention by me of President Ford launched Cheney into a detailed, fifteen-minute disquisition on the new Gerald R. Ford class of aircraft carriers and their innovative new suspension systems. Far from Darth Vader, my interlocutor was genial, wry, and talkative: good company.

At the end of lunch, as Cheney scribbled his private e-mail address on a slip of paper and handed it to me, he requested an outline of the subjects I proposed to cover in our oral history and the rough sequence in which I would raise them. He told me he would be busy for about three months and to "resurface" the idea on a date certain, which I did. He was, and is, an irregular e-mail correspondent, at least with me— sometimes it took resending the same e-mail a third time to prompt a reply. In the end, he approved my outline without change.

We would start, on Day One, with the personal side—his childhood, his expulsion from Yale, his relationships with Lynne and their daughters, his cardiac-induced brushes with mortality, and his personal views on life, death, and God—and then work our way through the presidents Cheney has known. On Day Two we would proceed to the foreign leaders he has known, Obama's foreign policy, energy development, the digital revolution, the Tea Party, immigration, and other current subjects. This session would also include an extended discussion of the intelligence community and how it has evolved over the course of his career. Cheney is one of the country's most famous consumers of classified intelligence, so I wanted to elicit his views on the good and bad intelligence that is central to his legacy. We would finish, on Day Three, with what I knew would be the touchiest subjects: 9/11 and its aftermath; the Iraq War; and a segment I called "Cheney Addresses His Critics," in which I planned to read to the former vice president the harshest criticism leveled at him and give him an opportunity to respond. With occasional digressions—such as any interesting dialogue will entail—we hewed closely to the outline, if not to the timeframe, we had agreed on.

When Cheney greeted me at the door to his spacious and brightly decorated home in McLean at eight thirty on Monday morning, the first of December, the sight of me on crutches elicited his characteristic lop-sided smile. Thirty-six hours earlier, I had stepped off a street curb the wrong way and shattered a bone in my right foot. I figured that if anyone in public life would be sympathetic to my plight, it would be Cheney, the survivor of five heart attacks who threw out his back while packing to leave the White House and had to attend the Obama inauguration in a wheelchair. True to form, Cheney over the next three days proved unfailingly courteous, providing an ottoman upon which I could prop up my bum leg and repeatedly asking if there was anything else he could do to mitigate my discomfort.

Behind a small desk in Cheney's sunlit study sits the chair he occupied in the White House for eight years as vice president, and above the white-trimmed fireplace hang three framed swords. One was a gift from the cadets at West Point when Cheney was secretary of defense; the second came from the U.S. Marine Corps commandant when Cheney was the guest of honor at the Marine Corps ball two months after 9/11; and the third belonged to Samuel Fletcher Cheney, the vice president's great-grandfather, who fought for the Union in the Civil War, enduring thirty-four battles only to lose part of his left hand in a sawmill accident after the war. Hugging the walls are approximately three hundred books, mostly military history and political biography, arranged in chronological order—the World War II books, proceeding clockwise, give way to the Eisenhower books, which yield to the Kennedy books, and so on—with all of the spines neatly aligned at shelf's edge. There is, in Cheney's private world, an orderliness that he must find sorely lacking outside the walls of his home.

On the audio recordings of *Cheney One on One*, made with state-of-the-art digital equipment, one can occasionally hear a heavy panting sound. This came from Nelson, the former vice president's sturdy and well-behaved yellow Labrador, who caused Cheney at one point to interject with a request for a break: "I gotta get my dog off to the doggie day care."

Also sitting in were two of Cheney's former aides. Jim Steen, a soft-spoken man about ten years younger than Cheney, has known or worked for the Boss, on and off, for the better part of four decades. He assists in the preparation of Cheney's books and speeches and serves as the unofficial archivist of Cheney's official papers, which are deposited at different research institutions around the country, from Washington, D.C., to Wyoming.

More familiar to me, from my days covering the Bush-Cheney White House, was John McConnell, the good-natured Wisconsinite who was a key member of the speechwriting teams of both President Bush and Vice President Cheney. Red-haired and boyish into his forties, McConnell had been with Cheney in the vice president's White House office when the second plane hit the World Trade Center. He watched as Cheney calmly picked up the telephone on his desk and said, "Get me the president." Occasionally, in the course of our discussions, Cheney would turn to Steen or McConnell for help remembering a name, or to elicit a contribution that he thought might help underscore a given point. Mostly, however, the two remained silent, except when Cheney's trademark wit got the better of them.

Six years after leaving the White House, Cheney remains the *bête noire* of the American Left. His gated driveway has seen more than its share of protesters chanting about "torture" and spray-painting the asphalt. Indeed, the only American politicians in modern times who have attracted more vitriol may be the man he served in the White House, to whom he refers, unsentimentally, as "43," and Richard Nixon. For the tumultuous era of 9/11 and Iraq, Cheney remains, in many minds, the malevolent power behind the throne—witness President Obama's joke about Cheney's being the worst president of his lifetime.

To many conservatives, however, Dick Cheney was, and remains, a bona fide hero, perhaps America's staunchest, most unapologetic defender of a muscular foreign policy abroad and fiscal restraint at home. While George W. Bush has followed his father's practice of not criticizing his successor in the Oval Office, Cheney has occasionally ventured forth from what passes for his retirement to fly the flag of resistance to the Obama presidency, particularly on foreign policy issues. Likewise, while Bush has spoken dismissively about Tea Party activists—"these movements come and go"—readers of *Cheney One on One* will find the former vice president not only praising the Tea Party but viscerally identifying with a movement that advocates for small government and American exceptionalism.

About a week after our sessions ended, Cheney—again, unlike Bush—returned to the public arena to defend the CIA's post-9/11 "enhanced interrogation techniques," which Democrats on the Senate Intelligence Committee had just branded "torture" in a densely documented but highly partisan report. And not long before Cheney's *Playboy* interview hit newsstands and the Internet, he headlined a fund-raiser for the National Republican Congressional Committee. Conservatives, for the most part, have even been forgiving of Cheney's lone notable departure from ideological orthodoxy—his early endorsement of same-sex marriage—seeing it as motivated by love of his daughter.

"When I was a congressman," Cheney told me, "I had one of the most conservative voting records in the Congress. If I were there today, I would still be pretty conservative—by anybody's standards." Whatever one thinks of his views, he is not one to bend them or break with them simply because shifts in public opinion make it politically convenient for him to do so.

———————

Spending time with Cheney in his study, I had to marvel at the extraordinary range of the man's knowledge of political, diplomatic, and military history. He has *read* all those books, and, blessed with a new heart and the outlook on life that can only come when you have cheated death several times over, he is aggressively plowing through more of them. When I arrived, he was halfway through Ed Cray's magisterial biography *General of the Army: George C. Marshall, Soldier and Statesman* (1990). "I don't know if you've ever read Cray's books," Cheney told me excitedly. "It's a great biography on Marshall—one of the best."

Cheney is constantly peering back in time to find parallels, or even rough analogues, to current events and to glean lessons from the past. He is, however, sufficiently convinced of the newness of America's geopolitical environment today, in which the anxieties of the nuclear age are compounded by the distinct threats of the twenty-first century, to wonder whether history can still yield useful guidance for policymakers.

Sometimes, he believes it can—provided the audience is receptive. During the debate over whether to launch air strikes on Al Kibar, he recalled, Condi Rice and Defense Secretary Robert Gates, himself a former CIA director, voiced doubt about whether the Israeli intelligence, even when buttressed by U.S. assessments, could be fully trusted. "Look," he recalled Rice and Gates arguing, "the intelligence we've got on Iraq WMD was flawed; how do we know this wasn't flawed, too?"

> [I]t shows to some extent sort of the legacy, the lasting effect inside the bureaucracy and among key policymakers, of that earlier failure, if you will, with respect to the intelligence community and WMD in Iraq. People had been snakebit. I always thought about it a bit and [looked for] an example when it *didn't* have that kind of problem, didn't have that lasting impact, where it was handled differently, and that was with respect to Pearl Harbor and Midway. I mean, our intelligence folks never picked up on the attack on Pearl Harbor. Six months later, [Admiral] Nimitz gets intelligence that the Japanese fleet is steaming for Midway and he bets the farm that it's good intelligence. Sends our only three carriers out there, sinks four Japanese carriers, changes the course of [the] war

in the Pacific. He didn't have—or he didn't let that earlier intelligence failure influence his judgment about the latest [intelligence].

At other times, however, Cheney projects a hint of despair as to whether Americans can still draw lessons and inspiration from their past triumphs and apply them today. "The world's changed dramatically," he said wearily. "Hard to find parallels.... There had been a time in our history when we had been able to go in and destroy our adversaries and then set up long-term governments that have turned into great friends and allies of the United States and major players on the world stage. But that was very different from the kind of situation that we were dealing with [in Iraq], and nobody was still alive who had been involved back in 1945."

> [W]hen tasked [in World War II], we clearly rose to the chal-
> lenge, to the tune of more than four hundred thousand dead
> Americans in that enterprise. Do we still have the capacity to
> do that kind of thing going forward? I don't know.

And isn't that worrisome?

Well, it *is* worrisome because, you know, it's sort of a key question.... I just think the kind of conflict and threats to the nation that we face today are pretty dramatically different. Spend time on cyberwarfare. The nature of the problems and conflicts we are faced with. It's not at all clear to me how all that's going to sort out, and what kind of steps are needed that we are going to have to take going forward in order to deal with those threats. It's not even clear we *understand* the threats.... You know, we clearly have had [the requisite will] in the past when it was needed. I hope we've got it now, going forward. But we've got to be able to define the threat. We've got to have good leadership. We've got to be able to develop the kind of national consensus that we've had in the past in order to be able to make the sacrifices that are required in order to succeed.

Cheney's passion for history occasioned the only regret I heard him express in the fifteen or so hours we spent together—over lunches, during meetings, and in the actual recording sessions—about the way he had lived his life. *9/11, Afghanistan, Iraq, Guantanamo, interrogations, wiretaps, campaigns, elections*—to the supreme irritation of his critics, Cheney regrets not a single decision in those sensitive and controversial areas, and will not, when asked about them, identify a single thing that, if granted the opportunity, he would do differently.

No, his lone regret is more personal, and it reaches back much further into the past. "As I look back on it now, and I've thought about it often over the years," the onetime political science major at the University of Wyoming told me, "in terms of my political career and my time in government, I would have benefited more from the study of history than the study of political science.... I don't think of politics as science. I think of it more as history, and the historical standpoint. And *people*, and the issues that are involved and so forth and the things you want to achieve— or oppose. It's the process by which we govern ourselves."

DAY ONE

JAMES ROSEN: **All right, today is December 1, 2014. We are sitting in Vice President Cheney's house in McLean, Virginia. And it's a great honor to be with you, and thank you very much for it.**

DICK CHENEY: Well, sounds like a worthwhile project. Took a while to get it organized but—

[laughs] Ten years!

[laughter] No, not ten—yeah, I guess it was. A trip that you missed the interview on.

Exactly, exactly.

Yeah. Forgot that.

So the first hour, as you may recall, is supposed to be oriented more towards personal things, and just "the man," and give people a sense of who you are. And so it occurred to me to begin very broadly by asking: Do you have a philosophy of life?

I don't know. I don't think of it in those terms. I've had a very interesting life, I've loved it. If I could design how I'd spent the last seventy years, I'd be hard put to improve on it. Just in terms of my personal satisfaction and family and Lynne and the kids. We just celebrated our fiftieth wedding anniversary in August.

Congratulations.

I look back over those years and they've been remarkable in every respect.

But have you approached it in some concerted way or from some philosophical point of view?

Well, I started out, I mean I had a great time growing up and going to high school in Casper, Wyoming. I was recruited to go to Yale. It didn't last about a total of about four semesters when we split, Yale and I did. It wasn't their fault; it was my fault. I didn't have any real reason why I was there. Somebody had suggested, "Why don't you go to Yale, and here is the fellowship?" And so I went. As I look back on it now, my life would have been very different if I had finished at Yale.

How so? I know that plunges us into the counterfactual, but have you given some thought to how life would, in fact, have been different?

Well, not a lot. It occurred to me from time to time. Well, the—[laughs]—one way to capture [it], I guess, is [to] tell the story George [W.] Bush told at commencement at Yale in '01. Of course, he was a graduate. And he said to the assembled multitude, the graduating class of 2001, he said, "You know, if you graduate from Yale with a gentleman's C, you can become president of the United States." He said, "If you get kicked out, you can become vice president." [laughter][1]

And that sort of captured the view of it. I could look at it at the time and say, "This is not good," but I really didn't like it, I didn't enjoy it. I frankly was having more time—more enjoyable time out building power line and transmission line. And it wasn't sort of a conscious career decision or anything like that. I hadn't really given much thought to what I wanted to do. But as I reflect back on it now, what happened to me, in effect, was that I reached a point where I had to recognize that I was headed down a bad road after I had been kicked out of Yale. I had been arrested twice for DUI. I was—when I guess, twenty-two, twenty-three—twenty-two years old. And Lynne had already graduated from college early, at the top of her class. My Yale classmates had all graduated. And I was in jail in Rocks Springs, Wyoming, just overnight, on a DUI charge, second one in a year. And that was a wake-up call, in effect.

I decided that I really needed to get my act together, and what I ended up doing was going back to school at the University of Wyoming. It was cheap: ninety-six bucks a semester for tuition. I could pay for everything out of my own pocket with what I earned summers, building power line as well as having a part-time job while I was going to school. I took a full class load, I think, the first semester. I had all As, I think, except for one C. And after that it was straight As. Academically, it turned out I was a pretty good student when I worked at it. And I valued what I was doing much more because I had to work for it.

In other words, in your own mind, life kind of begins with that realization that you're on a bad path and needed to do something about it and the wake-up call? Or, in other words, when you ask a person, "Do you have a philosophy of life?" or "Have you approached your life with some sort of philosophical underpinning?" some people might say the Golden Rule: Do unto others or,

you know. And I would imagine if that were true, that would have been true for you before Yale and after Yale.

Well, I didn't think about it in those terms. If I had reflected on how I spent those last few years, I'd had a great opportunity handed to me, all-expense-paid education at Yale and sort of blowing it off. And I hadn't really settled down and buckled down in terms of what I was going to do and why I wanted to do it. And it was a wake-up call. It was: "Look, if you continue the path you're on, you're going to come to a bad end."

Was that something that you were able to deal with entirely on your own, or was there something your parents said to you at that time that helped you process this as the wake-up call you needed?

Well, I can remember talking both with my folks as well as with Lynne.

Do you remember what they said to you?

I don't. If I did, it would have been private, anyway. So—they were disappointed.

Lynne made it clear that she did not intend to be married to a lineman for the county.

Lynne was not pleased with the way I was spending my time. [laughs] But I—no, it was a matter of sort of coming to a decision myself. And coming to making the decision that I was going to go to work, and—well, I can remember—I think I mention in the book[2] a guy I was traveling with in those days, a guy named Tom Ready, a journeyman lineman. Good guy. Part-time rodeoer from Riverton, Wyoming. But we'd worked about three jobs together and I went back to a place, the apartment he and I were sharing there in Rock Springs, and I packed up my gear. I was moving out on the job. I was going to stay out on the job. Stay out of the bars of Rock Springs and camp out on the job, which another guy was doing. And I told him that I was—I'm going to get my act together and try to make something of myself. And that was captured as much as anything. I wouldn't try to, you know, analyze that, dig into it. It was a pretty straightforward, simple proposition: If I continued doing what I'd *been* doing, I was going to come to a bad end. And I wanted to get out and see if I couldn't improve on that. And obviously, Lynne had a big influence on it.

How bad were the actual DUIs?

Not bad. I mean, I was driving at the time and I *had* been drinking. And—

Were you swerving out of the lane, or what was happening?

Uh—[pause]—I'll just leave it at that. I didn't hit anything. There were no accidents involved. I was drinking and driving, and there was no question I was guilty.

In all the narratives of your life, the Yale experience always appears as an unqualifiedly negative event, a cautionary tale of sorts.

Yeah.

Both for the excessive drinking and for the ultimate outcome: namely, that you flunked out. This raises for me two questions. First, while you clearly were on a self-destructive path, as you have called it—

Right.

—there must have been some funny as hell times associated even with that period.

[laughs] Oh, there were!

A classic prank or a hilarious drunken escapade.

Yeah.

And it seems to me that you have never allowed yourself the indulgence of relating one or two of those.

Of course not! [laughter]

[laughter] This is your chance!

Why would you want to do that? No. I—[pause]—the dean, at one point—I think I mention this in the book—wrote a letter to my dad saying that I had "fallen in with a group of very high-spirited young men." That was the way the dean described it. Yeah, I mean, we did a bunch of stupid stuff you do when you're in college. I've never dwelled on it or written about it, and I don't plan to—

That's why I'm asking!

I know, and I don't plan to talk about it now! No, I—when I think about Yale, I say that I can't think of my life and all that has transpired, and all that I have been able to do, without being aware of the fact that I had not taken advantage of that opportunity that Yale afforded me back in 19—what? '59 and '60. I always enjoyed the fact that after Desert Storm, when I was secretary of defense, I was invited back to Yale to speak to a large gathering of alums that was in the dining hall where I used to sling hash when I was a freshman. And there—I dunno—must have been over a thousand people there, and I was, you know, this was a period of time when the whole country is cheering: We won in Desert Storm, the troops are coming home, and so forth. When I went back, I was invited to come speak and did, and it was very well received. But I was never sure, and I've never asked, but I was never sure they knew they'd kicked me out thirty years before.

[laughter]

The subject never came up and—but I'm pretty certain at that point—you know, I was invited because I was secretary of defense and we had just been through Desert Storm, not because I had once been an undergraduate at Yale. No, if I had sort of gotten through and graduated with a gentleman's C, I don't know where the heck I would have ended up. But I don't think I would have had the motivation and the drive that ultimately led to, well, to a successful career.

Because you became very aware of time, in a sense?

No, not so much aware of time—I wanted to—when I made the decision to go back to school at the University of Wyoming, when I had to pay for it myself, when nobody was *giving* it to me, I had to go *earn* it, that meant a lot. And it said a lot about, I think, my motivation. And it was a fundamental change in attitude compared to what it had been before. And I think it stood me in good stead in all the years later, as I pursued the career that I ultimately led.

And in answering that wake-up call and in prevailing at that moment, it did not require for you a complete renunciation of alcohol, correct?

No.

I mean, you didn't become a teetotaler.

No.

And that's an interesting aspect of it to me because, for a lot of people, if they are feeling like, "This is the wake-up call and this is the problem," they would go cold turkey—that is one way to do it.

Yeah.

What was your thinking about, in that respect? In other words, "I can do this"?

Yeah, I didn't—[pause]—I *didn't* become a teetotaler; I mean, I still *drank*. I'm sure I was much more responsible at that point. I was asked a question—all of this came up in my confirmation hearing to be secretary of defense. And this was, of course, some years later. But if you remember the circumstances, John Tower had just been rejected. And John had been chairman of the committee that rejected him [the Senate Armed Services Committee]. That's never happened in the history of the republic. And he was rejected in part because of the reporting, that turned out to be true, of his womanizing and alcohol and so forth.

When his nomination was voted down, [President George H. W.] Bush immediately picked me, and I went through the confirmation process in seven or eight days; it went very fast. They had all my background information, of course. I'd been putting on my employment record since I'd first gone to work at the White House the fact that I had an arrest record. I always told that to Bush and, you know, everybody else I dealt with. But they—from the standpoint of the committee, it was—I think it was a little difficult for them to deal with, because they had just rejected Tower and here I am: misspent youth, you know, many years before.

So they had a closed-door session of the committee to talk about that subject and my FBI background and so forth, which may be typical for a lot of people. But I think it was [Senator] John Glenn who asked me, you know, he said: "How did you clean up your act?" And I said, "Well, I got married and I quit hanging out in bars." You know, that was as quick a summation as I could give to him. It got a bit of a laugh. I found out years later that [Senator] Sam Nunn had also had a DUI in years past. So I guess that was, as much as anything, sort of captured my attitude. I didn't think I had to give up alcohol; I had to give up my behavior and my sort of devil-may-care attitude towards life in general. And I had done that and, of course, by the time I'm being confirmed to be secretary of defense, I had already put a lot of miles behind me demonstrating pretty conclusively that I wasn't the kid I was back when I was eighteen, nineteen years old.

You've made clear at various points in your career and in our previous discussions that one of the few subjects you would prefer that your questioners not raise with you in depth would be religion.

Mm-hmm.

And without seeking to try to deprive you of that prerogative, I just wondered if you might explain why you are averse to that subject in interviews.

I just think it's a private matter. I was raised a Methodist. My family and my folks were very active in the church. Lynne and I were married in the Presbyterian Church because that's where she had gone as a youngster, and we, probably, if we go to any one particular church now more than any other, it's the Episcopal.

Why is that?

Because we like the Episcopal church in Jackson Hole, Wyoming.

The theology or the actual building?

It's, it's, it's the—[chuckles] the feeling. The place. It's a, um—[pauses]—it's just a church that we prefer.

You said your parents were "very active."

Mom sang in the choir. Dad was the treasurer of the church, kept track of all the funds. She was a pianist, played in the—they were very active in the Methodist church in Casper.

And so as a natural function of that—for you and your siblings—you, then, were active in that church, as a child.

Well—"active." I went to Sunday school when I was a kid. And I didn't—I wasn't all that active as a church member, certainly, as I got older. And my sister, to this day, her life almost parallels my mom's. She plays organ, she's very active in the church in Boise, Idaho. She is now a retired federal employee. But—so it was an important part of *their* lives. I think it would be fair to say I acquired a certain set of values and beliefs as a result of that experience. But I'll leave it at that.

That could also have been an answer to my very first question, "Do you have a philosophy of life?"

Mm-hmm.

And so this will be my last question on the subject matter. But—when you tell me that you did, in fact, absorb from that early period of churchgoing some values and attitudes and philosophies, what were they and can you remember a particular moment when they sort of struck you? Or this particular pastor who had that influence, or something like that?

No.

Okay. [laughter] This is the—

It's a private matter and I, you know, I have strong feelings. And I, you know, I'm a Christian. I believe in a life hereafter. And, um—[pauses]—but it is, for me, anyway, at least, a private matter. And that's the way I have always treated it.

This was the one moment so far where you played against type and actually rushed to fill the silence that you could have allowed me to squirm in uncomfortably! [laughter] "No."

Sure, that's right.

You're going to turn seventy-four soon.

January, yeah.

Simon and Garfunkel, in their song "Old Friends," sang: "How terribly strange to be seventy." And the song is about two friends on a park bench at that age.

Mm-hmm.

Does it feel strange to you to be in your seventies?

[pauses] Does it feel strange? I don't think of it in those terms—so much in terms of *age* or how *old* I am. I'm—I think probably partly because of my, uh—

Cardiac issues.

—heart problems and cardiac stuff over the years—

I mean, [the comedian] Jack Benny famously maintained that in his own mind he was perpetually thirty-nine.

Mm-hmm.

Is there an age for you—

I can't say perpetually thirty-nine, but certainly the experience with heart disease—five heart attacks, an episode of sudden cardiac arrest, end-stage heart failure—I've told you the story about the Cleveland Clinic having me up, because they were doing a conference on innovation in cardiology and they needed a patient to demonstrate that technology, and they discovered that I'd had virtually everything done that you could do to a heart patient. So they had me up for the day with my doctor. And they used my case to demonstrate the development of all that medicine: the technology and procedures that's reduced the incidence of death from heart disease by about 50 percent over that thirty-five-, forty-year period of time where I was dealing with it.

So I tend to think of it in terms of, "My God, I'm here! I'm alive! I feel good. I can do virtually anything I want to do," when there was a time, not long ago, when I thought I had reached the end of my days. And it was a, uh—[pauses]—I write about that period in my book, which is probably the best place to look for it. But when you get to the point where you've been through everything I'd been through, seventeen months after I had left the White House, the prognosis was pretty bleak. We'd pretty well exhausted virtually all the options. The only thing we *hadn't* done at that point was a transplant, and I never really thought I was eligible for a transplant. That's when we decided, reached the crisis point, where they went in one night and put in the pump, that ventricular assist device. But at that moment, in the run-up to that moment, I was convinced I'd reached the end of my days. I was nearly seventy years old. I'd had a tremendous life. Great family. And I was at peace with that.

The surgery to install the pump was the toughest I'd ever had. Some nine hours one night, over twenty units of blood. And when I came out from under that—the surgery—I was on a respirator for several weeks, heavily sedated, and when I emerged from all of that I had lost, I don't know, close to fifty pounds. I had lost virtually all control over virtually all bodily functions, except breathing; breathing was the only thing I could do without assistance, and there I had to practice several times a day with a little device they give you. So I went through that process of the LVAD [left ventricular assist device] surgery, the weeks in the ICU recovery process, and so forth, and came out the other side, went through thirty-five weeks of rehab, and then some twenty months after that surgery, I got a new heart. So when you say, "Gee, you know, doesn't age seventy sort of worry you?" or "You're going to be seventy-four next January"—

Or just feel incongruous, that's all. But in your sense—

No, I feel damn lucky that I'm alive, that I'm here, through the wonders of—

You've gotten a reprieve.

Yeah, I mean, I don't think I'm "old." I guess by a lot of standards are [*sic*]. That's not the dominant thought in my mind when I think about these things.

Given your experience.

I think, you know, I've had the tremendous good fortune, thanks to a donor, to the wonders of modern medicine, to my family, to the prayers of a lot of people, and I'm here. I'm doing this interview with *you*!

[laughs]

And probably stronger and feel better than I did when I was—when I *was* seventy.

I interviewed William F. Buckley Jr. on the occasion of his seventy-fifth birthday, and I just asked him, "How are you feeling?" He said [impersonating Buckley], "I'm decomposing."

[laughs]

You know, he went on, in his way, about how [impersonating Buckley], "You know, you don't swim as fast," and you know, he went—"or write as much." And I wonder if—you just sort of alluded to this when you say that you feel perhaps stronger and better than you did four years ago. But do you think that the caliber of your mental processes is where you would like it to be, or stronger than ever? In other words, does the mind suffer from aging?

Mmm, does the mind suffer from aging? I'm sure it must, to some extent. I don't think I'm as—[pauses]—as quick mentally as I was when I was younger. I think I'm *wiser*. Seen a lot more of life. There was a period in life when I thought my contribution to an enterprise was directly related to how many hours I spent at it and how little sleep I got, how much coffee I drank. I passed that up a long time ago. But I have got parts of my body that aren't as robust as my heart, like my right knee. And in terms of mental faculties, I don't *think* of it in those terms. I'm sure my—I am not as quick at recall as I was at times in the past.

That's why we have Jim [Steen] here.

Yeah. [laughter] Jim knows everything! But Jim's damn near as old as I am! So—

[laughter] Let the record reflect that Jim is rolling his eyes to the heavens.

[laughter from Cheney, Steen, and John McConnell]

But no, in terms of it affecting my mental ability, I don't think—well, the question always comes up in terms of: Does your heart disease affect your mind?

Sure.

And I have never been in a position where I felt the two were related, if I can put it in those terms. And there's, I think, ample evidence to indicate that that's—in my case, that hasn't been a problem. It *can* be a problem for people. But I had great medical care. The transplant's been very, very successful and so I—you know, you talk about all of that stuff. That's just not the way I look at it. I look at it as nothing short of miraculous, the fact that I am even here, able to enjoy life and all that goes with it. And that when I had every reason to expect, in fact *did* expect, that it would have been over some time ago.

You've written of your father that he was "reticent. Didn't give away a lot on a first meeting or a second or even a tenth."

[laughs]

Do you remember how old you were when you first took note of that trait in your father?

How old I was? No, frankly, I don't. I don't think I know.

In other words, when did it dawn on you, "This man doesn't waste many words"?

Well, he was *always* that way. I mean, I didn't—I didn't know any *other* way for a father. That's the way Dad was and the way he worked. I didn't think it was remarkable; I just thought that was *him*.

I ask because for some little boys that kind of reticence on the part of their father could conduce toward a kind of existential doubt, because if the father isn't saying as much, the child may not feel that—"Does he love me? Am I measuring up?" You know, you always want to seal the deal with your dad and sort of make sure that your dad approves of you and sees you as worthy in some way.

Mm-hmm.

And if a particular dad is very, very reticent and doesn't say much, a little boy could be given to doubt.

You're trying to psychoanalyze something here, pose some other kind of set—I had a great relationship with my dad. He *was* a man of few words.

So how did he communicate to you that he loved you?

Well, the time we spent together. I think he was proud of my accomplishments later in life. There were a few rocky years there, when he obviously didn't agree with the way I was spending my time. But he didn't chew me out. I knew he was unhappy. But it—[pause] in terms of his reticence, it wasn't a matter of he didn't approve of me or he didn't love me.

That was never in doubt?

That's too much psychobabble. That's not the way the relationship worked.

What traits that contributed to your success in life do you think you inherited from your mother?

Mmm! Mom was basically—[pauses]—optimistic. Um—[pauses]—both she and Dad were proud of what I—well, you know, when I played baseball and football and so forth. Mom had been on the girls softball team back in the thirties, in her hometown of Syracuse, Nebraska.

And they traveled, right?

Yeah, well they traveled all over the state. But, two years running, they went to the national finals. And those two years they finished second to the Cleveland Bloomer Girls [chuckles], who—they were the national champions. This is a big deal for a little town in Nebraska, to have a women's softball team that went that far. So she always had an interest in sports and athletics. Lots of times when, you know, when I wanted to practice pitching—I pitched some when I was in pony league and so forth—Mom'd catch me. It wasn't just Dad who was interested; she was *actively* interested in sports and so forth.

So would you describe yourself as an optimist?

Yeah.

And would you say that this kind of a competitive streak you inherited from her?

Hmm. Well, did I inherit—I suppose—

You mentioned sports.

Yeah.

I asked what—and, you know, you mentioned competition.

That's one of the things that stands out in my mind about her memory. I've got a—I *think* I've got a picture I put in my book of Mom and one of her teammates in Syracuse, Nebraska, in front of the family-owned café, Dickey's Café, when she was probably, oh, eighteen, nineteen years old.

Mr. Vice President, have you ever been in a fistfight?

[chuckles] Mmm, yes, I expect I have.

When was the last one? What's the one that sticks in memory?

Oh, my God. It's been a long time ago. Long, long time ago. When I was a kid.

Do you remember your first kiss with Lynne?

I do.

Can you—was it, was it on that first date, when you finally got the nerve to ask her out, to—

I'm not even talkin' about it! [laughter] That's very private! What was interesting about [chuckles] that relationship—I mean, after I screwed up my courage and invited her out, when we went to this—I don't think I put this in the book. We went to this formal dance, sort of a girls' sorority. And we double-dated with a friend of mine. And afterwards we went up on C Hill. C Hill was the hill in Casper on the south side of town that had a big C on it, and that's where you went to park. You could look out over the city of Casper and see the bright lights and so forth. And while we were up there, a couple of friends of ours snuck up on the car and let the air out of the tires.

[laughter]

They thought that was very funny.

[laughter from Steen and McConnell]

We had problems—you know, you didn't want to destroy the tires. We had to creep back down to the nearest filling station and get the air in the tires. But this whole thing made us late for curfew. I think she was due home at eleven, or something like that. And I was concerned, to put it mildly, that I was going to blow the deadline. So we finally got home and she [Lynne's mother] was there but she, you know, didn't really say much about it, didn't say much of anything. And then we found out—she didn't tell me this until some time later—she was, at that point, she was the secretary to the chief of police in Casper, Wyoming.

Lynne was?

No, Lynne's mother was.

Lynne's mother, okay.

And she got reports all night long from the various officers around Casper of where we were and what we were doing.

[laughs]

And I mean, you know, she just—they reported in.

It's the surveillance state run amok!

Exactly, as a forerunner to the NSA system!

But no, so we—she was always a great ally, Lynne's mother was. Her dad was much more standoffish and not as welcoming to this young man who showed up and started hanging out around the house.

Did there come a point where he kind of did confer his blessing on you or you sort of came to terms with each other?

Well, he, uh—[chuckles]—we came to terms, I guess is the way I'd put it. So—uh, "blessing"? He went to the wedding, paid for part of it. So, yeah [chuckles]—we [got] some degree of approval for it. But Lynne's mom was really the one who, no matter the transgression, she was always a fan and a supporter.

You've written about your teen years as having been "like a classic fifties movie," with you and Lynne as homecoming king and queen, and the jukebox at the canteen, the local hangout, playing Elvis and Fats Domino and the Everly Brothers. Were you among those who went to see _Rebel Without a Cause_, and was there any part of you that was attracted to the rebellion of rock and roll, the kind of underside to the fifties?

No.

But did you recognize that that was welling up in the society?

No.

Well, there must have been some kids even in Wyoming that were greasers, or sort of the "bad" part of the fifties that we talk about, right?

[chuckles] No. There wasn't. We'd talk about it, high school reunions— we just had our fifty-fifth high school reunion in August. And there were what we called "the car guys" and then the rest of us that were involved in sports and athletics and so forth. And those were distinct but not—I mean, there was nothing improper or inappropriate about or—nor did anybody look down on anybody else. I mean, Casper was, you know, by our standards it was a big town: the first- or second-largest city in Wyoming. Only thirty thousand people. We didn't have very many people in Wyoming. But to this day when we have these reunions, the second day is sort of always devoted to a picnic on Casper Mountain that focuses on the cars and the car guys. And one of my best friends, he's got, I think it's a '34 Ford. He and his wife ride a Harley to South Dakota every year for the annual rally. The car guys are still car guys! But it was never a—[pauses]—the sort of James Dean *Rebel without a Cause*. That was movie stuff. That wasn't real life, at least not in our town.

We've already talked about the Yale experience. The one other question I wanted to ask about it was: You have written about how you felt out of place there because you were from out West and suddenly you find yourself mixing with all these East Coast prep school kids.

No, and partly the physical setting, too.

Right, because previously you'd had a lot of big sky.

Yeah, exactly.

And here you are in New Haven. Can you recall a specific instance at Yale where you were subjected to snobbery or where you were made to feel by someone, in effect, "You don't belong here"?

No.

So this was all internal for you, it was just a kind of a perception—

Yeah, pretty much. And most of the guys I knew—[pauses]—most of the guys we hung out with were primarily public school–type. There's still the group of roommates, those of us that are left, still get together every couple of years. And just thinking back on one was the son of a Chicago police detective. Most of them went to public schools, public high schools.

You just sort of gravitated toward people like that.

Yeah, I mean, they were interested in sports. We had a couple of guys who were really bright, hard working, became very successful. A Wall Street lawyer. It was a group that sort of fit together. We ended up together after one year. We'd gotten to know each other—excuse me—that first year. First year, you're assigned to your roommates; second year, you get to choose. And we put together a group, I think there were twelve of us. And we had three suites. It was four, four—three suites, I guess. It was four people to a suite. And we took three suites and kind of put 'em all together. And then we doubled up and took one suite, and that was the party suite. That was turned into the [chuckles] living room and instead of two bedrooms I think one was—had a bar in it, and so forth. And then we all doubled up in the other places. But we—we pretty much had similar backgrounds.

I'm wondering about how it cohered in your mind that you don't quite like this place or that "I'm not *like* a lot of these people here."

Ehhh.

Is it a set of experiences, or—?

It wasn't people; it was more the place, the locale. Um—[pauses]—as I said, I write about in the book, this sense of a lack of space and openness that I had grown up with. I had been to Chicago before, but I had never been back East. And so, in terms of the relationships with others, in terms of whether they were prep school kids or public school kids, I ended up primarily with the public school kids. Those were the people I knew. We were the guys that were on scholarship, had jobs in the mess hall during hours, and so forth. Bob Tomain from Pittsburgh, who ended up running a big savings and loan in Atlanta. Bill Kranz, whose family owned a furniture factory in upstate New York, who was killed skiing in the Swiss Alps some time ago. You know, it was a group that we were really involved with—I mean, I'm trying to think of anybody—there was one guy who had been in prep school, but most of us were all public school products.

Your early career aspirations—and I think this is a point that is insufficiently remembered about you, for those seeking to understand you—

[chuckles]

—were to be an architectural engineer and then later a political scientist.

Well, the architecture stuff, engineering stuff, ended in the summer of 1958.

I said "early."

[laughter] Yeah, *really* early! No, I'd taken a drafting class when I was in junior high school and so forth and enjoyed math. And if somebody asked, "What do you want to be when you grow up?" I'd say, "Well, maybe I'd like to be an architect or an engineer." And then I spent five or six weeks at Northwestern. And I had been selected for that program. They brought, I think they call them "cherubs." I think they still run the program; every once in a while I run into someone who was one. And it was five weeks at Northwestern in the summertime. Partly, I'm sure it was a recruiting effort to encourage people to come to Northwestern; but it also gave you a lot of exposure, for example, if you were interested in engineering, to the engineering side of the house. And that pretty well persuaded me I didn't want to be an engineer.

Nonetheless, for example, just at our lunch in April—

Mm-hmm.

—a stray mention of Gerald R. Ford by me launched you into—and quite in contrast to the notion of you as this famously taciturn character—

Mm-hmm.

—into what I would estimate was a fifteen-minute disquisition on the new Gerald R. Ford class of nuclear submarines, is it?

Aircraft carrier.

Aircraft carrier. And you talked about the *suspension systems*. And it struck me that you have a real love of mechanics.

Mmm.

And I just wonder if it was your interest in structural mechanics that enabled you to master politics and government and various bureaucracies the way that you did.

That would be an overstatement [pauses]—in terms of [chuckles] indicating some deep interest in—[chuckles] I just think about—it's funny, because I just traded cars this past weekend. Saturday they delivered a new car to the house here and took the old one. The new one is just like the old one: exact same model, same color. It's a Lexus SUV. And as the guy was checking me out on the car and so forth, he opened the hood and we looked under the hood. I'd never looked under the hood of the old car. [laughs] Okay? There's not any—and I never had any *cause* to. You know, we reminisced about when I had a 1965 Volkswagen and you could pop open the back end of that thing and adjust the choke and so forth, the carburetor. But you know, I'm not consumed by—the thing that intrigued me from the standpoint of the Gerald R. Ford had more military aspects to it. I mean, I had an interest in—I had had for a long time—military issues and military matters when I was a member of Congress, when I was secretary of defense, and so forth. So there's a natural interest in aircraft carriers and how they work.

But you wouldn't say that, as a personality matter, you are attentive to systems and kind of structural mechanics of things? Not necessarily a car, but in institutions' mechanics or the points, the pressure points, at which something will bend, break, work, etc.?

Mm-hmm. I don't think of it in those terms.

Had you completed your studies to become a political scientist, did you have in mind what your dissertation would have been about?

Mm-hmm.

What was it?

Well, we'd started out, after Lynne and I got married. And I'd gone back—by then, I'd been back at school for a year, I'd focused on political science. There was a course I had taken at Yale that had piqued my interest—about the history of the Cold War, basically. This was, mind you now, the 19-early-60s timeframe, but it covered the period from the end of the war up till the present. And I'd read a lot of history. I had an interest in history. The courses that I enjoyed and the department I immediately gravitated to when I went to [the] University of Wyoming was political science.

So what would the dissertation have been about?

I finished my BA and my masters at Wyoming. Been an intern in the Wyoming Senate and the governor's office in Wisconsin. And then went to Congress for the congressional fellowship. But I'd made the decision, really had to make a decision between two fields: one was political science, the other was law. And I thought about the possibility of going to law school, but the big problem there was money. Didn't have money, and there were no fellowships available in those days. Whereas political science I could get fellowships, scholarships, and so forth, and to some extent, you know, teaching assistants [positions], those kinds of things, so that I could finance it. So that partly directed me in that direction, in terms of what was immediately available.

When I was working at Wisconsin for my major professor, a guy named Aage Clausen, he was working on, and got me started as his assistant working on, roll-call voting on the House and the Senate. And in those days it was a very quantitative kind of process: How are you going to explain the relationship between the constituency or party and how they vote on economic issues and so forth? And I was running multiple regression analysis on roll-call voting in the House and Senate over a twelve-year period of time. And he and I had actually published an article in the *American Political Science Review*, which was kind of him to give me coauthorship. Most professors wouldn't have done that.

It's highly sought after on eBay, I can tell you, that issue.

Oh, really? [laughter] I went back and looked at it some time ago, and it is—well, it doesn't fit with the world I lived in as a politician, a member of Congress. But I don't think that was its purpose. But basically, when I came to Washington, it was on a fellowship, with the intention—by then I had passed, finished my coursework and passed my exams for the PhD, the prelims. And what I had left was the dissertation. And I brought with me a great big huge box of computer printout—old style.

Right, Scantron, sort of.

Well, and you carried around punch cards, eighty-field punch cards, and that's how you input into the computer and so forth. I'd learned Fortran programming; this was a long time ago. But I was convinced what I was going to do based on the fellowship was work on the Hill but fold all of this into then returning back to Wisconsin, where I had an arrangement with my major professor to go back to work. And we'd do a book, and part of that would be my dissertation.

And so it would have been an analysis of voting patterns, in essence.

Explaining how members of Congress voted and the extent to which their constituency influenced them, or party and so forth, qualities of their individual districts. Explain their vote and try to explain that vote with that kind of analysis.

Many years later, you and Mrs. Cheney coauthored a book called *Kings of the Hill: Power and Personality in the House of Representatives* (1983), which was portraits of consequential Speakers of the House.

Plus Thaddeus Stevens.

Plus Thaddeus Stevens. Do you think that had you stayed a political scientist, that would have been a subject you would have come to? Or did that book originate as a function of your having served in the House?

Well, the book on speakers was history, biography. That's not what political science was about, at least in those days, or that part of it that I'd gotten involved in. There came a time, before I got to Washington, where I had an opportunity—just trying to think, this would have been probably '68—to run a congressional campaign in Wisconsin. I'd worked for the governor [Warren P. Knowles], and through my contacts in the governor's office, I was approached to run the campaign of the Republican candidate running for Congress in what was then the Second District in Wisconsin. It was the old [Robert P.] Kastenmeier seat. And it was attractive. I could use the money. They'd pay me a thousand dollars a month or some magnificent sum like that.

And I went to the department, talked to the chairman of the department, because it meant I'd have to postpone my prelims; instead of taking them in August, I'd have to postpone them until December. And he strongly recommended I not do that. And my immediate reaction was, "Gee, this is great, you know, I want to learn about Congress and so forth. What better experience to have than to go actually run a campaign for Congress?" And he said no. He said, "This will be looked upon as though you are not serious about an academic career." And so I accepted his advice and then some time after that the offer came along to come back here as a congressional fellow, which was sort of sanctioned activity by the *American Political Science Review* and so forth, and was taken as a definite plus from the standpoint of my long-term academic interest. But there's a split there between the academic profession and the real world, the real political world. And I was given the opportunity in fact to choose between which one of those I most enjoyed. And obviously I came down on the side that I would rather do it than teach about it.

As we survey the current landscape, I don't think that I could identify any of the richest or most accomplished political consultants and say, "Ah, there is a former political scientist."

[chuckles] Yeah. Most of 'em won't admit it!

Do you think, though, that your study of political science somehow propelled you in your political career?

It did to the extent that it was the setting in which I had access to the fellowships, to the internships. The thing that really moved me in that direction was the Wyoming State Senate, as an intern. Interned for the governor of Wisconsin, and staying on beyond the intern period. It was a six-month period, and he kept me on beyond that. I stayed on part-time when I started graduate school.

So in other words, the study of political science put you in contact with people who wound up facilitating your rise in politics.

Exactly.

But you wouldn't say that the study of political science gave you a kind of edge in the practice of politics.

Correct. Yeah, I think—as I look back on it now, and I've thought about it often over the years—in terms of my political career and my time in government, I would have benefited more from the study of history than the study of political science.

To the extent that you have been portrayed—as the most neutral word; "caricatured" might also be employed—but to the point that you have been portrayed as this supremely savvy manipulator of the process, this pusher of levers at just the right times and so forth, it would seem to me that your understanding of how things work, and also this exposure to political science might have contributed to that. That's where I'm going with all of that.

No. I don't think so. I'm trying to think—the only political scientist to be president was Woodrow Wilson. And I don't think he got there because he was a political scientist. [laughter] That was before my time, but no, they're very different. Political science is very different—as practiced today, especially the way we were doing it then, and again you're talking about a period that's forty years ago.

A very different discipline.

Yeah—well, I'd speak every year, a group comes down from West Point. There's a professor up there. And he arranges every year to bring down a group of cadets. He's got a couple of courses he teaches and one is on the presidency. And I can't remember what the other class was this year. But anyway, he's out of the political science department, or government, I don't know what they call it. But what they're interested in talking to me about is history. It's not political science. For most people who haven't spent a lot of time thinking about it, I don't think of politics as science. I think of it more as history, and the historical standpoint. And people, and the issues that are involved and so forth and the things you want to achieve—or oppose. It's the process by which we govern ourselves. And it's not really science in *my* mind; not the way you are using it.

A conservative view of the matter might hold that, in fact, there's really nothing new under the sun. And [William F.] Buckley used to use the term "patrimony," which was the inheritance of all that which had come before and had distilled itself in that which we know to be true objectively, without any need for resort to relativism, etc.

Mm-hmm.

Do you believe that there is nothing new under the sun and that's why history can be so instructive?

Mmm. No, I don't really believe that.

For example, one quarrel with that might say: Nuclear weapons are new. That's something that's new under the sun.

That's exactly right. And the kind of threats we face today. There's been such a dramatic change in technology. The extent to which we are vulnerable now to—more vulnerable, in some respects, *because* of our technology, because we are so dependent on it in so many areas. At the same time, we've reached the point where, you know, compare Pearl Harbor to 9/11. Pearl Harbor, the Japanese fleet descends on Pearl Harbor, and kills some—what?—twenty-eight-hundred people, sinks part of the fleet. 9/11, nineteen guys with airline tickets and box-cutters take down the World Trade Center, kill more people than we lost at Pearl Harbor, knock a big hole in the Pentagon. And we start to look beyond that at the kinds of threats that are out there in the WMD area, whether it's nukes or biological agents, or something like that. The world's changed dramatically. To say that there's nothing new, I don't buy that.

As a politician, as a public figure, as someone who is called upon to do a lot of public speaking, how would you characterize your own style of suasion?

Well, I don't think about it.

You had to, though; you have to make speeches.

Yeah, you do have to—I just get up and say what I feel and what I believe and say it the way I want to say it. To the extent good words have come out of my mouth, I've had a lot of help from Mr. McConnell here. But I don't think of my—I guess I don't analyze it. I don't know. John, what do you think? How would you describe?

JOHN McCONNELL: Logical, very direct.

Mm-hmm.

McCONNELL: You never hide the ball. It's always the thoughts of a man very clear and direct. Not a lot of ornamentation.

And is there anyone in your life that you could point to as saying: "My style of speech, my approach to rhetoric, probably is influenced by that person"?

No. I mean—the way I think of it, John has touched on it as, I get up and say what I want to say because this is what I believe. I don't think of it in terms of rhetorical flourishes and so forth.

Would someone who knew your father and you, for example, if there were a person here today who knew you both, would they be able to say, "Dick talks just like his father talked," or something like that?

Mmm, I've never heard that. We looked a lot alike, physically. I resemble him.

In other words, your manners of speech have to come from somewhere. And I'm sort of wondering where yours originated.

I never really thought about where they originated [chuckles], James.

I guess Wyoming or the West.

Well, I don't speak with a southern drawl. I'm not from New York.

For example, some public speakers might be inclined to use flourishes of humor. Or look at the Sorensonian approach for Kennedy; you know, that's a very different speaking style, right? You saw President Kennedy speak; we're going to talk about that in the next hour, when we talk about presidents.

Yeah.

But you know, yours, I think—as John has indicated—is a very simple and direct style. And I just wonder how that comes to be. Is it a function of the personality, ultimately?

I suppose that's part of it. Partly the way my mind works. [pauses] You know, I've had the benefit, and you've got to give some credit, obviously, to people like John, who have been—especially during my time as vice president—an integral part of the process.

But their job, in a sense, is to try to channel *you*, as they know you and understand you.

Right, but we'll sit down and talk about a subject. I mean, I think one of the best things we ever did was the eulogy for Jerry Ford. I still get comments about that, run into people in various places who bring it up. But writing speeches for somebody else is hard to do. Now, maybe that's because the guy I tried to write speeches for was [Donald] Rumsfeld. [laughs] He wasn't easy! And I got out of that as quickly as I could.

And a different style; a decidedly different style.

Well, Don, Don just was—I didn't think of it as style so much. He was a hard man to please. And nothing was ever finished. And having been through that process, I was convinced I did not want to be a speechwriter. It was my great good fortune, I found guys like John and his partner, Matt Scully, when I had to put together that speech, the acceptance speech for the convention in Philadelphia in 2000.

"It's time for them to go."

Yeah. And that was actually Lynne's line, which she stole from Al Gore or something. But it was a cooperative effort and the ability to work together. I could never do what John does. And I benefit enormously from being able to work with him on something, but generally we'll sit down and talk about a subject, talk about some of the ideas I want to try to convey. We'll get on the phone sometimes, John and Matt together. And—because Matt is still in California most of the time, he's not here.

McCONNELL: Arizona.

Arizona. And then they'll go away with what I have given them and come back and do a great job of it. But in terms of—I don't think about my style. I mean, I just—this is what I do. This is what I believe. This is what I want to say.

We are at the hour mark and so I want to wrap up. I have three more questions. Two of them are going to be the most sensitive I'll ask you in the whole [interview] but I feel that they are, first of all, respectful, and second of all, somewhat invited by the fact that you subtitled *In My Time* "*A Personal and Political Memoir*."

Mm-hmm.

And the third question is unrelated to this. But in the book you devoted two short sentences to the moment when [your daughter] Mary came out to you.

Mm-hmm.

You replied by saying very simply that you loved her very dearly and wanted only for her to be happy.

Mm-hmm.

The way I read the passage, it seemed to imply that when this happened, the news wasn't exactly a surprise to you; and probably for most parents in that situation, when that moment comes it really isn't a surprise. Assuming I am correct about that, and given your 1950s western upbringing and your general conservatism, I would think that most people would imagine that when you first *did* have the realization, it would have been, if not a disappointment, at least a time for some turmoil—inner turmoil—or reflection on your part. And for parents who are still in that stage, who might be struggling to get to the place where you were when Mary finally did have the conversation with you, and you were in a place where you could reply in the way that you did, for parents who may not be there yet, is there any advice you would offer about how to process that inner turmoil, or have that inner conversation with themselves, in a constructive way that can help them get to the place that you got to?

Well, it's not my business—I mean, for me to advise somebody else on how they should deal with those sets of circumstances.

In other words, you wrote the heart book [*Heart: An American Medical Odyssey* (2013)], right, to help people with cardiac issues.

Right.

When someone has that realization, a parent—to borrow terminology from another time—that's a heavy trip, right? And so they may look to someone who is a public figure, who has gone through it, and gotten through it in a very successful way and want to know: Is there anything you can tell me that can help me get to the same successful place that you did?

But I wrote a book about hearts. I didn't write a book about being a parent of a gay child.

No, but you did include this in what you called "a personal memoir."

Well, sure. I mean, it was important. It, it played a role in the first [vice presidential] debate [with Senator Joseph Lieberman in 2000], in the run for vice president, when I was front and center I had to explain my views, which I did. And it—in the second campaign, John Kerry tried to use it politically.

What did that say about him to you, to your mind?

Well, I thought Lynne captured it. She went out and spoke on behalf of the family and did it very effectively. [chuckles] We always talked about that afterwards as "the Mary Cheney bounce." It was a major mistake [chuckles] by Kerry to try to use something about a child in the political setting that way, while he was debating [George W.] Bush. And when the Kerry campaign manager [Mary Beth Cahill] went out and said, "Mary Cheney is fair game," I think that was a big mistake politically. And it would be, I think it would be—I don't think the book would have been complete without reference to that.

I see. Have you seen Kerry since then? Has he ever apologized to you?

No. Nope, never has.

Without reference to other people and helping other people necessarily, then, do you feel comfortable addressing how you came to peace with it in the way that you did, such that you were able to reply to her in the way that you did?

Well, I mean, I'm comfortable with what I believe. It's not one of those things you expect to deal with as a parent. But an awful lot of people do today, anyway. You know, we love Mary very much. She is a great part of the family. Just had Thanksgiving dinner with Mary and Heather and

.

k you might ever have arrived at that position as a public policy
there been no such personal connection to the issue? And should
essary, in other words?

w. That's not the situation I was faced with. I'm certain that
aughter you love very much, part of your family, and to find
rom her perspective, you know, the world looked very different
onventional, traditional view of marriage, or life in general.
es you to think about it, obviously—and which might not have
of front and center, something that you had to deal with if it
at smack dab in front of you. But no, I've said exactly what I
say and what I believed: that "we love you very much, Mary,"
know it was all right.

py when you're happy," in essence—

nt. Last question for this hour. Of your great-grandfather, Samuel
heney, who served with such great distinction in the Civil War,
the Union, a friend once wrote: "Cheney is clear grit."

.

nse that that is exactly the verdict you wish history to bestow upon
ey is clear grit."

heney is clear grit."

about that?

Sam and Sarah. And that's—[pauses]-
don't—I guess I don't *agonize* over it or

Was there a time when you did, I guess is

Well—

—when you struggled with this.

I always thought George Bush [the forty-
more than I did, when he informed m
constitutional amendment basically to ban g
And I can—I can [chuckles] remember hav
and he was trying to explain to me what he
he knew about Mary and that's partly what
worried that somehow I would be offended

I'm harkening back to the period when Mary
apparent to you. Was it a struggle for you to

No. And it, it was—and it was—*was* a s
something that, you know, was sort of th
about. Mary was very direct about it, came
we were in the airport in Denver. And
anticipated or contemplated before that.

You came to this position on same-sex marriag
connection to the issue.

Certainly, that helped, yeah.

And the same for Senator [Rob] Portman, for

Mm-hm

Do you t
matter h
that be

I don't
having
that, th
than th
And it
been s
wasn't
wante
and let

"We're

Exact

—as a
Fletch
fighti

Mm-

I get
you:

Hm

Am

That was said after the battle at Stones River, which was at the tail end of 1862, beginning of 1863, six months before Chickamauga.[3]

Is that what you would like your epitaph to be?

[chuckles] Well, it's not a bad one, actually. I had never thought about it as my epitaph. But, no—I think it was intended as high praise. And I would expect if he knew about it, he was probably pleased with it.

I know I said that was the last question but you can't trust reporters. I know you know this. As you look back on your life, is there anything you wish you had done differently? I guess you wouldn't even put Yale in that category, so—

I don't, I guess I don't run around thinking about, "Gee, I wish I had done this different" or "I wished I'd done that instead of this."

We all do.

Well—[pauses]—that's not the way I think about my life. And—[pauses]—it's just not—people always—well, reporters especially—a lot of your colleagues, I won't say it's [chuckles] necessarily representative of *you*. They're dying to get you to say—

"I made a mistake, X."

—"I made a mistake and I should have done it the way *you* think I should have done it." And I don't work that way.

When I asked [William F.] Buckley on the occasion of his seventy-fifth birthday, "Do you have any regrets? Is there anything you would have done differently?" And he thought for a moment and he said [impersonates

Buckley], "Well, certainly there are things that you—were a waste of time. If I could have known in trying to play the harpsichord all those hours I would never actually master it, then should I have done it at all?" That sort of thing—which I thought was kind of a glib response. I did ask him at one point—I think you will find this of interest—I said, "Mr. Buckley, when was the last time you felt insecure about something?" I said, "Emotionally insecure, financially insecure. Physically—in a bad neighborhood after dark. Anything at all." And he thinks for a moment and he says [impersonates Buckley], "Well, there have been some rather anxious moments at sea." He said, "I remember one squall that came through that was horrific, and I wasn't entirely sure I wasn't going to drown." This was 2000 when I had this conversation with him. And I said, "When was that, sir?" And without a trace of irony or anything he looks at me and says, "1958."

[chuckles] He knew.

Okay? So, to recap, I've just asked you when was the last time you felt a twinge of insecurity about anything under the sun at all and you have to dimly harken back forty-two years ago; that's a life well lived!

Mm-hmm.

Is there anything you look back on and say, aside from Yale, that, "I should have played the game better there" or "I would do this differently"? Or "I would—if I had a mulligan, I would take it"?

Well, that's not the way my mind works. You know, I can look at that first heart attack and see positive aspects of it. It was when I had that first heart attack—thirty-seven years old, in the middle of my first campaign for Congress—I quit smoking. Up until then I had been a heavy smoker. But something that I came with out of that heart attack was that I never touched a cigarette again—which probably saved my life; I'd have died much earlier and I wouldn't be here today at *all* if I had continued smoking after that. So I can look at a situation like that, that is, some people might say, you know, a life-altering event, having a heart attack. The things I take away from that, though, were (1) quit smoking, a definite plus; (2) I had a doc who, when I asked him if I had to give up my campaign, said, "Aww, hell, Dick, hard work never killed anybody." So I walked away from that experience not agonizing over the state of my health or "I'm going to die someday of a heart attack." I came away from it with what in essence were positive experiences for me, things that had positive meaning for me or led me to approach life with you might say a different attitude. I didn't run around worrying about if I go on with the campaign I am going to have a heart attack and die.

Right.

So, that's kind of the way I look at those kinds of events.

And Yale?

Yale I can look at and say, "Yeah, I blew an opportunity at a great education."

But it worked out, somehow.

Well, it worked out, and it turned out for me there were things that I got out of going to Wyoming that I never would have gotten out of Yale—when I had to pay for it. And I worked damned hard to pay for it and at the same time do what I did in order to get top-notch grades.

It seems, the way you are responding, that you look back at your life and you see turning points that helped get you to the next stage of life in some sense,

but you don't look back and say, "That's a mistake I wish I could do over again." Not even in the vice presidential years. There's nothing you would say, "I wish I would have played that differently."

Mm-hmm. No, I think that's generally true.

When I broke that bone in my foot on Saturday night, I thought, "Should I cancel?" you know, like, "How am I going to get there?" And you know, I thought to myself, "Hell, Dick, a little hard work never killed anybody."

[laughter]

So that's why I decided to continue.

Yeah—I don't know. Maybe another way that my heart disease and having to deal with that has affected that—after you have been through what I have been through—and thirty-some years of coronary artery disease, all those heart attacks, and so on and so forth, three open-heart surgeries, heart transplant, end-stage heart failure—when you get through that and come out the other side, one of the things you come away from it with is you don't sweat the little stuff. And nearly everything else is little stuff.

———————

The first president you saw in person was Harry Truman, but you were a child at the time.

Right.

Then as a college student you saw President Kennedy speak and ride in an open convertible when you were a student at the University of Wyoming in September 1963.

Correct.

Can you remember watching JFK speak and the impact he had on you as a speaker?

Well, I remember the event. [pauses] I'm just trying to—the Truman thing was the '48 campaign, and there was a hell of a rainstorm that night I recall, too—and he was doing his whistle-stop [tour] across America. The Kennedy thing, I was newly back to school. I mean, I had just started back at the school at the University of Wyoming in September and I went—nearly everybody in town went. I'm sure people from all over came to the big field house and that's where he spoke. I didn't recall until I went back and looked at it exactly what he said. It was just, "This is the president of the United States." That was a big deal. And it's hard to separate out from what struck me about that event from what happened in the immediate aftermath. You know, within a couple of months, he'd been assassinated in Dallas. And that stands out. I remember that very well. I went back and looked at his speech, as I recall, I think when we were doing the book, and we talked about—

The Greek concept of happiness.

Yes, and fulfilling—finding fulfilling, important work to do and so forth. But it wasn't something that I carried forward all those years, that I was aware of. I wasn't conscious, "Gee, Jack Kennedy said X."

Or he wasn't any kind of motivating factor in your going into a life of public service.

No, but he—I mean, I can't say he wasn't. I mean, there was a period of time there, having seen him, having watched and been through—like every other American did—the circumstances when he was assassinated and those days in the immediate aftermath of that: Oswald's assassinated, we have the funeral, and so forth. All of that is burned into my memory like it is for most other Americans.

Where were you when you learned that the president had been shot?

I had just finished a class at the college, at the university, and I was walking back. I had an apartment I shared with another guy in an alley, about—oh, it was four or five blocks from the building on campus where I had been to class. I don't remember what the class was. But I was walking back to the house and a stranger drove up in a car and stopped and had the window down. And he said, "Have you heard? The president's been shot." And I went over and I hadn't heard. That was the first I had heard of it. And he invited me to join him and we went back up to—I can remember *him*, I don't think he—he wasn't a friend or anything. But we went back up to the student union where they had television. And I can remember going into this room that was pretty well packed at that point, with people watching the television broadcast: Walter Cronkite and the announcement that the president was dead. This was on a—was it a Friday?

JIM STEEN: Yes. It was a Friday afternoon.

Yeah, because it was "the four days in Dallas," right? So—

Yeah, yeah. I'm thinking it over again. And what I did—I'd developed a pattern, it started just a few weeks before. Lynne was going to school at this point, working on her masters down at the University of Colorado at Boulder. And what I would do is on Friday after class, I would drive down to Boulder, which was maybe 150 miles, and spend the weekend with her in Boulder and then Sunday night I'd drive back up to Laramie. And I had to work nights in the job I had then, Mondays through Thursdays, reading to this blind air force veteran. The VA paid for it, but it was how—it was my part-time job. But so I remember driving on down that night, listening to all of this on the radio and so forth and then being in Denver with Lynne. I can remember being there. We had the radio turned on; she didn't have a television, either. And the radio [was] turned on and [we] listened as they were bringing Lee Harvey Oswald out of the jail or to arraignment, or whatever he was headed for, and hearing the actual live report, "He's shot. Lee Harvey Oswald's been shot." So it was a, you know, just a major—well, one of those events that sticks in your memory: you know where you were and what you were doing, like 9/11.

I was going to ask, and obviously a different part of our interview will cover 9/11 in detail.

Sure.

But when 9/11 happened, did it sort of bring up some kind of visceral memories of the Kennedy assassination or just that kind of feeling, the same feeling?

Well—

You were just so focused on what you had to do?

Well, I was, and life was different. And the things, the memories that were evoked by the events of 9/11 had to do with the continuity-of-

government program that I had been part of, which we'll talk about, I'm
sure, when we get to it. But [it was] a program I had been heavily involved
in, where the government prepared for, and practiced, what we would
do in the event of an all-out global nuclear war with the Soviets. And
then that's what triggered, in terms of preserving the legitimacy of the
constitutional government of the United States and so forth. I didn't think
of Kennedy directly, that immediately. I was also very much aware of
that we didn't want to get the president and I in the same location.

Right.

And the Secret Service was a reminder of that. That also was very much
front and center in my mind.

**Have you ever been interested in the questions surrounding JFK's death and
have you ever doubted, for example, that Lee Harvey Oswald was the sole
assassin?**

Interested enough. I never really doubted that theory. And the Warren
Commission, the work of the Warren Commission—

**Did you read about it a lot? I mean, did you follow the controversy over the
years—**

Sure. I read a lot about it. I remember the *TIME* and *LIFE* stories, the
magazine—special magazine stories that came out and so forth. It was
a subject of great interest. I also worked for Jerry Ford. And Jerry Ford
had been on the Warren Commission. And he had *very* strong feelings
about it. I remember talking to him about the Warren Commission and
the theories and him being, as I recall, somewhat contemptuous of the
people that would come along and say, "No, Lee Harvey Oswald didn't
do it" or had some contrasting, contradictory theory.

Did he, in talking about that experience with you, ever address the ways that the FBI and CIA dealt with the Warren Commission that in effect helped to fuel these conspiracy theories for the next thirty, forty years?

No, I don't recall it.

Is there anything else he told you about his service on the Warren Commission that sticks with you?

Well, I think he was proud of the service. [pauses] He referenced it a time or two. I don't remember him ever mentioning it in a speech or anything like that. There'd be private moments when something would come up. Was it the Stokes Committee on Capitol Hill [the House Select Committee on Assassinations, chaired by Rep. Louis Stokes] went through an exercise where they went back and reviewed all of the evidence, and—

Came to a different conclusion.

Exactly, yeah. Which I never gave great credence to.

You stood on the House floor when Lyndon Johnson delivered his final State of the Union address as president [on January 14, 1969], an event that you have recalled as a memory—

It was actually—I was in the gallery.

Oh, okay. Thank you. And you recalled that as a "melancholy" event. Do you remember what thoughts you had at that time, as you gazed upon this diminished and defeated figure, as to why LBJ's presidency had collapsed?

[pauses] I don't have any—I mean, I'm sure I had views of all the controversies that had surrounded him. I mean, this is—this would have

been January of '69. And we'd been through, up till then, of course, a time of considerable turmoil. The war in Vietnam, the antiwar protests at the University of Wisconsin, which were extensive.

Counterculture.

The counterculture developments. Then we'd had the Martin Luther King and Bobby Kennedy assassinations just a few months before. I mean, it was a general sense that stemmed back—I remember watching Johnson's speech the night he announced that he would not accept nor would he—

Right. The abdication speech [of March 31, 1968].

The abdication speech. We had a little black-and-white TV by then. We're living in student housing in the University of Wisconsin and had neighbors in, and we watched as Johnson gave his speech. He was, to some extent, a tragic figure by then.

And what did you understand the essence of the tragedy to be?

Well, part of it was caught up, obviously, in Vietnam. I think, and again it is difficult to separate out when I've learned since from what I knew—

From what you thought at that moment, right.

But that the job, in the end, had been too much for him. And it included, you know, riots in the cities in the aftermath of the assassinations of Kennedy and King. It wasn't a very happy time in America. It was the— well, starting in sort of January of '69 and earlier—well, it had been the previous spring. It was before the Kennedy assassination when I'd met with [Congressman] Joe Tydings. And he was the one who provided the fellowship that made it possible for me to be a congressional fellow. And having a beer with him on State Street in Madison, where he interviewed me about possibly becoming a congressional [fellow]. He was going to finance—this may not be in the book.

I don't think it is.

Basically, what had happened was Tydings liked the congressional fellows program. He had control over a fund, a scholarship fund, that had been left by—I think it was Joe Davies, who was his grandfather, or step-grandfather, who had been [President Franklin] Roosevelt's first ambassador to the Soviet Union. And that money had to be used to finance educational projects for Wisconsin students. He decided he wanted to take some of that money and use it to finance a congressional fellow under the *American Political Science Review* program. He'd called the president of the university; the president of the university had called the chairman of the Political Science Department. The chairman of the Political Science Department called me to see if I would be interested. And we agreed that I would meet Tydings when he came to the campus because he was there to recruit volunteers to go to Indiana to help Bobby Kennedy in the Indiana primary. So there was a big Democrat rally for Bobby Kennedy on campus, and I went to it, although I was a Republican; by then I was an avowed Republican. But he didn't know that; he never raised it. But I went to the rally where he recruited Kennedy volunteers, and then we went down and had a beer on State Street and he interviewed me. In the end he agreed that I would be selected by the [American Political Science Association] to hold this fellowship. He was always intrigued that I was recruited [chuckles] for that professional fellowship, you know, by Joe Tydings, a Democrat, out hard for Bobby Kennedy. It eventually got me back to Washington; it was obviously a major breakthrough in my career. I think I do write—I don't know whether I write about it in the book or not. There was a time later on in the newly elected vice president [period], and Lynne and I were at dinner at the house of the president of the University of Maryland. And Tydings was there that night and I went over and thanked him for what he had done for me all those years before. He didn't have a clue! [laughter] He had forgotten the experience!

Well, specifically I wonder if, at the time, you absorbed from LBJ's experience any lessons about the perils of waging a protracted war overseas without popular support at home.

No.

Did you regard that his tragedy was one of his own making? Because the way you have been talking about it just now—you spoke about external factors, and that the job was too much for him, in a sense. But in other words, wasn't his outcome a function of the choices he made? Guns and butter being one of them, for example or—

I wasn't thinking of it in those terms. I mean, I think what struck me at the time was, "My gosh, I'm in the chamber of the House of Representatives listening to the president of the United States give a farewell speech."

"This is cool!"

"This is pretty, pretty interesting!"

Were there ever times during the Iraq War where you got the sense that George W. Bush was being consumed by it the way that LBJ was torn up by Vietnam?

I did not.

The first president you met in person was Richard Nixon, when Don Rumsfeld introduced you—

Where I shook his hand, correct.

—in the Oval Office in 1970. Accounting for the fact that you wouldn't have with Nixon the depth of contact you would with his successor or other presidents to come, nonetheless I wonder if Nixon in person was more than the caricature of him that prevails today, this relentlessly brooding and paranoid figure. Was there more to Nixon than that?

Oh, yeah.

What was he really like?

Well, I can't—I was oftentimes a chart-flipper in the back of the room when Rumsfeld gave a briefing to the cabinet. I didn't have a personal relationship with him. I mean, I was down a couple of layers and did have an office in the West Wing, a closet I shared with another guy. But it was prime real estate. It was the West Wing. And this was the period, obviously, pre-Watergate. It was a period of time when—well, remember the tremendous victory Nixon won in '72. You know? Maybe the biggest or certainly one of the biggest in the history of the republic. I mean, we lost one state.

Right.

And that wasn't South Dakota. It was the District of Columbia or something [and Massachusetts].

I think people forget about Nixon that there are only two Americans in our history who have run on a national ticket five times. One is Franklin Roosevelt; one is Richard Nixon.

Yeah.

When John Kenneth Galbraith was asked once, in the aftermath of Watergate, "Don't you think there is a little Nixon in all of us?" he said, "The hell there is." But it seems to me that if you're running on a national ticket five times, that speaks to some core affinity with the American people. Does Nixon in your view deserve to be ranked at or near the bottom of the presidents, where historians tend to place him?

I think it's more complicated than that. And I'm very leery of the historical ratings system. I guess [Arthur M.] Schlesinger [Jr.] began this, or probably Schlesinger's father [Arthur M. Schlesinger Sr.] began this process years ago—

It's entirely politicized, in other words.

Yeah, I mean it's—

And subjective.

It's totally subjective, and you don't start with what I would necessarily consider to be a balanced view. This is how one particular group of people, who are "historians," evaluate the officeholders. But that's—

Was Nixon a good president?

I think he was, in some respects. I think he gets a lot of credit, and deserves it, for what he did in the international arena, especially with respect to Moscow and to Beijing. And I think those were—that he managed—that was his first love. But that he managed the foreign policy situation, in terms of China and Russia, with considerable skill and success. Having Henry Kissinger for his secretary of state. So I think he did a lot of positive things as a result of those activities. Now, everybody says you can never forget Watergate; well, fair enough. But he also, in the end, stepped down and resigned.

And surrendered the tapes.

And surrendered the tapes—

Along the way.

—rather than go through, you know, the ultimate, the trial in the Senate, over the—you know, you can say, "Well, that was an admission of guilt." Well, it was, and he left the presidency accordingly. So I'm not as—in terms of trying to say he's the worst president we ever had, I wouldn't say that. I'm also active—there's a group that reconvenes periodically; you may know about them, given your work with [a biography of John N.] Mitchell. We just had our annual gathering. And it started with the old—

Domestic policy—

—domestic policy staff. And it has expanded over the years. I have been going for years now. They extended honorary membership to Rumsfeld and me many years ago and—but there's sort of been a change from a situation where there was—there was a feeling of, you know, "Geez, here are a few survivors here and, and—"

Keep your head down.

"—keep your head down. We don't really want anybody to know we're meeting," to a situation now where it is a more positive thing. There is a broader sense of perspective in terms of that period of time. The group's busy now raising money to refurbish the [Nixon presidential] library out in Yorba Linda. This one we had this year put together sort of a West Coast group and an East Coast group. We got them all together this time around for dinner at [Patrick] Buchanan's the night before and the annual lunch we do at the Metropolitan Club.

I've attended those things and I've seen—the best time I ever saw the Rumsfeld-Cheney comedy act was at the Metropolitan Club there, a couple of years ago—

Yeah.

—where you guys just stood up there together and it was just—I really wish someone had recorded it.

[laughs]

Would you have advised Nixon to burn his tapes rather than turn them over?

Would I have advised Nixon to—I don't know, I mean—[pauses]—that's a hypothet—I'm not even going to deal with it.

All right.

I mean, you know, the story always was the reason there *was* a taping system was that he was physically inept and couldn't hang a ribbon around the neck of somebody he was decorating.

That's why there was a *voice-activated* system.

A voice-activated system. You know, having been involved over the years in a number of presidencies, I understand the need to have—or the *desire* to have—an accurate historical record. You know, you want to interview me today with a record, with the tapes [*sic*] turned on. You know, what goes on in the Oval Office to some extent certainly deserves an effort to try to preserve it for the important parts of it. We don't do as much now of that, probably, as we should, *because* of Watergate. But would I have advised Nixon to burn the tapes? I guess I would have advised him to have, you know, well—somebody should have had a sign that they flashed in front of him at the beginning of every meeting: "Mr. President, this meeting is being recorded." Like, you know, when you call to exercise a trade in stock. The broker you deal with, there will be a recording that comes on for accuracy purposes. They do that so often, that you'll be recorded.

It strikes me that Watergate—maybe even more so than you have even suggested about yourself—was truly a formative event for you.

Mm-hmm.

In that: So much of what you fought for in your later career—the restoration of power to the executive, particularly in the conduct of foreign policy and intelligence gathering—

Mm-hmm.

—but also the confidentiality of White House documents and decision making—seems to have grown out of your revulsion at watching a president, weakened by scandal, being forced to turn over his private tapes of his conversations and to accept deepening encroachments on his powers by a resurgent Congress.

Mm-hmm.

And it seems to me that Dick Cheney would not have taken the views he took if he didn't witness Watergate so up close, the way you did.

Mm-hmm. Yeah, I think there is a fair amount of truth to that. There's in my mind—separate for a minute my perception of what was happening—but I think, you know, the *record* shows there was a period of time when Congress really asserted itself—with the Budget Act, the War Powers Act, and so forth, that whole impeachment process—in ways that weakened the office of the presidency. And that part of my task, when I got involved in the positions to deal with it, was to try to recover some of that, if you will, to restore the legitimate power and authority of the presidency. And that things like the War Powers Act I still believe [are] unconstitutional. Most presidents who've had to serve under it believe it's unconstitutional; it's just never really been tested [in the courts]. So you have a tendency, and it's understandable, to want to sort of personalize it—"How did you feel?" But I did believe that the consequences of Vietnam and Watergate both served to weaken the presidency, and I felt strongly, as I served in a number of capacities, that I wanted to be an advocate for, supportive of, a strong executive with respect to the presidency.

And the record on that goes back long before your vice presidency.

Mm-hmm. Go back to Iran-Contra.

Iran-Contra and the piece you wrote for the—it was collected in a book—about congressional overreach in foreign policy ["Congressional Overreaching in Foreign Policy" (1989)]. Is it a mischaracterization of your views on the so-called unitary executive to suggest that those who hold that view basically argue for complete, untrammeled authority for the commander in chief in wartime?

Well, I hear that term used from time to time. It's never been clear to me what it *means*.

Which term?

"Unitary executive."

[David] Addington[4] used it more than anyone, I think.

Well, that may well be. I didn't always read his briefs. [chuckles] Most of the time. But "unitary" in the sense that the presidency stands alone? That there can't be any intrusion into his legitimate areas of authority and responsibility?

In other words, you are not arguing that?

Well, I want to make clear what we're—it's like the "neoconservative" approach.

Right. What does it actually mean?

Yeah. What does it mean? And lots of times, the—I think the word gets used implicitly with different purposes or different meanings.

So—

So what are we talking about here?

—to pare it down—

Yeah.

What kinds of checks and balances on the president's powers in wartime do you regard as legitimate?

Well, Congress still retains the control over the purse. That's about the limit.

So, in other words, if they can stop the funding for an executive action of military power in wartime, but beyond that, that's where their legislative ability should rest, in your view?

In wartime.

Mm-hmm.

As a general proposition, I think that's fair. I'm trying to think of other instances where—I suppose to some extent in Desert Storm we got around even that limitation. We had a sixty-billion-dollar war that only cost us five billion and the rest of it was paid for by allies and third parties. So even the power of the purse, in that particular and unique set of circumstances [can be limited]. The war was financed outside, if you will, the normal processes.

I'm going to mangle this quote. But Gerald Ford was once quoted in the Watergate era—he was asked what constitutes an impeachable offense.

Mm-hmm.

You'll remember this maybe better than I do. And I think his answer went along the lines of: "An impeachable offense is whatever the hell the House of Representatives decides it is."⁵

Mm-hmm.

Right?

And the Senate.

And the Senate; right, of course. Well—

He would have said the House, but—

Right. And so that answer puts forth a vision of the role of the legislature in the system as one that is basically what they make of it. And so the war powers of the legislature—

Yeah.

—in a sense come down to what the hell they decide it to be, right? In a sense?

Well, I'm just trying to think back [to the] real world, in terms of the role of the Congress.

To declare war, for example, right? That's one big one.

Yes, but we often operate without a declaration of war in a formal sense. You know, we've kind of—

Does that bother you, that we do that?

No, it doesn't. We've come up with AUMF, authorization for the use of military force. Now, is that a declaration of war in a technical, legal sense? Maybe not. On the other hand, if you go to the Congress and get them to approve legislation that authorizes the president to use military force to take down al Qaeda, or some other appropriate action, that's a—that's not a declaration of war. In a technical sense, we haven't really had a declaration of war. I guess—what? We certainly had one on December eighth of 1941.

The Gulf of Tonkin is another of these kind of authorizations that's not really a declaration of war.

Right. But I can also recall—I'm just thinking about two *real*-world experiences, both in—I mean, in Desert Storm with [Bush] 41. We had all the authority we needed. The UN's charter had been ratified by the United States Senate, and under Article 51, Kuwait as a member was perfectly—their government—the U.S. government was perfectly justified in responding to a request from a member state that had been invaded to come to their assistance. Didn't need any votes. We went and *got* 'em—Bush did, 41, because he thought it would be useful from the standpoint of his purposes to have a clear demonstration to the country that Congress was behind what we were doing.

It's a lowercase "p," political decision, in that sense.

Well, yeah. It's a—it was a decision he made. We had an argument about it. I argued against it. I argued that we had all the authority we needed, and that if we went and asked for it and didn't get it, that we'd be in big trouble. We still would have no choice but to go forward with our military action because we had, you know, half a million troops in the desert, and you couldn't leave them there indefinitely.

Did you feel the same way after 9/11? Here we were, unmistakably and objectively attacked—

Mm-hmm.

—in a kind of a state of war.

Mm-hmm.

Did we need to—

Not "a kind of." An actual, real state of war.

Okay. A different kind of war than we were used to, perhaps.

Mm-hmm.

Was it your feeling then that we didn't need an AUMF because: "War exists. I don't need you to declare it for me in order for the president to be required, as a matter of his office, to be responding effectively to it"?

Yeah, I don't think you needed it from a legal standpoint. I thought it was very useful to have, partly because I believed that one of the signal events represented by 9/11 was a change from looking on terrorist attacks as a law enforcement problem to a recognition of the attacks of 9/11 as an act of war. And having the Congress on record saying that, in effect, made it even clearer that we were in a position where we had all the authority we needed, including the approval of the Congress, to go forward and use our military assets, our intelligence assets, all of the other means at our disposal, to go get the guys that had done it as well as to use it to prevent that next attack. So it was valuable to have. Now, was it legally required by the Constitution? I don't think so.

It was a useful predicate, of sorts.

Yeah. It was a way in part to rally the country. The Congress wanted to be involved. We *wanted* them involved. But—[pauses]—I thought, you know, both Bushes—in one case when I was secretary of defense, one case when I was vice president—felt the need to go forward and seek the approval of the Congress in support of those policies.

You became the youngest White House chief of staff, under Gerald Ford. It still bothers you that the *Saturday Night Live* caricature of him prevails in the public imagination.

Mm-hmm.

How is it wrong?

Well, they tried to—it sort of was a play on what Lyndon Johnson had said about Ford, that he had "played too much football without a helmet," kind of thing. I always thought it was a cheap shot, that Jerry Ford was probably one of the finest athletes ever to occupy the Oval Office. That was reality; that was the truth. This was a guy who had been an all-conference center at the University of Michigan. He was, even in his sixties, he was a great skier. He'd fall down on the slopes—you're sitting here with a cast on your leg because you tripped over a curb and busted your leg.

[laughs]

He never was as badly injured as you are right now!

[laughs]

And yet, Chevy Chase, I guess in particular, was somebody that I— bothered me about it. Ford, it didn't bother him nearly as much as it bothered me.

Do you think it actually contributed to his electoral difficulties?

Mmm, I can't say that it did. I mean, there were other, bigger items involved, like the Watergate part and so forth, that certainly had an effect. But it bothered me to some extent—there was another element that figured in there, too. I was always uncomfortable when members of Congress would come down and talk to Jerry, and that happened frequently. And he wasn't "Jerry." They knew him, he had been the House Republican leader for years.

The quintessential Man of the House, in a sense.

Exactly. And they all looked at him as their friend Jerry, and he campaigned for them, and he'd been in the leadership up there for twenty years or whatever it was. But he was *the president*, and I wanted them to *address* him as the president. And a lot of them did, but some of them didn't. And I always felt that was inappropriate, that that was partly respect for the office. And that what the comedians do—now, this was—you know, I can't say I haven't laughed [chuckles] at the way they portray other presidents or the way *I've* been portrayed over the years, but—

But those things have resonance, right? Popular culture *matters*.

They do. But there was something special about Ford that it bothered me. Because it was such a distortion of who he really was. And, you know, he had to live with it. We actually took steps.

So the caricature of you is *less* of a distortion from who you really are—

Well, I wouldn't—I wouldn't want to say *that*. [laughs] But it depends on which characterization you're talking about! But with Ford we—well, we went to the extent that in '76, when it was time to brief the budget, he did it himself. No president had done that since Harry Truman. He knew it so well; he had been on the Appropriations Committee forever. And we did the annual bit where the Washington press corps goes into the State Department auditorium and up on the stage you've got the entire cabinet arrayed, and the director of OMB, and there's Ford. And he did the whole damn brief all by himself: answered all of the questions, did the whole thing. And that was a remarkable performance. I don't think we ever got to a point where you could say—where it was treated appropriately by the press.

So it didn't seem to bother him. And maybe just because he's the first president I ever worked that closely for. Because I admired and respected him. But I really thought it was over the top.

I don't want to spend too much time on this, but I have a question that relates to the Nixon pardon: Was thought, as far as you know, ever given to pardoning

not just former President Nixon—was thought ever given to pardoning the others who were on trial at that time? Mitchell, [H. R.] Haldeman, [John] Ehrlichman?

Not to my knowledge. Now, I wasn't there for the actual pardon. I mean, I was there for a couple of weeks after he [Ford] came in—I think he came in [on] August ninth [1974]—and then I went back to my company and Rumsfeld went back to Brussels, and on the ninth [*sic*; the eighth] of September the pardon was issued. And we didn't get back until about the middle of September, about a week after that, so I was not involved in the discussions before the decision was made.

You credit President Ford with an important demonstration of American resolve post-Watergate in the *Mayaguez* incident. Tell me about that and why that was important.

Well, it came almost immediately on the heels of the withdrawal from Vietnam. And we'd been through the evacuation, as I recall the timing, when we had been lifting Americans and some Vietnamese off the roof of our embassy in Saigon. The North had invaded, Saigon was falling, and we were trying to get our people out. And within a matter of days after that—which was clearly a defeat for the United States, militarily and politically. You could have all kinds of discussions about that, but where it was easy—well, that's not the right way to put it. There was concern that this signal that the United States no longer was the great power that we had been—that Vietnam had been a defeat and so forth—then along came the *Mayaguez*, Cambodian pirates hijack an American ship on the high seas, and the president responded decisively. That led ultimately to the release of the ship and the release of the crew. And that it was a demonstration, if you will, of U.S. commitment and so forth: certain things and principles hadn't changed just because we were withdrawing from Vietnam.

Sometime around 2004, former President Ford said of you to Tom DeFrank—with the understanding that none of his remarks would be published until Ford was gone—"Dick has not been the asset to George W. Bush I expected." Do you remember that comment?

Mm-mm ["no"].

It's in the book by Tom DeFrank [*Write It When I'm Gone: Remarkable Off-the-Record Conversations with Gerald R. Ford* (2008)].

I've never read the book.

Did Ford ever express to you any sense of disappointment with your conduct of your vice presidency?

No. He was always rather proud of it. Took delight in telling me it was the worst job he ever had, and "Dick, I don't know how you ever took the job," and so forth. No, he never expressed any dissatisfaction to me.

One individual I want to address with you who is not a president but still looms large, even today, is Henry Kissinger. And you have described him as a singularly impressive public official. But the Joint Chiefs of Staff during the Nixon era, and others such as James Angleton at CIA, viewed Kissinger with grave suspicion. And in his 1976 memoir, *On Watch*, Admiral [Elmo] Zumwalt, the former chief of naval operations, quoted from his personal notes of a conversation he had had with Kissinger in which Kissinger told him, "The U.S. has passed its historic high point like so many earlier civilizations," and that it was his job, as Nixon's national security advisor, "to persuade the Russians to give us the best deal we can get recognizing that the historical forces favor them." This is Zumwalt quoting Kissinger as saying that to him. What do you make of all that?

I have never read it. I mean—that's not been my experience with Henry.

You know that he has attracted over the years a certain amount of suspicion from conservatives and from the military and from the intelligence community.

Oh, yeah. No, I, I was there [chuckles]—

Why do you suppose that is?

Well, I remember it surfacing in '76, in the—partly in the battle of the nomination.

The platform, as well.

The platform fight, yeah. It was a situation where we'd won the battle over 16-C, the rules change that the [Ronald] Reagan forces tried [on] us.[6] It was a test vote of who was going to win the nomination, and we won. But it was followed by the Helms amendment, and after we did 16-C in the rules, we had to do the platform. The platform had an amendment, foreign policy amendment, authored by [Senator] Jesse Helms [of North Carolina] that basically dumped on everything Henry had ever done but never [chuckles] mentioned him by name. And I love the story. We gathered in Ford's suite at the hotel, and the argument was whether or not we fight the platform plank, the amendment to the platform. And Henry was demanding that we had to fight it or else it would destroy him and so forth. [Vice President Nelson] Rockefeller was there backing up Henry, and I was there, [William] Timmons and [Tom] Korologos were there. I'm sure Stu Spencer was probably there. And this is when Henry finally sat down, and he said, "If you don't oppose this amendment and defeat it, I quit." And Korologos said, "Henry, if you're going to quit, for Christ sakes, do it now. We need the votes."

[laughter]

And Henry never after that—I told this story in front of Henry a couple of times. We basically just approved the amendment on a voice vote and there wasn't—we didn't have the votes to win on it.

From whence emanated this enduring suspicion of Kissinger?

Well, it went back to, I think, Henry's strong support for détente; his strong support of the arms control with the Soviets; his reluctance, for example, to have [Soviet dissident Aleksandr] Solzhenitsyn come visit Ford in the White House.

What were your feelings about détente?

Well, I basically supported it. I thought it was a move in the right direction. I didn't disagree with it. I did want to see Solzhenitsyn come to the White House. I argued *for* that.

Because you realize that latter-day conservatives kind of pose—almost as a binary choice—[that] you can either have favored détente, like Nixon and Kissinger and Ford did, which is on the "wrong" side of history; or you could have been like Ronald Reagan, who said, "Tear down this wall," and who called the Soviet Union an "evil empire," and who is credited, rightly or wrongly, with bringing down the Soviet Union. And so I wonder what you make of that dichotomy.

I think it is a false dichotomy. I look on the Helsinki Accords, for example, as something that was positive. That took human rights and put it front and center in the relationship between the United States and the Soviet Union. I think that was a significant achievement. And I know it is something that the president and Henry both felt strongly about. But Ford—part of it, with Ford, came out of his work on the captive nations movement back during the Cold War, when there were a significant group of Republican members of Congress who were concerned about the captive nations held behind the Iron Curtain and so forth—the Baltics, etc. And I think from the standpoint of détente, I am hard put to see a distinction between the way Reagan dealt with Gorbachev and the way Ford would have dealt with Gorbachev.

Or Nixon and Brezhnev.

Or Nixon and Brezhnev. You can find places to argue about it. But I'm a conservative. I ran against the Panama Canal Treaty when I ran for Congress—just like Ronald Reagan was against the Panama Canal Treaty. But I think it's a false dichotomy. Henry was a lightning rod during those years. Part of it might have been his past association with Nelson Rockefeller. I think that had something to do with it as well. But you know, Reagan did a very crafty thing in the '76 campaign. I mean, you know, we whipped him in New Hampshire—close, but we beat him in New Hampshire, we beat him in Florida, we beat him in—I don't know—Wisconsin or wherever it was. And then we ended up in North Carolina and he turned the tables around and beat us, and he did it on the Panama Canal.[7] Partly, I think Jesse Helms had a lot to do with that. But it became a gift to the Reagan campaign. And I think if they hadn't had that, if they hadn't carried North Carolina, they might well have been finished. But it was all wrapped around this notion of, you know, Henry's a left-winger, Ford supports Kissinger, and so forth.

I love the televised debate that [former Senator] Sam Ervin moderated in 1978 about the Panama Canal, where Reagan was opposed by Bill Buckley, and Reagan stands up and he says [impersonates Reagan], "Bill, I just don't understand why you haven't rushed over here yet to tell me you have seen the

light." And Buckley rises and says [impersonates Buckley], "Because I fear that were I to approach you, the force of my illumination might blind you."

[laughter]

There is only one communicator who might get the better of Ronald Reagan, I think.

Yeah. It would be him.

Did you ever meet Buckley?

Yeah.

Under what circumstances, do you remember?

I think Rumsfeld and I went and had lunch with him once in his office there in New York.

Whereabouts in time?

Oh, God. Hmm. [pauses] Must have been when I was working for Rumsfeld. So it would have been back—[pauses]—

In the early seventies.

Yeah, early seventies. I'm trying to think [of whether it was] in the Ford administration. I think it was before that. Would have been a time when I basically—I traveled with Don. I was doing a lot of stuff with him. So my guess is it was—

You were never a guest on *Firing Line*?

That I don't remember. I remember *Firing Line*.

Did you ever have any dealings with Nixon after he left office, when he would summon foreign policy analysts and members of Congress and so forth to his home in Saddle River, New Jersey?

I had one memorable session with him when I was in Congress and it was an election year. And I'm trying to remember which election. I want to say maybe '84. He came to town, to the Jefferson Hotel, and he invited a few of us from the Congress to come down and have a drink with him. And we went down and spent a couple of hours with him late one afternoon. I don't remember who all else was there, but you know, a relative handful.

STEEN: Gribbin was there.

Was Dave there?

Dave Gribbin.[8]

And he proceeded to sort of run through the country state by state, and how various states were going to go and so forth. And it was damn near perfect. I mean, it was spot on. Very, very impressive performance. And it was a sort of—I think he liked the idea of being able to come down and talk about that stuff. And I'm not sure why they put together the particular group they did. But that's one that stands out in my memory as a time when he returned and performed and was—you know, knew his business.

We are making our way through the presidents with diminishing time.

That's all right; go ahead.

Let's talk about Ronald Reagan for a moment. You didn't work for him directly, but you interacted with him. What should people understand about Reagan as a politician, as a leader, as someone you worked with, given that his legacy is so widely appropriated and misappropriated for so many different agendas today?

Well, I'm a Reagan fan. I worked my fanny off to beat him in '76, and we did. The last time he ever lost anything. When he came to town, the same time he came to town, I became chairman of the House Republican Policy Committee—number four slot [in the House Republican leadership]. And during his years I was either the policy chairman or later on the conference chair, chairman of the caucus. And as he was leaving, I got elected whip. But I was involved in most of the leadership meetings with the president.

One of the things that stands out is Iran-Contra, because I was the ranking Republican on the Iran-Contra committee [the House Select Committee to Investigate Covert Arms Transactions with Iran]. And that was basically started for us sort of late '86, right after the '86 election as I recall, was when the C-130 over Panama, someplace down there [*sic*; Nicaragua], had been shot down, and they were smuggling arms to the Contras and so forth. And then most of '87 was taken up with that. I was sort of looking at the seamier side of things, and the interaction with Reagan in that sense was after the fact, when we were all through with the report and wrapped up the hearings and so forth. I was home here in Washington on a Saturday, and I got a phone call from Camp David, and it was Nancy [Reagan] on the phone, and then she put the president on the phone, and they both thanked me for what I had done in managing that whole process.

You know, there is a similarity with the caricatures of Ford, in that where LBJ had said of Ford he played football one too many times without a helmet, I

think it was Clark Clifford who said of Ronald Reagan he was an "amiable dunce."

Yeah, that was a cheap shot.

What did you observe about Reagan's mental acuity and his intellect and just his bearing?

Well, he—[pauses]—I would describe him as masterful in the way he operated, politically. One of the first times—well, I had seen him when I worked for Ford. The first time I had been in his presence, we went to his hotel suite in Los Angeles at the Century Plaza. And Ford was there to speak, do a big fund-raiser downstairs. And Reagan was there, and the two of them met. I was the only other person in the room. Big black-tie dinner, and we're looking out over the landscape of Los Angeles at night from the presidential suite at the—I think it was the Century Plaza. And I can remember thinking not about what Reagan said, but just looking at him, his presence, the way he carried himself. The guy *looked* like a president. I mean, he was right out of central casting in terms of the—sort of the physical attributes and appearances. And the two of them sitting there together, talking—but what struck me about the meeting was, you know, this guy was *for real*. And this would have been probably '74, fall or late '74.

In terms of dealing with him, I can remember when, after he had been elected [president in 1980], but this was before the inauguration, he came up to the Hill for a meeting with the congressional leadership, and I was involved; by then I was chairman of the policy committee. But there must have been ten or twelve chairs in a big circle and I think we were in the, maybe in the Senate, behind the lobby there, off the floor, in one of the side rooms. And Tip O'Neill was presiding as sort of the senior man present. And there was an empty chair. Reagan came in, walked around the circle and shook hands with everybody, sat down.

And then Tip started off, and he had a list of items that he wanted to bring up, sort of policy issues: tax policy and budgets and so forth. And he got all through and he turned to Reagan, expecting him to respond to some of his comments and queries. And Reagan didn't answer the question—he told a joke about some Irish movie actor! Broke the place up! But he never did answer the question. But he sort of dominated, and he paid us a significant honor by coming up to our territory to sit down for this first meeting. And his humor was exactly the right touch, in the sense that you weren't going to sit there and hammer out the details of the tax bill in that, sort of that first meeting.

And that speaks to a certain savvy.

Yeah—and understanding of how to work the crowd, in a sense, if you want. I can remember—I think I probably tell the story in the book. This was when we had a battle going over the tax bill, and we'd killed the rule on the tax bill. The president wanted us to pass the bill. The Senate [was] controlled by Republicans, the House controlled by the Democrats. What we had to vote on in the House was the [Dan] Rostenkowski Democrat tax bill, which we didn't like, but the White House wanted it passed. So we sent it over to the Senate, and the Senate Republicans, to clean it up and so forth. But a number of us—myself, [Congressman] Trent Lott, and others—were opposed, didn't want to vote for that House Democrat bill. So we killed the rule. When the rule came up, we killed it. And that created consternation on the part of my friend Jim Baker and [chuckles] some of the others downtown. I think Jim was at Treasury then.

Reagan then decided he wanted to come up and speak to the troops. But before he came up to the meeting there'd been a [military] plane crash up in Newfoundland, flying back from duty in the desert. They had been over in Sinai for a while. And they crashed on landing or takeoff [after takeoff, on December 12, 1985] from Newfoundland, killed everybody on board. And they had a big service for them down at—I think it was

Fort Campbell. And he had gone down that morning, gone to the service, and then he came up to the Hill to talk to the House Republicans. When he came in, though, he didn't say a word about the tax bill. He talked about patriotism and sacrifice and what it meant to be an American and about the troops that we just lost. Finished with all that, he said, "Now, gentlemen," he said, "about that tax bill." That's all he had to say. [Congressman] Henry Hyde jumped to his feet, and he yelled, "I am with you, Mr. President! You can count on me!" And guys are jumping up all over the room. He turned around, I'm guessing, something like seventy votes—just like that. Without ever saying word one about the tax bill except, "Gentleman, about that tax bill."

What does that tell you?

Leadership. Knew what he needed. He didn't get down to the nitty-gritty about what the rate on capital gains was going to be or anything like that. But he knew what he had to say to turn that crowd on. It was totally appropriate. The impact on the audience was amazing and changed enough votes that we brought the bill back to the [House] floor, passed the rule, and did exactly what he wanted us to do. Part of it was stimulated by the assassination attempt. And I always felt the fact of the attempt, so soon after he had been inaugurated, the way he dealt with it, the humor he brought to the case—I remember when they wheeled him into the operating room and he's severely wounded and [a] very, very serious situation, and he tells the doctors he hopes they are all Republicans. Just the way he dealt with that gave him a stature and a status not just with the Republicans and not just with politicians, but with the country. It put him on a level that most presidents would aspire to and most of them never reach. And he was—it made it more—well, it set a tone and created an atmosphere, I felt, both for the country as well as with the Congress that's relatively unique in modern times, in terms of a president being able to lead and to get the country to do difficult things.

You told a television interviewer one time, "Look"—I'm paraphrasing, but pretty faithfully—"I've been in Washington forty years. There have been times when I have been praised when I didn't deserve it and there have been times I have been criticized and I didn't deserve it." With that kind of rough, back-of-the-envelope accounting in mind, is too much credit accorded to Ronald Reagan for the collapse of the Soviet Union, for "winning" the Cold War?

Not in my mind.

What did he do to "win" the Cold War?

Well, he—[pauses]—he did a very clear job of understanding, you know, the good guys and the bad guys. These are our enemy, this is our adversary. Call a spade a spade kind of thing. I think what he did with respect to the defense budget, which was significant. We had economic problems of various kinds, deficit and so forth, but the commitments he made in defense, especially with commitment to Star Wars [the Strategic Defense Initiative], I think there was no question in my mind that the course of action he chose with respect to defense spending placed the Soviets under pressure that they hadn't faced up till that time.

And part of it was based on something that never gets mentioned, but it's true. We had bought, the intelligence community had basically accepted, the Soviet interpretation of their economic data: how well they were performing, how big the economy was, etc. And they had grossly overestimated it, distorted and misrepresented. And what that meant was their economy was really smaller than we thought based on what we were reading about their projections. And that meant that instead of spending 15 percent of their GDP on defense, they were spending 25 or 30 percent. The guy who had done a lot of this analysis worked for me over at the Pentagon. I'm trying to remember his name now. He became the assistant secretary of defense. He worked in the policy area. I'm sure we can dig out his name.[9] He had a belief that the

Soviets were lying about their economy and he was right. And he was proven right in part with this. But I always thought part of what was happening here wasn't just that [Reagan][10] was seeing to it that, you know, we were buying the F-15s and the Abrams tanks and the Bradley infantry fighting vehicles and increasing the defense budget. But we were also doing it at a time when the Soviets, to the extent that they had lied to themselves and everybody else, found it increasingly difficult to match what we were doing. And especially when you started to get into the new technology areas and the space-based missile defense and so forth, where it was, I think, the way he dealt with that, as well as his openness and willingness to deal with a guy like Gorbachev. But we got a confluence of events there that I think he gets some of the credit.

One last question about Reagan. Reagan is always held up by latter-day conservatives and Republicans as an emblem of strength on the world stage. When you were vice president, you would sometimes recite a litany of terrorist incidents that had occurred across the 1980s and 1990s and which the United States had responded to weakly or not at all.

Mm-hmm.

And you argued that that allowed groups like al Qaeda to believe that they could attack America with impunity. And that that in turn accounted for some of the boldness that al Qaeda showed on 9/11.

One of those early events you always cited in the litany was the bombing of our Marine barracks in Beirut by Hezbollah in 1983. And you cite the nonresponse by the United States to that event. Should not that episode, then, color our perceptions of Ronald Reagan as a commander in chief?

Mmmm. I think we were still in the mindset then that a terrorist attack was a law enforcement problem. And partly I recited that litany to show that this was a problem that had been going on for quite some time.

Except that when the discotheque attack occurred [in Berlin in April 1986], Reagan responded with—

In Libya.

—in Libya with jets, and aiming directly at [Muammar] Qaddafi and his family, and that was not a law enforcement response.

Yeah.

So, in other words, doesn't Reagan bear some of the responsibility for the way America allowed terrorism to fester and grow as a problem, since you cite that very instance in the litany? You remember the speech I'm talking about?

Oh, yeah. No, I've cited that example many times, and cited the Marine barracks many times. And it also went along about the same time as Grenada, where we did respond with military force. Yeah, I suppose you could make that argument. I mean—what came out of the Marine barracks bombing by way of policy change really was Goldwater-Nichols.[11]

And also [Bobby Ray] Inman, right? Wasn't the Inman standards[12] for security of overseas facilities? I think that might date to that.

I don't remember the Inman standards. I do remember that the examples of Goldwater-Nichols and Grenada both happened around the same time, where issues that were tried—we tried to address in Goldwater-Nichols. But no, I won't argue with you about that. No. I think, coming back to Reagan again, there was a place where he got into some difficulty, and we talked about this in connection with the Iran-Contra affair. That the NSC apparatus that he had in place in the first term was pretty good. And that's more the staff operation of the White House, [James] Baker in charge of running the operation. By the time you get to the second [term] and you get into Iran-Contra, I think we ended up—over eight years, we had something like seven different national security advisors. I mean, it wasn't well managed and well run. There were internal problems. Part of it [derived from] I suppose the swap, when Jim [Baker] left and [Donald] Regan took over. So there are places where there were—I don't want to portray the Reagan administration as flawless in everything they did. But I think on the big issues that I cared about, I thought they were pretty good. And I always remember, and I've told this story (I think I do in the book, too), after Desert Storm, of calling the president to thank him for what he had done to make possible what we did. I mean, his policies in terms of defense spending and the military and so forth, in the early eighties, made it possible for us to do what we did in '90 and '91 in Kuwait.

You worked closely with both Presidents Bush. What were the most significant differences you observed between them as men and leaders?

Hmm! Well, one, I liked them both. I was grateful for the opportunities they provided. I think of them as very different people. You know, we always talked about [the fact] that 43 was a lot more like his mother in terms of personality and so forth, with a quick wit and a sharp tongue on occasion. That politically, in some respects, he was more successful because he got reelected. That, uh—[pauses]—they were different obviously, they came with very different backgrounds in the sense of their political experience.

Military experience.

Yeah, but 43 arrived as a successful two-term governor of one of our biggest states. Heavy emphasis on the domestic side of the ledger. And from my standpoint, in part, that's why he wanted me—because I brought my own background and experience on the international side. His dad, on the other hand, came with, you know, all the credentials of a guy who had been a naval aviator in World War II and director of the CIA and ambassador to the United Nations and ambassador to China, member of the House and so forth. So totally different backgrounds in terms of how they arrived at the—

Did you find one easier to work with than the other?

Uh—you know, the experiences were so different.

Being sec-def [secretary of defense] versus being vice president.

Yeah. And there were other differences, too. I always thought the national security team we had under 41 was especially effective. With Baker and [National Security Advisor Brent] Scowcroft, as well as the president, obviously, myself, [Chairman of the Joint Chiefs of Staff General Colin] Powell; it was a group that worked well together. That wasn't as smooth an operation by the time you get to 43. But again, my perspective on it was different, because in one case I'm the secretary of defense and the other I'm vice president. You know, everybody always wants to compare across administrations. Political side, I spent a lot of time on exactly those types of questions. After you have been there and spent the time at it and worked in the different circumstances that I did, you find what strikes you is the differences, not the similarities.

In an oral history that was released recently, you were quoted as wondering whether George Herbert Walker Bush "had the balls" to call up the reserves for the first Gulf War. Why were you in doubt about that?

That was one of the issues that was important, as we got into Desert Storm, because [of] the legacy of Vietnam. And the Defense Department in those days—this would have been back in 1990—most of your senior officers had gotten their start back during the Vietnam period, and there was a culture, a set of beliefs, that the politicians had blown Vietnam, not the military. And to some extent it was true. And it was a willingness in terms of operating on the basis that we are going to deploy as units and come home as units. We are not having individual replacements in and out of units deployed to the field. That we're going to send a force large enough at the very outset to win. Give them the whole load right away. We were going to call up the reserves, and [Lyndon] Johnson had always been reluctant to do that. There was a set of propositions like that that we consciously handled in a different fashion. The stop-loss order, you know—nobody is going out until we finish the job. Those were important questions that needed to be answered from the standpoint of the department, and 41 answered every single one of them in the affirmative.

Okay, to your relationship with George W. Bush. The account goes that you famously told Dan Quayle, "I have a different understanding with the president" about the role that you would play as vice president.

Mm-hmm.

And when Quayle asked you, "Did you get that directly from Bush?" your answer consisted directly of the word "yes." Where and when, exactly, did you and George W. Bush hash out this understanding of the role you would play?

Oh, you know, it had grown over time. I can't say, well, let's see, at two o'clock on the fourteenth of March. No, it didn't work out that way at all. What had happened, in effect, was he had asked me to help him find somebody to be vice president. And walking through that process over a period of months, talking about various individuals and the traits and attributes he was interested in and what he needed, I developed an understanding of what he was looking for. And when we got through that whole process he concluded by saying, "You're the solution to my problem." And I think it's through that process, it would be more appropriate than saying there was one particular point in time when he said A, B, C, and D.

In other words, there is one account that quotes him as having said at a certain point, "Dick is going to have the intelligence portfolio." Was there ever a conversation between you, prior to Inauguration Day, where the two of you sort of laid out what large areas that you would tackle as vice president and how your authority would be structured?

You're overthinking it. You really are. It was the kind of situation where he wanted me because of my background in national security: secretary of defense, intelligence, on the [House] Intelligence Committee, in charge of a big chunk of the intelligence community *as* secretary of defense, and so forth. I mean, you go through all that litany of credentials and we began at the very beginning of the process. You know, he's the one who sent me to Washington to start working on the transition, in terms of recruiting candidates for it. He obviously had firm ideas of what he wanted to do in some areas. But we talked about functions and so forth. There, from my perspective, one of the things I wanted to do, and told him I planned to do, with his approval, obviously, was as soon as I could I wanted to dig back into the intelligence community—because I had been out of the loop for eight years. And so I spent those early weeks visiting the Defense Intelligence Agency, National Security Agency, the Central Intelligence Agency, etc. Went through all of them, visited all of them, got to know the top leadership in all of them, spoke to groups of their employees, spent an awful lot of time getting back up to speed on intelligence at the outset of our time in office. That's partly what he wanted me to do.

One of the distinct features of your vice presidency was that some of your aides in the vice president's office held dual hats, whereby they were also part of the president's staff. Was that something for which you needed to seek his approval in advance?

Of course. One of the things I was concerned about [was] I had seen other relationships between presidents and vice presidents not work out. And usually that started at the staff level, not at the principals' level. Jerry Ford always got along great with Nelson Rockefeller. But obviously, in the end, Rockefeller had to go, and it didn't go as smoothly as had been hoped. What I wanted to do was, if we could have some dual-hatting of certain people: Scooter Libby, for example, was one, who had both a commission from me and from the president. Mary Matalin, same thing. Dave Addington used to meet every morning at the outset with the entire legal staff. Oh, the congressional relations shop, lots of times, was run by people who had worked for me before they worked for the president. Everything we could do to tie the staffs together would strengthen the operation. That, plus the fact that I wasn't running for president myself. I didn't aspire to the job, I didn't have my own agenda. There was only one agenda, and that was the president's. All of those kinds of things were important in terms of melding together the two operations. And I was going to be more successful as vice president, in doing what he wanted to have done and what I wanted to do, if in fact we did that. And so those kinds of dual-hatting arrangements were part and parcel of that.

STEEN: McConnell was one. Weren't you, John?

Is that right?

Yeah, John did both.

McCONNELL: Yeah.

In the first term, did Vice President Cheney ever approach the business of presidential decision making in ways that Chief of Staff Dick Cheney would have regarded as unacceptable, in terms of the proper flow of paper and ideas to the president?

Why don't we save that for—till tomorrow? Let me, let me think about it.

Okay.

DAY TWO

All right. Today is December 2, 2014. We are back in the vice president's study, and thank you again for your time. We closed out yesterday discussing your relationship with Bush 43, and we'll deal with some of the signal events of this tremendously consequential presidency in tomorrow's session. But I did want to conclude our discussion of presidents you have known by addressing certain aspects of the relationship that I think are important and [by] getting your take on a lot of what has been said and written about it.

And I start with a question about your working habits. In the literature of the Bush-Cheney era, we are continually reading about alternately passionate, angry, detailed, lengthy memos that Don Rumsfeld or Colin Powell or Condoleezza Rice or Steve Hadley sent to the president, or this recipient or that recipient, or this or that set of recipients. Conversely, we *never* seem to read of a memo that Vice President Cheney sent to anyone. Were you not in the habit of sending memos?

DICK CHENEY: That's correct. [chuckles] I was not in the habit of sending memos. What I would do frequently, in terms of helping me work through a problem or think about it, was sit down and make notes to myself, kind of thing. It wasn't anything I would send to somebody. But I can remember, oh, the night of 9/11, when Lynne and I had been evacuated—and Liz and the family—evacuated to Camp David. And they put us in Aspen Lodge, the president's lodge, because that was the most secure [location] and at that point Secret Service didn't know how extensive the attack might be. But sitting up most of the night watching the reruns on television of what had happened that day, of the towers coming down, and writing notes to myself as I thought through the process of: What does this mean in terms of policy? And: How do we find out who did this? And notions such as: We're going to hold accountable not just the terrorists but those who sponsor terror or provide sanctuary and safe harbor for terror, what came to be called the Bush Doctrine. So I would do that sort of thing or be on a trip—I can remember coming back, I think it was—well, first of all, on the way to the Gulf back in '90, when I was going over to see [Saudi] King Fahd and [Egyptian President Hosni] Mubarak about deploying troops, writing out what I wanted to say, what the important message was and so forth.

I did *not* write memos and send [them] to people, as a general proposition. If you go to the Ford library, up in Ann Arbor, I don't know whether you've ever been up there and looked in my file; it's a *very* thin file. Part of that was because that was the Watergate era. And as I was taking over and operating and functioning as the deputy and then the number one [chief of staff] in the White House, all kinds of bad things were happening because of recordings of conversations in the Oval Office and memos that had been written and so forth. So I sort of began my career operating at that level, very leery of writing extensive memos. I didn't keep a lot of notes. I suppose maybe history suffers because of that. On the other hand, it was just my style of operation. And I would refrain from expressing myself in words on paper most of the time. There were probably a few exceptions to that. But generally I did not write long, extensive memos.

There's a saying: "Make love by paper, make war by phone."

[chuckles] Well, there's another saying that [House Speaker] Sam Rayburn had, which was: "You never get in trouble for what you don't say." And I was always very much aware of that.

So how large a body of official papers did you leave behind as vice president?

Well, there's a considerable body just because of the flow of all of the stuff I got and the memos that would come to me. But I would work—we had a session on domestic policy for a while. Neil Patel was in charge of that piece of the business. He would come in probably once a week and bring the four or five key people that were working the various policy issues. We'd sit and discuss, and I'd talk and express myself. They'd brief me. There probably were papers prepared in advance. But in terms of my actually producing, you know, a decision memo, that wasn't the way I would work. I'd tell 'em what I wanted to do. But the papers are pretty extensive. Jim [Steen] spent a lot of time on them over the years. I've got papers—my congressional papers are basically at the University of Wyoming, at the archives, the library there. I've got papers at the Ford facility up in Ann Arbor. [Materials from the] Ford [era are] split between University of Michigan and Grand Rapids Museum. I've got papers down at College Station [in Texas] that relate to my time as secretary of defense.

Why there?

Because that's where the Bush 41 library is.

Okay.

And all of those, especially the classified stuff, all that. Those purple binders up there on the second shelf [in Cheney's study], those are all of the speeches and press interviews that I did during my four years as secretary of defense. But there's also—

Proclamations and sort of the public papers of the—

Public papers. I'm sure I used to do regular memos for 41. One of the ways he liked to operate was to receive a memo about once a week on just what's going on with the department. So there are a fair amount of papers there, but they are scattered. My vice presidential papers at this point are at the National Archives here in town. That's the place where they had to go when we left office; there wasn't any other alternative. I'm told there's space for them down at the Bush library at SMU [Southern Methodist University in Dallas]. I haven't decided where I am going to put 'em yet; that's an option. Or another option is to leave 'em at the National Archives. They are interested up here in Washington or possibly the Library of Congress. So I just haven't decided where they will go eventually.

Again, returning to your relationship with President Bush—

Which Bush?

Bush 43; these are all Bush 43. Is it true that you would review, and sometimes have amendments made to, the President's Daily Brief each morning before the president himself would read it?

Mmm, I wouldn't put it in those terms. I always saw it in advance. That was just because of the way the clock worked. When I got up in the morning, I would be visited at the vice president's residence by my CIA briefer. And I had a—evolution over time. I probably had four or five CIA briefers over the eight years. But they would come and they would bring the PDB, the same thing that was going to the president.

Now right away, right there—was that typical for the vice president of the United States to see the president's PDB?

I don't know. It's the way *we* worked.

Was there ever a discussion between you and George W. Bush about that—that "I want you in on the PDB"?

Well, he obviously did. I can't remember a discussion about it. What we did was, I would get the brief at home in the morning and then it always had a tab. And behind the tab were things I was personally interested in, whereas the PDB was coming up from the [intelligence] community—from the [Central Intelligence] Agency, primarily—and might well have stuff in it that the president had asked about. Behind the tab were things that *I* had asked about, or things they knew I had a continued interest in. I had more time to spend on that subject than he did. You know, he's having to pardon a turkey at Thanksgiving and a lot of ceremonial duties [chuckles] and responsibilities. I don't mean to [chuckles] diminish the post at all, but I was able to spend as much time as I wanted on, especially on intelligence, and it was a special area for me. And so we developed this habit of "in front of the tab" and "behind the tab," and occasionally I would see a piece that had been done for me or that I had asked about, that would come in and have something I thought especially significant in it that I thought the president ought to see. And then I would recommend that that ought to go into the president's brief or it ought to be presented to him. I don't recall I ever recommended taking something *out*. You know, occasionally, I think Condi occasionally would take things out in her capacity as NSC advisor.

Do you know why?

I don't. I mean, just her judgment on her part. She may have known about something else that was going on that wasn't conveyed in that or had had reasons of her own to modify that.

So in other words, she also saw the PDB before he would?

I assume she did, yeah; I'm *sure* she did. But then we'd end up in the Oval Office, he and I would, usually with the national security advisor and the CIA briefer. He had briefers assigned to him as well, too. And certainly, in the first term, also George Tenet, the director of the [Central Intelligence] Agency, was there. This is all before we reorganized after 9/11 and so forth and created Homeland Security and rearranged all those things. But our mornings always began with he and I sitting side by side in front of the fireplace. National security advisor over on the couch to the left, originally Condi, later on Steve [Hadley]. And on the right-hand couch, as I looked at it, would be the briefer and Tenet. Now, that changed and evolved over time, and the second term we did more in-depth stuff, in terms of—

Threat matrix?

—bringing in analysts, for example, who weren't ordinarily part of briefing the president but were experts in a particular area and we wanted that covered. The community wanted to bring that to the president. The role of the CIA director was diminished to some extent after we reorganized and created the new director of national intelligence post and so forth. So there were those kinds of changes. But every day— *nearly* every day, there were exceptions, but even when I was on the road—I would carry—I can remember carrying with me to south Texas on a quail hunt a battery solar-powered station that linked up to a satellite, secure, that would produce for me and my quarters, wherever they might be, a connection back to the Sit[uation] Room in the White House. And the president would go down to the Sit Room on those days, and he'd have the usual collection of people there, and I would participate in going through the PD Brief even though I might be in California or someplace else. Overseas it was a little harder to do.

I always had a briefer with me wherever I went. I can remember fishing at the south fork of the Snake [River], along the Wyoming-Idaho border, doing an overnight in the canyon there, and my briefer would come down in the morning about six a.m., with the next shift of Secret Service agents, and he would have my morning brief with me. And I wasn't plugged in at that point. The president—we weren't doing it jointly, but I would be going through my daily brief just as he was, even though I'm sitting on the back of the south fork of the Snake, getting ready to go fishing; so it was something we pretty religiously stuck to. Exceptions would be when he was out of town: I'd still receive the brief but we didn't meet *together* on the brief. And that's how we started every day. In the first term, when Scooter [Libby] was still with us, he took the morning brief at my house with me most of the time. He didn't go into the meeting with the president, but he was aware of [the substance], and had the necessary clearances and so forth, and he would receive the brief usually with me at the house before we went to work in the morning.

To finish this: Do you regard that President Bush *understood* that you had already seen or received this PDB each morning before he did? In other words, when you would sit in with him in the Oval, that "Dick has already seen this," did you think he understood that?

Oh, I'm sure he did, yeah; nothing secretive about it.

Okay.

The thing that I've found—well, I asked a lot more questions but partly [because] I had the *time* to ask more questions, and I had the background to do it. And he asked a lot of questions, too. I mean, he was very much an active participant in the briefing process. And I read about Barack Obama, who doesn't read the morning brief, or there was always the joke about Bill Clinton, when the plane crashed into the White House [in September 1994]—some guy stole or hijacked a Piper Cub and flew it in—and the joke was, that was the CIA director trying to get in to brief the president. Not all presidents displayed that much interest in the intelligence material. George Bush was an *avid* consumer of the product. It was a very important part of his day, and [he] asked a lot of questions and generated a lot of the [paper] flow by the nature of the questions he asked.

And that mitigates against the caricature of him as intellectually incurious, right?

Absolutely. It's just totally not true.

This is the question that we ended on yesterday: namely, whether in the first term Vice President Cheney worked to shape presidential decisions in ways that Chief of Staff Dick Cheney would have regarded as unacceptable in terms of the proper flow of paper to the president. You said you wanted to think about it.

Yeah. Again, I come back to this proposition: presidents are very different in terms of their personalities, their experiences, what they like, the way they like to operate, who they like to deal with. The circumstances under which they govern are very different, too. I mean, Katrina hits, the president is going to be spending a hell of a lot of time on Hurricane Katrina and the aftermath in New Orleans and so forth. You get 9/11, and that's going to shift your whole focus there. So when you say, did I do things differently as vice president than I would have recommended or accepted as chief of staff, you can't really sort of dig down into that without saying, well, this is how Ford worked, this is how Bush worked, this is what he was interested [in], these are the issues we had to deal with. It's a different world. It's also a different perspective. I think I probably benefited, and had more influence and ability to operate as vice president, because I had been chief of staff. My chief of staff experience was important in my thinking about how to operate as vice president in terms of avoiding some of the pitfalls, some of the ways that relationship I'd seen damaged over the years. Jerry Ford never tired of telling me how much he hated the job as vice president. I'd watched Nelson Rockefeller himself, who was reputed once to have said the only way he'd be vice president in the second term was if he could also be chief of staff.

[laughs]

It's a true story, supposedly. I think it's in the new book on Rockefeller, the biography.[1] I'd never seen anybody really happy in the post, and all of that thinking had dominated my response the first time the idea came up: Would I agree to be considered to be vice president?

So the things I did as vice president and the way I operated I think were certainly significantly influenced [by] what I had seen and experienced as chief of staff in my own right. And you know, that led to certain decisions. One, I wasn't going to run for president in my own right. And the president *knew* that when he picked me. I had looked at running for president back in the early nineties, and I had decided *not* to do it. Nothing had ever changed. Now that was very important. I wasn't making decisions or offering advice based upon how it was going to affect my fate in the Iowa caucuses four years hence. And it's important to emphasize that, because I think most vice presidents, when they find themselves in those positions, that's really the only reason that they are there, is the hope it'll give them a leg up on the nomination, and that was never an issue for me—and the president knew that.

There was the whole question of integrating the staffs, to the extent possible. I talked about that yesterday. John McConnell came to me from the president's speechwriting staff. He did and oversaw virtually all of my operation, but also, at the same time, he was an integral part of the presidential speechwriting staff. Things like that helped enormously. [David] Addington's role as my counsel and [White House Counsel] Al Gonzales's office, working with the president's counsels. Very close working relationships with congressional relations, etc. All of those things were designed in part to minimize the extent to which there was friction that would develop between the staffs. Participation in various meetings and so forth.

Andy Card [White House chief of staff 2001–2006] and I were very close. We'd known each other a long time. And there wasn't virtually anything Andy and I couldn't talk about. The relationship between the chief of staff and the vice president in the Rockefeller era, you know, I was—oh, just one indicator of how rocky that was [chuckles]: The official residence of the vice president, it didn't exist before Ford. When Ford became vice president, his buddies on the Hill were determined to get him official quarters, and they ended up getting the [chief of naval operations'] quarters over at the [Naval] Observatory on Massachusetts Avenue. Ford never lived there because before he could move in, he moved to the White House when Nixon resigned. So that meant that the first occupant, if you will, of the VPR as vice president was Nelson Rockefeller. Nelson never lived there because he had a bigger house down on Foxhall Road—you know, his own personal digs. But he used the vice president's residence to entertain, and when he got it into the shape that he wanted, he had a series of parties for the Congress and the press and the Executive Branch and the cabinet and so forth, just about everybody in town who was anybody—except me. I never got [chuckles] invited to the vice president's residence till Walter Mondale was vice president in the Carter years.

So I was sensitive to those relationships, and the relationship I thought that I had with Andy Card—and I think Andy would say the same thing—was a very close one. We worked together, we knew each other, we had been involved back in the first Bush administration. And our ability to talk freely with one another, and our offices right next to each other, was instrumental in shaping how my office—and me, personally—worked and operated with the presidential staff. That doesn't mean there weren't points of friction between staffs—probably more with the communicators than on the presidential staff. But it was a deliberate effort on my part, and I think supported by the president and by Andy, that we were going, to the extent we could, to avoid the kind of frictions in the past that had really damaged the working relationship between presidents and vice presidents. So that's the way I think of that first experience as chief of staff influencing how I functioned as the vice president.

Were there occasions where you as vice president brought paper, or were responsible for paper being brought, to Bush that bypassed the normal systems and the staff secretary and so forth?

Yes.

That's what I was getting at when I asked if Vice President Cheney ever approached the business of presidential decision making in ways that Chief of Staff Cheney would have found unacceptable. And so can you explain what would have been the criteria for you to do that?

Well, to every rule there's an exception. [laughs] And there was one in particular, as I recall. [pauses] Well, in the early days after 9/11, I would end up trying to deal with the problems that people had brought to me. For example: this whole question of the Terrorist Surveillance Program. That evolved out of a meeting I had with Mike Hayden, who was at the NSA, and Tenet, who was at CIA. We talked about whether or not there were additional things we could do with the NSA capability if Mike had more authority, more presidential authority, to operate. And he came back and said yes, indeed, there were, and I took, as I recall, Tenet and Hayden in to see the president. And we got his approval for what we wanted to do. He gave us some very explicit instruction about safeguards and he wanted to be in the loop. He wanted to personally approve the extension of the program every thirty or forty-five days. But I pushed hard to get that approved early on and to get that program up and running. Now, you know, eventually everybody else—well, not everybody else; a few other people were involved and knowledgeable about it. Condi would have been knowledgeable about it, but it didn't come up through her. Rumsfeld was knowledgeable about it. We wanted the attorney general to sign off on it before the president would approve the extension, Rumsfeld to sign off on it. They had to approve it each time before it got reauthorized. [The] CIA director and Hayden obviously both had to sign off on it, too. Dave Addington in my office was the keeper of the documents—and that was, I suppose you could say, out of the ordinary. But on the other hand, Dave was a CIA-trained attorney. He'd spent a lot of time on, and in, the intelligence business. He was the guy who kept the documents in his safe and every thirty to forty-five days would get them circulated, authorized, and signed off on by the right people and then get them to the president. And Andy would be involved in that process. So a unique kind of an arrangement was set up. Part of it was because of the sensitivity of the program: We couldn't read anybody into that program without the president's personal approval.

So that was different, I suppose, than the way we would have operated back in the Ford days. In those days, Kissinger would have dealt directly with the president—but that was a different time and a different set of circumstances as well, too. And I didn't see it as violating, you know, good procedure; I did see it as a unique kind of arrangement that recognized the extreme sensitivity of what we were doing but also the importance that we could get it done fast. We didn't have six months to sit around and argue through the bureaucracy about who's going to do what to whom. We had a major problem; we expected a follow-on attack. We'd just been hit and lost three thousand people. And we had, we felt, the capacity to act, and then I saw myself as being in a position, because of my background and experience and the confidence the president had placed in me, is that I could grab it and run with it and make sure everybody was heading in the right direction and get presidential sign-off. And—so that's the way I functioned. But Andy knew what I was doing.

Another example that I am sure you are familiar with—and which is pre-9/11—is the Kyoto letter [a letter President Bush sent to U.S. lawmakers in March 2001, drafted by Cheney's office and presented to the president for signature directly by Cheney, announcing the administration's intention to withdraw from international environmental protocols reached in 1997].

Kyoto letter? Oh this was on the—the Kyoto agreement on the [imposition] of carbon caps, yeah.

And the letter that went to some members on the Hill.

Yeah.

And the way it's written is that you personally took this to the president, had him sign it—*asked* him to sign it—he signed it, and this was before the EPA [Environmental Protection Agency] administrator knew about it.

Mm-hmm.

And this is cited as another example of Vice President Cheney—

Short-circuiting the system.

If you will.

Yeah. I did.

Now, there was no exigent circumstance there in the same sense as we can readily discern in an event like 9/11.

Well, I don't remember all the specific details, but there was *some* degree of time [sensitivity] on this involved in it, in terms of getting a response [from the president]. I can't remember exactly how the sequence went, but getting a response to senators who had written a letter to the president asking for clarification.

Right.

And the issue was whether or not—I'm trying to think how it worked. Now, he had made a statement—

In the [2000 presidential] campaign.

—in the campaign. Was it about carbon dioxide?

It was about carbon caps, I think.

Carbon caps—about whether or not it was a pollutant, as I recall.

In essence, this involved him walking back a campaign pledge.

Right.

And there *was* some time sensitivity to it.

And I thought it was important to walk that back. He did not disagree with that. It wasn't a tough sell. It was timely, and I did step in and use my access to get that done.

Is it fair to say, as the consensus in the literature records, that your influence on Bush's decision making waned in the second term?

"Waned in the second term." Well, the second—it changed, obviously. The second term, by then he's a much more experienced hand. In the first term, 9/11 and the early months of the administration, he's still feeling his way, in terms of getting comfortable with what we are dealing with and so forth. By the second term, you know, he's a much more experienced hand. He's got all of those years behind him of dealing with problems. He's got relationships that he's developed not only within the government but with respect to other governments. And the way I think of it is, he was more *confident* of what he wanted to do and how he wanted to do it. I didn't win all the arguments. I didn't win all the arguments on things like oh, bombing the North Korean–built Syrian reactor. I had strong feelings about that. I still think it was the right thing to do. I lost that argument. The president made the decision, but, you know, I don't find that surprising. That's exactly what I would have expected.

The Six-Party Talks [multilateral negotiations held with North Korea, aimed at persuading that country to dismantle its nuclear programs] was another area—a related area.

Well, the Six-Party Talks, as long as they were six-party talks, were consistent with decisions he'd made early on about how we were going to try to get China involved in North Korea. What happened was, the State Department totally circumvented the process on [the] Six-Party Talks. And we could spend—I don't know whether you want to do it right now or not, you can spend a lot of time on the question of North

Korea and the North Korean–built Syrian reactor and North Korean nukes proliferation.

The sets of challenges they presented are complex, I understand.

Yeah, I write about it pretty extensively in my book. But things changed a fair amount. Of course, we changed cabinets, pretty extensive change in the cabinets. Hadley was in as NSC advisor and Condi was over at State by then. So it was different, and you know, did I have less influence? Probably had less influence in the second term than I had in the first.

And so here is the question that is raised for me. The question is why greater experience and confidence on the part of George W. Bush, rather than *cementing* his faith in your counsel, should have led him to *reject* your counsel more frequently. Why do you suppose that was?

I didn't see it as rejecting my counsel.

Well, if he chooses the option advocated by this advisor and not the option advocated by you, that is in some sense a rejection of [your] counsel.

Well, I didn't *think* of it in those terms. I mean, he never guaranteed me that he was going to always do what I wanted him to do.

[laughs]

I always was free to dig into whatever I wanted to dig into, basically, to offer up any advice that I wanted to offer up. If you go back to the Syrian reactor example, we were in a situation where we—well, questions had been raised. *I* had raised questions myself, when we received briefings that suggested that a senior North Korean official associated with the nuclear program was traveling to Damascus on a regular basis. And on more than one occasion I questioned that: "What's going on here?" And what would come back was: "There's no evidence of any cooperation between the North Koreans and the Syrians on nuclear matters." That was sort of the standard pat response that came back. At one point we had a report that in a case of—over a period of—and the numbers are [unreliable here]—that over a period of [something like] eighteen months, this guy had made [something like] seven trips.

Something like that.

Yeah. And I can remember asking if he had a girlfriend in Damascus. I mean, why the hell is he *doin'* it?

[laughs]

We came to find out, thanks to the Israelis some months later, that in fact the North Koreans had built a nuclear reactor for the Syrians in the Syrian desert at Al Kibar. This guy was in charge of that program. He was also part of the Six-Party Talks, representing North Korea, about getting rid of their nuclear program. The way *we* found out about it was Meir Dagan showed up—the head of the Israeli Mossad—with pictures. And he met with Steve [Hadley] and I; we sat down in Steve's office. He wanted to see the president. He had to settle for Hadley and Cheney.

[laughs]

But [Dagan was] showing color photographs taken *inside the reactor* that the North Koreans had built.

Not just aerial.

No—*inside the reactor*! I mean, it was not [laughs]—it was about as solid, guaranteed, valid intelligence as you're ever going to see. And that led, of course, to discussions about how we were going to deal with it. The Israelis, having brought it to us, we dug into it and were able to verify a lot of what they'd provided. But the Israelis basically wanted us to take it out. They obviously didn't want it to go hot; the fuel hadn't been loaded into it yet. I felt strongly that *we* should take it out. And that's what the Israelis wanted. I didn't feel that way *because* the Israelis wanted that, but it reinforced my notion. I think they were—they definitely wanted to get rid of it. I think they were concerned that if they did it, it was more likely to result in a broader conflict, whereas if the United States did it—and certainly, at that point, we had a major presence in the region— that it was less likely to precipitate their questions.

So we had the debate internally; the debate was well handled. Hadley basically ran the debate, the NSC. We had a couple of opportunities that I made my case to the president. We ended up in a meeting in the upstairs oval office—not Oval Office, but it's a big living room on the second floor [the Yellow Oval Room]. And basically, the National Security Council and staff were there. And I made my pitch that this was something that had to be done, that proliferation of nuclear weapons was one of our biggest concerns, especially [by] the terror-sponsoring states. The president had made a statement when the North Koreans first tested [a nuclear device], back in [October] '06, that a red line was proliferation to any terrorist-sponsoring state, and this was exactly a case of that. At the time they tested, they had also been building this reactor for the [Syrians]. And [I argued] that we could send a very strong signal if we'd take it out, that it was a very straightforward operation from a military standpoint, and that I thought it was a great opportunity. When I got through, the president asked if anybody else agreed with the vice president. And nobody did; I was the only one who was advocating this course of action. And that's when he opted to go to the United Nations, which is what the State Department was recommending. I was confident there was no way the Israelis were going to turn the matter over to the United Nations. When they called [Ehud] Olmert, who was then the [Israeli] prime minister, then said that's what he wanted to do, the Israelis said, "Thanks, but no thanks," and took it out themselves—which was the right answer.

But we missed a golden opportunity. And it also, the way we had managed it, it created problems in the sense that the North Koreans were never held to account for what they had done. We ended up, later on in '07 and '08, lifting the designation of North Korea as a—the sanctions that had [been] imposed on them as a terror-sponsoring state.

They were delisted.

Delisted. I thought that was a big mistake. We also—the Syrians paid no price for it at all. That was partly because State was trying to do what State *always* does: leave a legacy of peace in the Middle East, to try to have a conference of which the Israelis and the Arabs and the Palestinians come together and solve the age-old conflict. This was going to be the conference at Annapolis, and—

I was there.

You were there at the conference? [chuckles] Condi was trying very hard to get the Syrians to send a delegation and therefore didn't want to call them out on having built [a] North Korean–built, –designed nuclear reactor. You know, I thought it was badly handled, still do today; I devoted a chapter in my book to it. I had my chance to make my pitch. I never felt that somehow I had made a mistake. I thought I was doing what exactly I should be doing. I think we made a mistake as an administration when we didn't take it out. I think we were lucky that the Israelis did, because later on, obviously, ISIS controls the territory where the nuclear reactor was. Fortunately, the Israelis had taken it out before that happened.

And there was no wider conflict.

Right.

Was it your observation that George W. Bush was more sensitive to public opinion in the second term? How do you assess the change in his decision making? Not just with respect to the Syrian reactor but in general: on the Six-Party Talks, or a lot of different things.

I'd rather focus on specifics, rather than some sort of generic assessment. The specifics in this case. To some extent, he had taken a *lot* of flak—incoming, if you will—with respect to Iraq and operations in Iraq. At this point, we were in the early stages of the surge. There had been a period of time, even in the run-up on the surge, where he had authorized some contingency planning, if you will. Especially, [the] communicators were interested in doing that. This is during the period of time, it would have been spring, when efforts were underway. Occasionally, there would be a leak out of the White House that we were looking at "Plan B," sort of in the offhand chance that the surge doesn't work. And some of that he had instigated himself. There was another thread that ran through some of this, and that was on intelligence itself. And one of the arguments that was made by those who disagreed with the notion that we should go strike the Syrian reactor—I think [Defense Secretary Robert] Gates made it, Condi may have shared in it, too—was, "Look, the intelligence we've got on Iraq WMD was flawed; how do we know this wasn't flawed, too?"

Which is a kind of a crippling doubt to entertain.

Well, yeah. But it shows to some extent sort of the legacy, the lasting effect inside the bureaucracy and among key policymakers, of that earlier failure, if you will, with respect to the intelligence community and WMD in Iraq. People had been snakebit. I always thought about it a bit, and an example when it *didn't* have that kind of problem, didn't have that lasting impact, where it was handled differently, and that was with respect to Pearl Harbor and Midway. I mean, our intelligence folks never picked up on the attack on Pearl Harbor. Six months later, [Admiral Chester W.] Nimitz gets intelligence that the Japanese fleet is steaming for Midway, and he bets the farm that it's good intelligence. Sends our only three carriers out there, sinks four Japanese carriers, changes the course of [the] war in the Pacific. He didn't let that earlier intelligence failure influence his judgment about the latest—

And you think Bush was susceptible to this?

I didn't say Bush made the argument; I said staff made the argument.

Well, I'm asking.

Or cabinet members. The president made the decision he made; it's what he wanted to do; he was comfortable with it. And I still think that one of the biggest threats we face to this day is the development of nuclear weapons in the hands of terrorists or terrorist-sponsoring states, that we did a good job when we took down Saddam [Hussein] because we put him out of business for that. You can argue about whether or not he had a stockpile. We knew he had twice previously tried to produce nuclear materials: the Israelis hit him in '81 [in air strikes targeting Iraqi nuclear facilities at Osirak]; we hit him in '91 [in the Gulf War]. But whatever else you can say about that operation, Saddam was no longer in business. When we took down Saddam, Muammar Qaddafi got religion. Five days after we captured Saddam, he [Qaddafi] announced that he was going to surrender his [WMD] materials—and he did. The centrifuges, the uranium feedstock, the weapons design. That led us, in turn, to take down A. Q. Khan, the black marketeer who was supplying the Libyans; they were his best customer. And so, you know, we made some significant progress against the problem of proliferation. But here was a case where we could have, you know, driven another nail in the coffin and made it very, very clear that that was one of our top priorities, that we were prepared to use military force to stop proliferation, and we were prepared to send a very strong signal to the Iranians. The only time the Iranians stopped, and had a pause in their nuclear program, was when we took down Saddam Hussein. They quit, for a period of months, activities with respect to their nuclear program. So I think we, we were not as good as we should have been if we had adopted the course that I had advocated; but I was alone at that point in the operation. The Israelis agreed with me, but in the end the president made the decision not to do it. That was his call.

I've only got a few more questions about your relationship with Bush and we'll move on. Peter Baker wrote in *Days of Fire* [*Days of Fire: Bush and Cheney in the White House* (2013)] that by the fall of 2006 the relationship between you and President Bush "had grown strained." True?

No, I wouldn't consider it strained at all. Um—[pauses]—when it got strained, obviously, was towards the very end, with respect to [Bush's refusal, in early 2007, to issue a full pardon for Cheney's convicted former aide] Scooter Libby. No, in '06, no, we were pretty much—we were in sync, for example, on the surge. That was a period of time when we were reassessing our strategy [in Iraq]. This was the period of time when he decided to replace Rumsfeld. There had been a debate about that earlier, and I had argued against it. This time around, he informed me. It was clear he wasn't seeking my advice; he had made a decision. And Don had come to me in the spring of '06 and made it clear that he was perfectly prepared to step aside, that he knew, recognized he was carrying a lot of baggage, and if there was ever any point at which it was deemed a wise move or that it would help the president and so forth, he was perfectly happy to step down. That was several months before.

Then the president made the decision right around the time of the '06 election. Then he asked me if I wanted to be the one to deliver the word to Don, and I said, "Yes, I would," which I did. And I mean, there's no—it was a very smooth [transition]—it was what Rumsfeld understood was going to happen, and he was a real trooper about it. That, you know, was a point that the president sought. I don't think that our relationship was strained at all by that. It was a legitimate decision by the president. It might have been different than the one I would have made, but it was—there were occasions when I was asked to take on those kinds of assignments: [another was the request for the resignation of Treasury Secretary] Paul O'Neill. And so I think that continued to function.

If I may venture a hypothesis here—

Sure.

If there was a rift, I see it developing prior to the Libby issue. I would identify this clash with the Department of Justice, over the reauthorization of the NSA programs in March of '04, that culminates in the dramatic and famous and much-discussed hospital room visit [with ailing Attorney General John Ashcroft]. After that episode had passed, after the president had effectively acceded to [Deputy Attorney General James] Comey and [FBI director Robert] Mueller's demands and amended his March 11 order, did he ever discuss that episode with you?

No. I mean, I was aware of it when he met with them. I was in the—we had done a morning brief at the Oval, and then he met with, I guess it was Comey right afterwards, separately, where Comey told him that there was consternation over in the Justice Department. But that was the first I'd heard of it. I mean, I didn't learn about problems in the Justice [Department] any earlier than he did.

I ask because in *Decision Points* (2010), the president wrote of that episode that he "made clear to my advisors that I never wanted to be blindsided like that again." Did he ever convey that sentiment to you?

No. No, and I think, in fairness to him, was I look at what transpired and—and I am trying to remember the exact sequence. Part of being "blindsided" was he had no idea that Ashcroft was no longer active as attorney general, that he had turned over his authority, delegated all of it, to Comey, which was a total surprise to everybody in the White House. The president didn't know about it; I didn't know about it; Andy Card didn't know about it. It wasn't a subject, as far as I know, that anybody in the White House was aware of until Andy went over—Addington was there, carrying the papers, and Gonzales was along, too, Al Gonzales—went to Ashcroft's hospital room, and Ashcroft, who had previously signed some twenty times for the extension of this program, all of a sudden switched, and took himself out of the loop, said that he'd delegated his authority to Comey. And I wasn't present in the meeting at the hospital, but that was, in terms of someone being blindsided, that's what I took to mean, that was really *being* blindsided: The attorney general who's signed up for this program twenty times all of a sudden decides he is not going to do it anymore, and turns it over to Comey, who was—that was the one that was especially troublesome.

We are going to talk more about Iraq in tomorrow's session. But since we just were on the subject, I figured I might close out this area by asking about that period when the administration was debating a surge. And it has been suggested that you were less forceful than you might ordinarily have been in advocating for a surge, even though that *was* your view, because your good friend Don Rumsfeld was opposed to it and kept putting forth the "bicycle seat" metaphor [the idea that the U.S. needed to force the Iraqis to assume complete responsibility for their own security, like an adult ceasing to steady a child who is learning to ride a bicycle]. Is there any truth to that? Or was it

a source of some *pain* to you that Rumsfeld was on the wrong side of that issue?

No, I don't think so. I mean, Don was—[pauses]—he's a pro. He's the guy—he'd been around the track many times himself. It was his second tour of secretary of defense. He was recruited to the post. It wasn't a job he'd ever sought. He loved doing it again. It was important, and I thought he did a good job of it, and I was a defender of Rumsfeld. But at the same time, in '06, as I recall, I think—or that summer—we'd begun a discussion inside, internally, within the administration, about our strategy in Iraq. We had, as I recall—well, I've got the rock right [points to a brick displayed on a nearby shelf in his study] there. AMZ: Abu Musab al-Zarqawi. That's taken out of the wall in the building where we killed Zarqawi. I think it was June. Yeah, June seventh of '06. That was a major success. We got the leader of al Qaeda in Iraq. But it also occurred about a time—because we're still having—that there's a sense that we need to do something different. And there were discussions; I can remember one, I think it was held over at the Defense Department, where—and also I can remember a couple in the Oval Office—where the subject was brought up deliberately, and people brought to participate, with respect to what was the right thing to do in Iraq. Should we change strategy? If so, how, and what direction did we want to go? There was a view—I think it wasn't just on Don's part. I think it was held by [U.S. Army] General [George W.] Casey, who was then in charge in Iraq.

And [U.S. Army General John P.] Abizaid.

Abizaid, who was the CENTCOM[2] commander. And then I think probably if you were to poll the [Joint] Chiefs generally they would have believed that the key was to get out of Iraq as soon as possible and turn it over to the Iraqis. There were contrary views. We had a discussion in the Oval Office one day. The president was there. Jack Keane[3] was there. Wayne Downing, who was the Joint Special Operations commander, had been—I mean he no longer was, but he was a consultant involved in this—half a dozen of us talking about that. There were conversations—I had conversations, separately and apart, along that same time period with Jack Keane and my friend Fred Kagan from the American Enterprise Institute and West Point and so forth.[4] And—

And Stephen Biddle[5] and Eliot Cohen[6] and all these—there's a certain number of people, outside advisors who were—

There were several groups working, I guess I would say, some sort of officially sanctioned, some of them outside, some of them inside. All of this accelerated as we went through the '06 year and up to the election. To some extent, it was an issue in some of the elections, the congressional elections, that year, where we're looking at various options and alternatives. We had the surge proposition that Keane and Kagan were big advocates of. There was a congressionally mandated commission that [James] Baker—

The Iraq Study Group.

The study group. And I can remember sessions in the Roosevelt Room with that group as they came forward with their recommendations. They never—the surge wasn't high on their list of possibilities, although there was some reference to it in their recommendations.

A fleeting reference.

Yeah. And Gates had been part of that group, working group. Steve was working internally, Steve Hadley, with a study group. Pete Pace, then chairman of the Joint Chiefs, was involved. They brought back, created, I think, a group called the Colonels.

The Council of Colonels.

The Council of Colonels. And oh, I'm trying to remember the name of the guy now.

Is it [Colonel H. R.] McMaster you're talking about?

McMaster, yeah, McMaster, McMaster. And he was brought in as part of that group. I had him over to the house, just by himself, because he'd come highly recommended, and I knew of him, and I spent a couple of hours with him over at the VPR one afternoon. This was just as the colonel—Council of Colonels was getting started. And he was an advocate of changing strategy, sort of outside what the chain of command wanted.

But I don't think—I mean, I was always solicitous, obviously, of Rumsfeld's views; he was in charge of the department. From the very beginning I was cautious, as a former sec-def, about sticking my oar into what were major responsibilities that Rumsfeld had. But I was pretty much that way. You know, I would have different views, I'd express them and so forth. But I was cautious about, just as vice president, in terms of how I dealt with cabinet members, and tried to avoid getting into a situation where I was undercutting State or Defense or whoever else it might be. There were times when I did operate independently, but in that general area I was cautious—but I don't think overly so. And I spent a lot of time, when we get into the surge, once we started on the surge, started implementing it in the beginning of '07, I operated on the basis—I'd been a strong supporter of the surge. When we, the president and I, went over—this was late '06, Rumsfeld is still secretary and Gates is not on board yet—we had a meeting in the tank [a secure conference room inside the Pentagon] with the Chiefs, and at which I argued, I can remember Schoomaker, Pete Schoomaker—I am a big fan of Schoomaker's, by the way. But the Chiefs' mission had changed. They were no longer in the chain of command. The Goldwater-Nichols [Act of 1986] made them the guys who raised and trained and equipped the force. Their legitimate role was to be concerned about maintaining the force, and they expressed those views when we started to talk about the surge. The notion of turning everything over to the Iraqis I questioned, on the grounds that they weren't ready for it, and that it would be a big mistake for us to assume we were going to solve our problem if we turned everything over to the Iraqis. They *weren't* ready, and [if] we ended up with a significant al Qaeda victory in Iraq, that was a risk that wasn't worth taking.

There is a portrait of Rumsfeld that has emerged with respect to the Iraq War: that once [Ambassador Paul] Bremer was appointed [as administrator of the Coalition Provisional Authority of Iraq, in May 2003], and it seemed as if Bremer had a reporting relationship directly to the president, that Rumsfeld kind of withdrew from Iraq as a subject, and was kind of hands-off. I'm sure you have seen these narratives.

Well, I haven't read all the narratives. I know Bremer. Once Bremer was invited upstairs by the president—for a workout session, as I recall, he went over and [they] worked out—Bremer then wasn't really willing to deal with anybody else except the president, which was—it was unfortunate, frankly. But one of the arguments or themes along here was there was always the feeling on the part of the Pentagon that the State Department wasn't carrying its fair share of the load. That—

There should be more civilians in Iraq.

Yeah, you needed to get more civilians in Iraq, and what you were trying to do in terms of building a government and so forth. Rehabilitating the economy wasn't really a DOD function, but DOD ended up carrying the ball because State hadn't been up to the task. There was an element of that involved. But if you come back to the surge, after we had that session in the tank—and it was a good session. They did raise, the Chiefs did raise the possibility of breaking the force. You know, what the surge required us to do was to go from twelve-month to fifteen-month deployments. And to get to the force there you wanted in place, you had to extend people who were there beyond what they had expected in terms of coming home, and you had to accelerate the deployment of others. And—

The surge of five brigades, in fact, exercises an impact on fifteen brigades.

Exactly. And the Chiefs, I can remember Pete in particular raising those concerns, which was their responsibility to do.

A guy who was instrumental in reassuring us that the force could take the strain was Jack Keane. And Jack had been vice chief of the army; we'd tried to make him the army chief of staff. But he said, "Look, nothing is going to break the force quicker than losing a war," and "We can do it. Maybe there will be problems," and so forth—and he was right. I took him in to see the president. We established something of a back channel because [U.S. Army General David] Petraeus figured prominently in all of this. He'd been the guy out rewriting the army manual on counterinsurgency. Part of the decision was to replace Casey with Petraeus in-country. And Petraeus's mentor was Jack Keane. They had a relationship that went back to their days when Keane was commanding the 101st [Airborne Division], and they had that story of them being out on the firing line one day and Petraeus being accidentally shot, and being evacuated by helicopter, Jack Keane on board, to Nashville. And when they landed on top of the hospital, the guy who got him off was [future Senate majority leader] Bill Frist. This is before Frist got involved in politics, but he was the heart surgeon who saved Petraeus's life. It was a close relationship between Petraeus and Keane, and Jack on a regular basis would travel over to Iraq, spend time over there with Petraeus, in terms of what was going on, and then report back. He would report back in the building [the Pentagon], but he'd also then come see me. And the president made it clear he wanted to preserve that back channel. At one point he came down, he knew Jack was coming to see me on a particular day, and he showed up in the middle of the meeting in my office and made it clear he knew what Jack was doing, he appreciated it, and wanted to maintain it. It created some tensions over across the river [at the Pentagon]. Part of the [chuckles]—well, [with then–Chief of Naval Operations] Admiral [Mike] Mullen, in particular. There was an effort made to try to cramp down on Keane's travels to the region that wasn't successful.

So I was a strong supporter of the surge. I thought it was the right thing to do. I think that you can argue about whether Casey and Rumsfeld and so forth were correct. Casey eventually went along with the idea of maybe a one-brigade surge. That would not have been adequate. On the other hand, the president liked Casey, thought it made sense to make him the army chief, which is the post he moved into. So I never thought of [this] as anything that [didn't] sort of ordinarily come up during the course of events of managing a problem, *big* problem in this case, obviously. But—

Did it take too long, the whole debate?

Ah, I don't think so. I think, given what was at stake, it was the kind of policy that took time to implement. The debate was pretty well resolved by the end of '06. And it was kicked around at fairly senior levels inside the West Wing. There were debates I can remember between Pace and Condi. Condi at one point said we should only get involved with our forces—this is when we were talking about counterinsurgency—when it's clear that there's a Srebrenica[7] facing us. And Pace and I made the arguments, you know, how do you translate that into—

An order.

—an order to the guys in the field? How will they know they can start shooting now because this is "another Srebrenica"? It didn't make any sense, and Pace was articulate in making that point. So we had those kinds of debates. This is along December of '06. The president pretty well decided he wanted to do it, but he wanted to wait until Gates had been on board and Gates had had a chance to travel out to the region and come back. And then sort of the tail end of that story was, as we got into spring, there were—I'm trying to think how to describe it. There were those in the West Wing who had doubts about the policy and tended to be more on the political side of the house, the communications side of the business. And I remember getting a call once from Steve [Hadley]—I was on my plane on the way back from Wyoming—that there had been meetings among a staff group in the White House, talking about alternatives to the surge, which was—

This was after it had been announced [on January 10, 2007]?

After it had been announced. And so we're along in the May–June timeframe. [Senate Minority Leader] Mitch McConnell was nervous. There were some senators, I think Dick Lugar [Republican of Indiana, ranking member of the Foreign Relations Committee] was one of them, went to Henry Kissinger and asked Kissinger to take a position different than support for the surge and the administration, to give the guys on the Hill some maneuvering room. It was an election year. A lot of them were looking for a way to put some distance between themselves [and the Bush administration]. And there was a point at which—I think I mentioned in my book—there was a story [that David] Sanger—I don't—or maybe [Peter] Baker, Sanger—wrote a piece in the *New York Times* about planning in the White House for a fallback alternative B. I can remember raising a stink about it in the morning meeting, and Steve came in to see me after the morning meeting to tell me that he'd been the source, but he did it at the direction of the president.[8] The president wanted it out there. So, you know, it was—

Kind of a feint by the president, if you will.

Well, it was, I think he'd been persuaded by the communicators that he needed to appear flexible, and it wasn't enough for us just to sort of stand fast and continue down the path we were on with respect to the surge. What we had to do was to get to the fall. If you remember, there was going to be the August recess, and then we'd have Petraeus and our ambassador, Ryan Crocker, back before the Congress when Congress reconvened in September, able to report on the surge, which then would have been in place for some period of time, and to give a report on the success, which they were able to do.

But in the meantime we had to keep Congress from doing something foolish or backing off the policy or trying to adopt an amendment on appropriations that would interfere with or limit what we were trying to do with the surge. And I had been contacted by Mitch [McConnell], who was concerned that we didn't have the votes, and there were the rumbling[s], if you will, in the West Wing, hearing concerns that we needed to be more flexible and have a fallback. I had [Senate Minority Whip] Trent Lott do a whip check in the Senate, and Trent came back and said we were okay; we could hold any vote. And shortly after that, Mitch came to me. Well, I had a group of senators to dinner down at the VPR about that time, Republican senators. And it was the same night Trent had gotten back to me on his whip check. And Mitch was there, and Mitch came to me and said, "We're going to be okay, we can hold the vote." And that pretty well ended the squishiness, if you will, in the West Wing, in terms of carrying through on the surge.

I know that yesterday I asked you whether you were ever able to observe George W. Bush succumbing to a kind of Lyndon Johnson strain in the conduct of the war, and you said no, you didn't.

Mm-hmm.

But the literature records many, many observations by people who were friends—personal friends—of the Bushes and so forth, that it *was* really eating him up and that he seemed consumed by it. How would you characterize his demeanor as wartime commander in chief over time and whether he at any point seemed truly consumed by this?

Well, I think he was clearly focused on it. I mean, who the hell wouldn't be? This is a major policy. Lives are at stake. He's carrying out his responsibility as commander in chief. And [he] believed in the policy, and he carried that burden, there's no question about it. But I don't find that surprising. Nor do I see it as Lyndon Johnson–like. I mean, I think he knew what he had to do. He was willing to make some tough decisions, and he did. There may have been outsiders who didn't see him on a regular basis, on a daily basis, dealing with the issues. And you know, I know he felt deeply the difficulties and the pain of dealing with the families of those who had been killed in action. We did some of that together. But I never felt that he was in a position where he wasn't up to the task or where he was overwhelmed by the responsibility.

I think if you talk to him today he will say it was one of the most difficult aspects of the job: you have to make those life-and-death decisions about sending our servicepeople into harm's way, and you know some of them aren't going to come home again. He was well aware of that, and he lived with it on a daily basis. But every president I've ever worked for has, and I think he handled it as well as any of them. So the notion [that] some outsiders are writing "this was really weighing heavily on him," I wouldn't describe it in those terms. I think it was very serious business. He thought about it a lot; he spent a lot of time on it. But during the same period of time, he spent a lot of time on Katrina and the aftermath of Katrina, which was along in the '05 timeframe. And that was a major responsibility for him as well.

How often do you and he speak today?

Umm—[pauses]—well, we had dinner with he and Laura a few months ago when we were down in Dallas, went to the library, Lynne and I did. And she made a presentation on her book on James Madison.[9] And before we did the presentation we went upstairs, just the four of us, and had a private dinner. So we talk occasionally.

Do you miss him?

Do I miss him? [chuckles] No, I have a feeling I can reach out and touch him anytime I want. I mean, it's an interesting relationship. I would say it was always primarily professional and not personal. We weren't buddy-buddies in that sense. We fished together a few times, down on the pond on the ranch at Crawford. And, you know, so, I mean—and I look back on that time I served as vice president with a sense that I am glad I had the opportunity. That it was a remarkable period in our history. If I were to look for a way to end my career in public service, that wasn't a bad way to do it, and that I appreciated very much the fact that, in the end, he persuaded me to take on the job and that I was a part of all that. It's a very important part of American history, and I think it was a consequential presidency and vice presidency. So I'm deeply grateful for the opportunity that he provided me. We didn't agree all the time, but, you know, welcome to the NFL! I mean, I always got the opportunity to present my point of view, and I think on the big issues we were pretty much in accord. There clearly were times when there were differences, but I wouldn't have expected anything else.

Have you ever had an extended discussion with Barack Obama?

No. [laughs] No. I saw him—on my history with Barack Obama, I campaigned for his opponent, when he had an opponent in the Senate race in Illinois [Republican Jack Ryan]. But then somebody in the—I think it was probably the Democratic political machine in Chicago, leaked sensitive matters from the divorce proceeding that our candidate had been involved in previously. And that's why he dropped out of the race. And Obama basically ran unopposed for the United States Senate in Illinois.[10] And this would have been '04. I didn't meet him then. That's the first time I sort of became aware of him. I think that's when he gave the speech at the [Democratic National] Convention as well, and [that] sort of put him on the map.

I swore him in when he came to Washington as a new senator. Vice presidents swear in all the new senators. There's always the big ceremony, you get two or three of them at a time down in the well, but then afterwards there is a photo shoot in the old Senate chamber for each new senator and his family. And I had small talk with him at that point. Didn't see or hear anything of him in the next two years until '06, and all of a sudden he is running for president. I had no dealings with him during the campaign. I did the morning of the twentieth of January of '09, as we were leaving office. We had the traditional joint coffee between the incoming crew and the outgoing crew.

[laughs] "Crew."

"Crew." [chuckles] I've got a picture—there's a picture someplace; I think maybe it's in my book—of he and [Vice President Joe] Biden and me talking at that coffee. I'm in a wheelchair with a cane. And this is when I told Joe this is what he was going to look like when he finished [chuckles] his tour as vice president. The next time I saw him [Obama] would have been when—this was last year, when we dedicated the Bush library down at

SMU. And they had a special tour for the previous presidents, and I was attached to the tour as a previous vice president. There's about a thirty-minute walk through the library. And during the course of that walk, I basically said hello to him, we shook hands, and that was it. We didn't talk or spend any time together. Those were the only times I have been around him.

Do you feel as though Obama, either intentionally or inadvertently or by some combination of the two, has undone some of the important work that you and President Bush did?

Oh, absolutely.

What?

Well, where do you start? I think with respect to the situation in Iraq, his precipitous withdrawal and refusal to leave any stay-behind forces to negotiate a status of forces agreement with the Iraqis was a huge mistake; we are paying a price for it now. He's having to go back in now, and the guy who campaigned on the basis of "bring the boys home and get out of Iraq" is now redeploying forces to Iraq. I think his apology tour, [when] he went to Cairo in the summer of '09 and said the U.S. overreacted to the events of 9/11, was a huge mistake. I don't think he ever bought into the notion that we're at war in terms of a war on terrorism. I think he always wanted to treat it as a law enforcement problem.

I think he's done enormous damage to the military. I think what's happened to the military in terms of morale, in terms of financing, budget, and so forth is just devastating. And I think he is doing—I think we obviously use the military extensively. But I think the way Obama is functioning now, he's crippling the capacity of future presidents to deal with future crises. It takes a long time to build up that military force. And I am absolutely convinced there will be a future president—two or three times down the road, perhaps—and he will be faced with a major crisis and he will not have the military capability he needs to deal with it. We are limiting the options of future presidents because of what is happening to the defense budget today. It's a—well, you want—I can go on for hours.

But [chuckles] I think—in energy. You know, we've had enormous success, a lot of it due to the private sector, in terms of becoming self-sufficient on energy. That is a huge development for the United States and affecting our situation globally around the world. Here we are now, we are getting, becoming self-sufficient in energy. He's doing everything he can to shut down the coal industry. Unilaterally. Congress rejected the carbon caps; he is doing it through the EPA by executive authority. We will not build the Keystone Pipeline. Really he hasn't got any good reason why he doesn't want to.

Or why it should take this administration longer to decide against it than it took to—

We could've *built* it! To be done! I think we ought to be aggressively promoting the fact and developing self-sufficiency in energy, and we ought to be using that. For example, instead of shutting down the coal industry and trying to fill the gap of gas, you know, they tried to appoint a guy who was head of the federal power commission who was anti-gas [Ron Binz], even. That was rejected. But we ought to be using that to develop capacity, to support the European gas market for U.S. exports. The Baltics should not have to get 100 percent of their gas from Russia. You can put a real cramp in Putin's economy and activities, and his eagerness to create problems for us in Europe, if we would take advantage of what we've got by way of our capacity to produce gas. And instead of shutting down our own coal industry, leave it alone and take those surpluses and reestablish a dominant position in terms of "we're the major exporters. We're

going to fill the energy needs, especially of our friends in Europe."
Put some backbone into NATO. And put a crimp in Vladimir Putin's
economy.

**You've anticipated ten or so of my questions. I was going to ask about shale,
I was going to ask you about Putin.**

But it's a big deal. The other thing that he's done—I have never seen, in
all my years now—I came to town, what? Forty years ago. More than
that; forty-five years ago. Well, '68. Now, what's sixty-eight—

I was born in '68 and I am forty-six, I am sad to report to you, sir. [laughs]

Okay. That's how long I've been involved. To travel, to deal with people
I have known in some cases for a quarter of a century, foreign leaders,
especially in the Middle East—they are so terribly frustrated, angry,
frightened. "Whatever happened to the United States?" A conviction
they can't count on us, that our word doesn't mean anything.

The Syria red line having been a particularly damaging episode?

Classic example, where he got everybody stood up to do something about
Syria and then at the last minute pulled the plug. I had a prominent
Mideast leader talk to me when I was there last spring. First time I'd ever
heard him say this; he's always been very self-confident and very much
in command. He said, "You know, you assume there is no political price
to be paid for those of us over here who support the United States. Wrong
assumption. It is sometimes a real question of leadership these days
whether or not it's smart, politically, for us, with our people, to be
friendly to the United States." General el-Sisi, new president of Egypt:
he's been to Moscow; he hasn't been to the United States. It's not because
he loves Russians; it's because the political price he would have to pay

domestically, inside Egypt, to come to the United States and be seen with Barack Obama would be very damaging for him.

We're to the point where our—I've said it repeatedly, not an original thought, but—our friends no longer trust us and our adversaries no longer fear us. We've created a huge vacuum in that part of the world, and ISIS has moved in, big-time. Now we have a caliphate in Syria and Iraq. We have had a massive spread in the number of al Qaeda–type organizations. The RAND study that came out last summer said between 2010 and 2013 there had been a 58 percent increase worldwide in the number of al Qaeda–type organizations.[11] We used to worry, at 9/11, just about Afghanistan; now it stretches from Mali and Nigeria in West Africa, across North Africa, through the Middle East, all around into Indonesia, where you'll find potential sanctuaries and safe harbors for Salafi Islamists, the terrorists, the al Qaeda types. It's a *very*, very, I think, dangerous situation. I think the threat is growing steadily, and I think our capacity to deal with it is rapidly diminishing.

I look at Barack Obama and I see the worst president in my lifetime without question—and that's saying something. I used to have significant criticism of Jimmy Carter but, you know, compared to Barack Obama and the damage he is doing to the nation, it's a tragedy, a real tragedy, and we are gonna pay a hell of a price just trying to dig out from under his presidency.

At different points, Obama and Attorney General Holder have suggested that racism is a factor in criticism of them. Is there any truth in that—or is it Obama and Holder who are the ones playing the race card, in your view?

I think they're playing the race card, in my view. We ought to be— certainly we haven't given up, nor should we give up, the right to criticize an administration and public officials. To say that we criticize, or that I criticize, Barack Obama or Holder because of race, I just think it's obviously not true. And I think, you know, my view of it is the criticism is merited because of performance—or *lack* of performance, because of *incompetence*. Hasn't got anything to do with race.

Before we take a break, there were five foreign leaders I wanted to ask you about. And maybe we can sort of zip through them quickly, just to get you on the record about these people, sort of under the big rubric of [chuckles] "presidents you have known." I didn't say they'd all be American! But, very quickly: [Afghan President Hamid] Karzai.

[pauses] He was there when we needed him. It was *very* important, when we went into Afghanistan, that we be able to help them establish a government as quickly as possible. And Karzai was very much on the map. He was living in Pakistan but he had been actively involved in—counterattacked Taliban operations inside Afghanistan. And after—it was the *loya jirga* process that we went through, he emerged as a most likely leader, prospect, to take over. And in my dealings with him I found him generally to be straightforward.

You know that the stories about him are legion, and colorful.

About corruption and—yeah. I was there when we swore in the new parliament with him. I've got a picture in the book about spending time with him, and I made a number of trips over there. I can remember sitting in the session when the president decided we were going to get Karzai and [Pakistani President Pervez] Musharraf together—the Afghans and the Pakistanis—and we had a little private dinner upstairs in the White House, in the family dining room. Condi was there and I think Steve Hadley, myself—and the two of *them*. [laughs] It was not a very successful enterprise. Very hard to get the two of them to come together, because of age-old conflicts and the view I think on the part of both of them that the other was providing a safe harbor for their adversaries and their enemies. So I, you know, Karzai is gone from the scene now. I think one of the things that we did reasonably well, you know, when Ryan Crocker was involved there, for example, before he went to Iraq, and—[pauses]—I'm trying to think, he's our neighbor here [in McLean], worked for me in the Pentagon, later became our ambassador in Afghanistan.

[Zalmay] Khalilzad.

Zal.

Yeah.

Who was very effective, I felt, at dealing with Karzai.

Was Karzai corrupt?

Quite possibly. But that wouldn't be the first corrupt individual in that part of the world that you have to deal with. But, but we were better off with him than we would have been without him. We had to have *some*body, and Karzai was the best we could get at the time.

What would you say of Musharraf?

Liked him. He's visited me here in my home since he left office, since we both left office. Again, I found him, in his dealings, my dealings with him, straightforward. I liked working with him. I thought he was a friend of the United States.

Was the problem of infiltration of ISI, the Pakistani intelligence service, one that Musharraf had the ability to do something about? Because it seems that even in successive administrations, that issue, of the intelligence services of Pakistan

being somewhat comprised by infiltration of Taliban or the wrong element, seems to recur.

Yeah.

And so the question is whether someone like Musharraf would have been in a position to do something about that, or it's just kind of a permanent feature of life in that part of the world.

Well, there is sort of a third interpretation, which would be: It's deliberate. They need to have a foot in both camps. And that where Pakistan is concerned—I'm trying to remember, you know, we got into a situation with them, after they tested their nuclear capability, where we pretty well suspended the military-to-military relationship between the United States and Pakistan. And the Paks, obviously because of history, naturally spend a lot of time worrying about India. They look at Afghanistan and they see Afghanistan as a potential safe haven for the Indians to use as a base to come after them. When you look at it within the overall context and the problems they've got, the part of the world they live in, the difficulties they face, it's not surprising that you will find ISI, or their intelligence service, with ties or connections on both sides of the border, working sometimes in ways that [are] not necessarily consistent with our interest. But on the other hand, we haven't always been solid, reliable allies for them. And I think sometimes they feel, and other countries do, that again, the United States hasn't been an absolutely reliable ally, and we've got to understand the world that they live in, the pressures that they operate under, the concerns they have, the problems they have to deal with. I can remember going up into Pakistan [in December 2005] when there was a major earthquake over there [October 8], and the president asked me to go; Lynne went with me. And we spent time up in the northern part of Pakistan, in the difficult areas, and set up a MASH unit, one of our military hospitals up there.

I was with you on that trip.

Yeah. Great trip. But you get back up into that country, you know, and [there's] nothing more than goat trails. I mean, there aren't roads, and it's an extraordinarily difficult part of the world to operate in. And I think sometimes we Americans are a little heavy-handed, not all that sympathetic, not consistent administration to administration. And some of our folks in that part of the world, including somebody like Musharraf who's operating in Pakistan, he's got problems across the border in Afghanistan. He's been the host for an awful lot of, well, Karzai and a lot of the others who fled the Taliban in Afghanistan. He's always worried about India and China. It's a complicated, difficult part of the world. And I think the Pakistani intelligence service reflects the needs and desires of the Pakistani leadership, and that oftentimes involves them having relationships with people that are not necessarily our friends.

[Iraqi Prime Minister Nouri al-]Maliki.

Uh—[sighs]—disappointment. Problem. Again, when we had Crocker and Zal and Petraeus, when we had a top-notch team over there, Maliki was fairly malleable. I think when we left and when the troops, all of our troops left, and there was no SOFA [status of forces agreement], no stay-behind agreement, that—what was it? About two, two and a half years there, where there was no U.S. military presence to speak of—and—that Maliki, I think, did some very stupid things in terms of purging Sunni generals—

Colonels and generals. Down to the colonel level, I think.

—yeah, out of the military. The Sunnis—one of the great things that went with the surge, that occurred simultaneously and was partly related to [it], [was] the awakening out in Anbar province. And the Sunnis really signed on. I think they believed that we had demonstrated, "we" the United States, that we were in for the long haul and we were seeking victory. The surge was a part of that. But when Maliki had his chance—and he did when we turned our back, the Obama administration, and demonstrated repeatedly that we were leaving and that we weren't going to negotiate a stay-behind agreement—I think Maliki began to move in ways that were designed to take advantage, to get rid of his adversaries, and that included Sunnis, both politically and militarily.

Do you regard that Maliki was kind of an agent for the Iranian government, as has been suggested from time to time?

Well—[pauses]—you've got so many cross-cutting currents. I mean, he'd found refuge in Iran when he fled Saddam Hussein in Iraq. We were told—at one point I can remember the State Department, I think it was, arguing that we couldn't allow anybody in the government in Baghdad that had been an expatriate, had gone, left the country. But if you look at what happened, virtually everybody that ended up in the government, in positions of responsibility, had fled the country. If they hadn't, Saddam probably would have killed them. Maliki fell in that category, and he did find safe haven and sanctuary in Iran. He wasn't the only one.

But you've also got cross-cutting interests now. The United States, as far as Iraq is concerned, under the Obama administration, [has] been actively and aggressively involved in withdrawing. If he looks around that part of the world, Iran is a neighbor. It's also a dominant Shia regime in that part of the world. I don't find it surprising that he's got some relationships with the Iranians. But, again, to some extent, we did it to ourselves: We created the vacuum. The Obama administration has created a vacuum, and it's pretty clear, based on what ISIS has been able to do, coming back in from Syria, that it's not surprising that you would see somebody like Maliki reaching out wherever he can to find help and assistance.

I'll say his behavior was much more consistent with what we needed and expected when the president was on the secure video to him on a regular basis, when we had regular conversations between the Situation Room and the West Wing and Petraeus and Crocker and so forth in Baghdad, and occasionally direct contacts and conversations. You haven't seen anything like that out of this administration. I think we turned our back on them, and that's contributed to the fact that Maliki was no longer in a position to be able to continue to work with the United States. And he's gone now, so.

Two other leaders and then we will take a break. I do want to pose to you the question about Margaret Thatcher. You called that meeting with her in the run-up to the Gulf War the "most valuable" session you had in that period because she imparted to you, as you recounted, "lessons both in military strategy and how to build and maintain public support." Can you recall what she told you?

Well, it was interesting. I was a fan of hers. On this particular day I was on my way to Moscow to find out if the Russians had given any weapons to Saddam Hussein we didn't know about. We were getting ready to liberate Kuwait and to go up against the Iraqi military. But en route I stopped and did some business in the UK, and Tom King, who was my counterpart, who was the UK defense minister, and I paid a call on Prime Minister Thatcher. She kicked out all of the staffs, and just the three of us just sat there for a long time that afternoon, and she harked back to her experience in the Falklands. And talked to the sort of in the—[pauses]—thought of herself very much as a U.S. ally in terms of what we were getting ready to do. She had been, when I called back—first weekend of the crisis, the Gulf crisis, the president [George H. W. Bush] sent me out to get permission to deploy the force in Saudi Arabia. And when I got that approval and called back to the White House to tell him that I had their agreement and I was ready to deploy the force and wanted to sign off, Maggie Thatcher was in the Oval Office with him. She'd come back with him from Colorado. So she was sort of a feature as we went through this process. And when I got to her this must have been October, maybe November—October, November timeframe in the fall of '90, shortly before she left office. But she talked at great length about her Falklands experience, about marshaling public opinion, about building support for what she had to do in the Falklands, which was a fairly risky venture from the standpoint of the Brits.

Did she say how she was able to succeed at that or impart some counsel?

No, I think it was more of just sharing those experiences with us, sort of a real-world experience. A few years before, obviously: It was back in '82 when she had done it. And of course, we had been going through the process of building the coalition, getting people to sign on and so forth. But there was considerable wisdom there backed up by her own personal experience.

Lastly: Vladimir Putin. President Bush famously said he looked into Vladimir Putin's eyes and got a sense of his soul as a man that business could be done with. You wrote in *In My Time* that when you looked in Putin's eyes, you saw an old KGB hand.

That's true.

Did you ever tell the president that you disagreed with him about Putin?

Mmmm, well, I never felt so much that it was a disagreement, I guess. I question the assumption because he saw him and said he saw him as somebody that he could do business with—I think that's almost what he *had* to say if he wanted to—especially after the first meeting. He's trying to build a relationship; you got things you'd like to do *vis-à-vis* the Russians. He might well have shared my exact view that this guy is KGB. I mean, that's where he came from, that's his background, that's the experiences of his life. So I don't take it—I never, at least it never—in terms of our conversations between the president and myself, [as] a sort of a fundamental difference of opinion.

So you don't think that he fundamentally misjudged Putin?

[long pauses] I can't say that he did misjudge him. Now, you know, I think he obviously learned over time—everybody did. Putin was a relatively new commodity when we got there in 2000. I had been skeptical of [Mikhail] Gorbachev. I mean, one of the first things I did when I got to be secretary of defense was make a prediction on the [Rowland] Evans and [Robert] Novak television show that Gorbachev would fail and in the end be succeeded by somebody a lot more like the old Soviet leaders than like Gorbachev. I got a phone call from my buddy Jim Baker, who was at State and made it very clear to me I had transgressed into his turf—and he was right. But I think I was right, too [chuckles], long-term. But no, I—[pauses]—I'm not critical of the president for the way he dealt with Putin. I think he handled it pretty well.

What could the Obama administration be doing, with or without the backing of our European allies, right now to repel Putin in Eastern Ukraine and, more fundamentally, to force him to make the choice that you say in your book Russia "must" make between its current conduct and being a responsible international stakeholder?

What, what should our policy be?

What are we doing—what could we be doing that we are not now to roll him back from Eastern Ukraine, if not Crimea, and more fundamentally, to get

him to make the choice that you say in your book, "Russia must make a choice." How do we *make* them make that choice?

Well, I think you've got to repair the damage that's been done. I start in just about every one of these issues you talk about: first and foremost, we've got to rebuild the military. You cannot tolerate the course we are on from the period of time—[Robert] Gates really put out the last budget that was sort of a product of the Defense Department. I think the base was back in—it was for, maybe fiscal year '12. Since then, we have been running on sequesters. I think the level of spending now on defense is about a trillion dollars that we've dropped, not spent, over that period of time. You're not going to be able to do anything long-term if your diplomacy's not credible, and your diplomacy's not going to be credible if you don't restore U.S. military capability—and we are going in exactly the opposite direction. So whether we're talking about China fooling around in the South China Sea, or the vacuum that's being created in the Middle East and a loss of confidence on the part of our allies, or Putin's willingness to throw his weight around in Europe, we've got to demonstrate that we're an administration that believes that we—if we can *get* such an administration—that believes that the U.S. has a major role to play in the world as the leader; that it's backed up by significant military capability; that we're prepared to keep our commitments in various places around the world; and make it very clear to friend and adversary alike that the U.S. is going to be the kind of formidable player we have been for most of the last seventy years.

When I look at Barack Obama I see a guy who is not part of the consensus that has governed Republican and Democratic administrations alike since Harry Truman's day. Whether you are talking about—you can argue about Carter and how committed he was, but there's been a basic fundamental belief since the end of World War II that United States leadership in the world produces a far more peaceful, less hostile world, greater prosperity. The U.S. has to play a leadership role. And it's going to take a lot to rebuild the damage that has been done over the last few years, because we've actively conveyed to the world the notion—this president has—that we no longer believe that. That speech he made to the United Nations, talking about no system that elevates one nation above others can be tolerated; sort of sending Winston Churchill's bust back to the British Embassy when he first gets back into office; looking upon the United States, I think, sometimes as a colonial power rather than, you know, the most powerful nation in the world that's done basically good, good works with our power and influence over the years.

I had an interesting comment when I was in Israel this spring. A prominent official said to me—and it wasn't the prime minister, it was somebody else—he said Obama distinguishes between victims and victimizers. He divides the world up into victims and victimizers. That the Israelis were victims during the Holocaust and therefore deserved help and assistance. Now the Israelis are victimizers because of the way they treat the Palestinians. And that he looks upon, if you look at his, sort of his basic fundamental attitude, I don't think he shares the consensus that Republican and Democratic president alike have shared, whether you are talking about Jack Kennedy and Harry Truman and Lyndon Johnson, or Dwight Eisenhower and the Bushes and Ronald Reagan, about the U.S. role in the world. I just think he's got a fundamentally different concept in his head. He's got no qualms at all with rapidly diminishing the size [and] capabilities of the U.S. military, withdrawing from the Middle East, creating a vacuum there.

I think in terms of dealing with Putin and trying to rein him in, you've got to make NATO *mean* something again. And you can say, well, it's NATO's responsibility. NATO works when the United States provides the real leadership and the muscle behind it; it's always worked that way. We ought to be able to persuade our NATO allies that they need to make their commitments, from a spending standpoint, in terms of the percentage of GDP they spend on defense. Hell, we are not even coming close ourselves anymore. They—we ought to be able to actively support our friends in the Baltics. There ought to be beefed-up military exercises in Poland, joint ventures and exercises of various kinds with the U.S. If you want to get Putin's attention, you really ought to whack him economically, and that's not just a matter of sanctions; it's also a matter of going after his energy stuff. What's happening to oil prices now frankly is a blessing for us because it really puts the screws to Putin. He's so dependent on oil, in terms of his economy, that we ought to do everything we can to encourage that. So it's a mindset, you know, that is, I think, totally lacking in this administration. I don't know where the president gets his guidance. I don't know who he talks to. I don't know who he listens to. He has gone through defense secretaries; you know, he sort of spits them out and chews them up. I don't have any concept that he has a worldview that's sort of the traditional worldview that most American presidents have adhered to for seventy years.

One final question on Putin. Most accounts portray him as an omnipotent figure, unchecked by any other forces in Russia. Is that an accurate view? Or should we see Putin as a powerful figure, to be sure, but one who nonetheless operates within a given framework and who is buffeted to some extent, as all leaders are, by various institutional actors, external forces, and so on?

Well, I think he is clearly buffeted to some extent by external forces and so on. But he has, I think, because of his background and experience, because of his worldview, there is a strain of nationalism that runs through the Russian mindset. I think he really believed it when he said one of the worst disasters to befall the twentieth century was the demise of the old Soviet Union. Now, most of the rest of the world looked at that and said, "Hot damn, that's a positive development." You're going to have the near-abroad, free and independent states that no longer are going to have Russian troops stationed throughout Europe. The Cold War is over, the good guys won! I think he has got a pretty significant positive standing in the polls these days, sort of based on the notion he's reclaiming Russia's rightful place as a major world power.

And a completely propagandistic media.

Exactly. He owns the media and—now, how long can he sustain that? I don't know. But Europe's in a weakened position, I think, at this point. Part of that's their dependence on Russia for energy. Part of it is the fact that the United States is weak, and we appear weak, and we haven't followed through on our commitments. I talked to a couple of British members of Parliament. They were all up on the step, as well, on the Syrian red line on chemical weapons. They're not about to stick their necks out again, you know, for what Obama is trying to do now, in trying to get others to volunteer ground forces to go fight ISIS in the caliphate.

Again, I think our—we're viewed as so weak and indecisive that it is not likely we can marshal the resources or provide the leadership that the Europeans need if they are in fact going to confront and stand up to Putin. I think Putin sees an opportunity here. I think he believes he's got a window of about two years in which he can pretty much throw his weight around and do what he wants to do—and I think we haven't heard the last of him yet. I think we'll see him actively, if not anything else, doing everything he can to undermine NATO and to persuade Ukraine, for example, that they really don't want to be part of the European economic community, they really want to be associated with the Russians.

In the Baltics, I can see him bringing pressure to bear to suggest, perhaps, that one or more of them might want to withdraw from NATO. That would be a very significant political move, would demonstrate his strength. And, you know, if you spent time in Lithuania and Latvia and Estonia, they're very, very worried. They've got a significant Russian minority population, and they live right next door to "the bear," and it doesn't take very much to create major difficulties for them, if you're 100 percent [dependent] on Russia for your gas, if you're vulnerable to cyberattack, as they have been. I can see him, without ever sending troops across the border, wielding a heavy hand to undermine the cohesion, the European allies of NATO, of the U.S. position in that part of the world. And I don't think this president has a clue about how to deal with it. He's doing exactly the opposite—for example, in the energy area—from what he ought to be doing.

———————

You have been a consumer of the product of our intelligence community dating back at least to your membership on our House Intelligence Committee. Am I correct about that, or were you a consumer as chief of staff?

No, I first [served] as a consumer when I was chief of staff for Ford and then the deputy, really, before that.

Okay.

There was a—this was not the PDB itself—there was a next-higher level that was more widely distributed that I started receiving when I was the deputy chief of staff. And then I would get involved. There were problems that would come up that would involve intelligence matters that I would get involved in. We had, oh—I'm trying to remember. We had the Rockefeller commission looking at CIA activities, allegations of wrongdoing by the Central Intelligence Agency.[12]

[There were similar inquiries led by Senator Frank] Church and [Congressman Otis] Pike.

Yup. The Church and Pike Committees. [CIA Director] Bill Colby was there. Ford replaced him, obviously, with George [H. W.] Bush. And I would get—well, [White House Counselor] Jack Marsh was a close friend; he was part of the Ford operation. Jack was a former Democratic congressman from Virginia, had been in congressional relations at the Pentagon, at one point; close to Ford because, I guess, he was a conservative Democrat. But I worked closely with Jack, and Jack would keep me up to speed, for example, because he was doing the Church and the Pike Committees. And I'd get involved in the political issues and the policy issues and so forth. And then I got a daily brief, but it wasn't the PD Brief; it was a cut below that.

Without casting aspersions on the legions of dedicated patriots who work in the intelligence community, how would you assess the *caliber* of the intelligence product that you have received across the span of your career? Have you seen the caliber change, fluctuate, evolve in any discernible way?

Hmm! [pauses] Well, it's—it's changed a lot, in part to reflect the, the changing nature of the threat. And back in the seventies, you know, we were really Cold War–oriented, ballistic missile–oriented. We wanted to know how many ICBMs the Russians had, and did we have an accurate count, and so forth. When we were targeted on governments—lots of times we're interested, obviously, in individual leaders and what they were doing and saying and what kind of policies they were pursuing. What was pretty much missing was the non-state actors. We didn't have that much of it back in those days. You know, when you come forward into the second Bush administration you had—of course, then all of a sudden we are interested in al Qaeda, terrorist attacks, the kinds of—it's a different target. And our natural skill that we developed over the years, in terms of our technical capability, our overheads, our capacity to count missile silos and so forth, and to know precisely what the Soviets had or didn't have—that used to be the heart and soul of what we did. And by the time of the second Bush administration, that was still important but it was a lot more important to try to figure out, you know, what al Qaeda was up to. And that was a very different target.

In between we went through several iterations. I mean, in terms of my own experience, I took the job on the Intel Committee. [House Minority Leader] Bob Michel offered it. Actually, membership on the Intel Committee is determined by the speaker, but the speaker always talks to the minority about representation from that side of the House. The Intel Committee was fascinating. It was the best committee assignment I had during my time on the Hill. Lee Hamilton was chairman for a while, and he and I got to be close friends. He is the only Democrat I can think of that I ever sent a campaign contribution to.

But when I went on the committee, it was fascinating in part because, you know, I'd had some exposure to it before, but it was also an interesting time. It was one of the most nonpartisan activities you could engage in in the Congress. And I saw it as a tremendous opportunity to learn. And there were people in the [intelligence] community who were eager to share what they were doing with somebody in a position of responsibility. And I worked—I spent a lot of hours up in the closed, in the secure spaces, reading all of the materials coming through. Most members never did. But I was intrigued by the business. There's a story I love to tell about—[pauses]—oh, the guy who was convinced everybody in the agency was [a mole]—

[CIA counterintelligence chief James Jesus] Angleton.

Yes, Angleton.

This is in your book.

Yeah. And every once in a while I think of him because he had called and set up a meeting for something he absolutely had to tell me. And

Henry Hyde and I got all set to have dinner with him, and he died. And we never did find out what he wanted to tell us. [laughs]

I could see the little smile on your face yesterday when I happened to mention Angleton, briefly.

Yeah, yeah. But it is a fascinating part of the business of what we do. Most members, even the ones on the committee, don't aggressively dig into it. They tend to treat it like other committees. But what I found was my own interest, some great staff people, a couple of guys that I later took with me. Marty—oh, not Marty Anderson.

JIM STEEN: Faga?

Faga. Marty later became—I put him in charge pretty much of our whole satellite operation. So I picked up staff. Addington came originally from the Intelligence Committee. But once I'd demonstrated interest, I was inundated with the opportunity to go get actively involved in the business. And they love nothing better than getting somebody who had a legitimate right to know and had the clearances and the interest to show them what we were doing.

Appetite for the product.

Exactly. And so I spent a lot of time on it as a member of Congress. And then when I went to Defense, I had jurisdiction over more of the community than the CIA director did when he looked at bodies and budgets, because all of the defense-related intelligence stuff came to me. And I worked closely with Bill Webster, who was CIA director a good part of that time. We used to have breakfast once a week, just to stay close and keep everything knitted together. And intelligence was very important then, not only in terms of keeping track with what was happening in the Soviet Union—this is a period when the [Berlin] Wall is coming down, the Cold War is ending and so forth. I used to have Saturday seminars in the Pentagon where we'd bring in outside experts. We'd get one or two guys from the agency, a couple of academic types, and about once a month I'd sit down and I'd spend a Saturday morning then focused just on the Soviet Union. So I was out drummin' up activities as well, because of my interest, and I thought it was important to be actively involved. Desert Storm: heavy, heavy involvement in the intelligence community and especially the military side of the business, DIA [Defense Intelligence Agency], and so forth. So it was something I spent a lot of time on and was, was deeply interested in.

The reason I ask is because in *In My Time*, almost every reference that you make to U.S. intelligence product that you were receiving at the time you were secretary of defense is faintly negative in one way or another. And it suggests that you were seeing intelligence failures long before 2002. Hear me out.

Mm-hmm.

In the Gulf War period alone, you recalled how the Israelis had determined by July 1990 that Saddam Hussein had a nuclear program that was, as you put it, "much further advanced than the one portrayed in our intelligence estimates." You wrote of the period of August 1990: "Having missed Saddam's invasion of Kuwait, our intelligence analysts now seemed to see signs everywhere of his invading Saudi Arabia." A few pages later, you wrote: "CIA estimates of numbers of tanks destroyed varied widely from the CENTCOM estimates." And by the end of the Gulf War you noted (and this is all just in a page range of about sixty, seventy pages): "We were told repeatedly by our own intelligence services that Saddam would never survive after the blow the coalition had delivered. But he was able to turn the fact that he had stood up to and survived a massive assault into a personal victory." So right there, in a fairly compact frame of reference—

Mm-hmm.

—you are averring to a series of intelligence failures. And so it seems that you have long taken a somewhat jaundiced view of the caliber of the product you have been receiving.

Yeah, those are all accurate statements. I don't move from there to say I have a very negative view about intelligence. When we talk about, oh, in the run-up to the Gulf War and the conflict between the agency and the military, one got it right. In that case it was DIA and the military. We *had* an accurate portrayal of what was going on. But I think, as oftentimes happens in the business, the policymakers will sometimes be faced with conflicting reports from inside their own intelligence community. They don't guarantee unanimity of view coming forward.

Seldom, in fact, does that occur. But you see how I could draw that inference based on what I was reading in your book?

Sure. But I can't remember how much I did it in there. I've known some really tremendously able, capable people in the intelligence business who have done some remarkable things. Some of which I can't talk about, because the real success stories oftentimes never see the light of day—and there *are* some of those. So the reason I portrayed it in there, intelligence was important obviously in what we were doing. And there were times that, places where, we have fallen short—and one of them has been our ability, or our *in*ability, to predict when a particular state is going to achieve nuclear status. And we're usually behind the curve. In the case of the Iraqis, we had—I mention in there, I think, the briefing I had from [senior Israeli officials] Ehud Barak and Moshe Arens in the summer of '90, before Saddam invaded Kuwait, where they basically came and talked about their assessment of where the Iraqis were on nuclear matters, and believed that they were much closer than we thought. And we found out afterwards, when the International Atomic Energy Agency got in after the war was over with and reviewed it, they agreed with the Israelis, not with *our* intelligence community, which had anticipated it was some years off. So—

I think the estimate was six months.

Well—

Something like that; pretty close.

—it was within a year, yeah. Point being, again, yeah, our guys have missed it from time to time; no question about it. On the other hand, compared to other intelligence services, you know, we've got such a big world that we are interested in and involved with. The Israelis are very, very good at their particular target. Their target's a lot smaller than ours in terms of the geographical area [of] interest that they have.

So I'm intrigued by the business. The fact that they sometimes are wrong I attribute, as much to anything, to—sometimes it's failure of imagination. Oftentimes it involves the fact that your target's very, very good at hiding what they're doing. But I wouldn't want to be branded as someone who is, you know, hostile to the intelligence community or anything. I can be critical at times; I think you *have* to be, to be a good consumer. You gotta ask the tough questions. And I always tried to do that—but I also spent a lot of time defending the community, working to get them additional resources when they were needed. That's one of the things I did as vice president. George Tenet on a couple of occasions would come and he was coming up short on his budget, and I would help him get the money he needed off the Hill.

We'll talk more about Tenet and the Iraq WMD assessment tomorrow in the Iraq portion of our discussion. But just to finish on this subject of intelligence and the kind of—with a *professional* view of it. In the period surrounding Iraq

and the failure to find WMDs, we heard frequently the charge that intelligence had become "politicized."

Mm-hmm.

Now, in fact, there were those who said that around the time of Watergate, and—the attempt, for example, to rope [then–CIA director Richard] Helms into the Watergate cover-up, in the very early portion of it, for example.

Mm-hmm.

But I just wonder if you, who have seen these areas up close, and as a high-level consumer of intelligence, if you can identify a period at any point along the way where you believe that intelligence really *did* become "politicized." By the way, I would simply add, too, that there were those who watched the vice presidential debate between Biden and Paul Ryan, where Biden seemed to throw the intelligence community under the bus with respect to Benghazi. And I did some reporting on Benghazi at that time where I had a former CIA person and someone who was brought in on a contract basis to evaluate some of the evidence in Benghazi tell me that "the intelligence, I've never seen it more politicized than it is today." And so to this question of the "politicization" of intelligence: Was there a period where that came to be so? Is it enduring? Is it fluctuating?

What do you mean by "politicization"?

Well, I guess where—another example, by the way. I was brought down as part of a group of reporters to a nondescript building downtown in [November] 2007 to be briefed on background by [name redacted] and [name redacted] and some other folks. These were the guys who had—they were basically briefing us on the executive summary of the Iran NIE [National Intelligence Estimate] that concluded that—

Yeah, yeah. I know what you mean. Yeah.

—there had been a halt in the effort toward a nuclear weapon.[13] Now even the conclusions of that NIE itself, which were suspect in some ways, those conclusions themselves were widely misunderstood and misreported. It wasn't that the entire nuclear program had come to a halt; it was *asserted*, whether rightly or wrongly, that just the work on weaponization had been halted. And people like [former UN Ambassador] John Bolton and others were telling me at the time, "You cannot believe how politicized that NIE was," that the guys who wrote it were opponents of the Iran policy and so on. In that briefing, [name redacted] said something that was so shocking to me to hear that I made sure that Bret Baier, who was at that time our White House correspondent, reported it. I said, "You have *got* to—because we're going to be the only ones." Okay? [*New York Times* intelligence correspondent] Mark Mazzetti was at that briefing, a lot of people.

Mm-hmm.

And as it turned out, we were the only people to report this.[14] [Name redacted] said at that briefing—as "a senior administration official," of course, it was a background thing; so we'll make sure this doesn't violate that—but he said, "Well, of course we, we still believe that it remains Iran's latent goal to build a bomb." And that statement wasn't in the ten summary points. Now, when you're telling us they halted some aspect of their program, if you had included the point in there that "it remains our judgment that it remains Iran's latent goal to build a bomb," that would put a very different cast on the whole NIE, right?

Yeah.

I'm not accusing [name redacted] of politicization; but that report was one example of, I think, *rank* politicization of the intelligence products. When you ask me, "What do you mean by [politicization]?"—

It's a good example. Yeah.

—that's one example, okay. So the point is: Can we look back historically and sort of identify the point at which intelligence *did* start to become "politicized," if that's true to say?

Hmmm! [pauses] Well, the way I think about it—I remember that report, and it created a *hell* of a problem for us because of the way it was perceived, even inside the community and by the policymakers. As you say, it clearly created the notion that they'd stopped their effort to acquire nukes, if you wanted to put it in those terms. But there was an added complicating factor here. This was in the aftermath of Iraq WMD, of the charge "Bush lied, people died." And nobody was quite certain what the hell to do with this report. And I remember when they came to brief me on that report you are talking about. I made sure I had two other guys, my staff guys, in the room with me, all that time, so that nobody could allege, you know, that I had tried to change it or twist it or done anything other than simply receive the report. I *still* don't understand to this day exactly what all transpired; everybody was afraid to even *talk* about it. And part of that was on the basis of what had happened with respect to the original, you know, NIE back in '02 on Iraq WMD and the—I'm trying to think how the process unfolded.

My recollection is that there was some SIGINT [signals intelligence] that we had that suggested that some fairly mid-level Iranians who were involved in the nuclear program could be overheard receiving the news that they were to halt their work with great dismay from higher-ups. And that was a key part that provided the foundation for that conclusion. But again: If it is your view that it remains Iran's "latent goal" to build the bomb, that's a pretty significant point that's not in the executive summary and not briefed to the world.

Yeah. But you could have said the same thing about the Iraq WMD. We didn't find these stockpiles, but they clearly retained the intention to build the nukes.

And [weapons inspector Charles] Duelfer did make that clear in his report.

Yeah. But in what is politicization, in terms of how you define it, start off, the charge was made that we had *manipulated* the intelligence on Iraq WMD—which we did not do. I think it was probably the first intel report I received after the election in 2000 that warned about Iraq WMD. And it was some twenty-seven months of reporting on that. And yet the story now today, all these years later, is: Bush and Cheney manipulated the intelligence. We never manipulated the intelligence. We never *tried* to manipulate the intelligence. The Silberman-Robb Commission[15] reviewed the whole thing and found absolutely no evidence of any effort to manipulate the intelligence. And yet that, that's *doctrine* out there. That's politicization, if you will, of intelligence in a sense.

It's taking, well, in that case the truth and distorting it for political ends or political purposes. I'm not sure how you keep it out, how you prevent it. Well, look at the whole Valerie Plame crap, you know, where there were suggestions at times that I was out trying to get a different outcome in terms of what the community was reporting, when what I was doing—and I thought it was part of my job to do that. I'd go out and get a briefing and say, "I want to be briefed on X," or "Send a team in and brief me on it," and I'd ask a hell of a lot of tough questions. I felt that was my job and that was the way I could be an effective consumer. They say when all is said and done, when Robb-Silberman went afterwards and tried to find somebody, whoever felt that those sessions had been an effort to manipulate or warp the outcome, they couldn't find a single person who would validate that.

I guess maybe it's *always* been there, to some extent; the consequences of it are so great, of success or failure. And I can't think of a particular moment sort of when it started to be political in terms of—and you have to be a little careful about the "politicization" of intelligence in the context that you mean.

I mean, probably we could go back to the Cold War period and find fairly passionate interagency disputes about given assessments of intentions on the part of the Soviet Union or the Communist Chinese, or what have you, and I'm sure that there were political colorations to those disputes, too.

Mm-hmm.

So it may be inherent in the process, as you say.

Yeah. It's something you try to guard against but—[sighs]—it's very hard. So you trust individuals that you work with and you get a sense. You try to develop multiple sources. I had a policy, for example, when I was at the Pentagon in terms of how I worked with the Joint Staff and specifically with the chairman, with Powell. And Powell likes to have everything coming up through him; he'd been used to being the secretary's military assistant back in the [Caspar] Weinberger days. And he liked to control everything coming up to the secretary, and that gave him great power and influence. And that's, you know, a tough, aggressive guy—it's a natural, normal kind of thing to do. I didn't want that at *all*. My commitment to him was in terms of giving orders to the troops and operating, I'd always go through the chairman. But I never wanted to be in a position where that was my only source of information about what was going on in the building and so forth. So I developed all of these separate channels, if you will. And you have to do some of that in the intelligence area.

And you wrote in your book that Powell made clear he didn't like that, or he chewed out some of the guys who were—the service chiefs.

Yeah, when I'd send my guys out to run the traps. I'd find out afterwards that he had expressed dissatisfaction. But I made it very clear to him what I wanted, and that's the way we worked. But it's not—as I think back about it, in terms of the guys I've worked with, you do—if you work with people enough over a period of time, you get a sense of who you can trust, who you can rely on, who will give you the straight skinny; and those are the people you want to spend time with. And you have to be careful of sort of the bureaucratic processes that operate in the community and you get, you know, two different views out of the CIA on whether or not Saddam Hussein would ever do business with al Qaeda. One branch says he is secular, they're religious; never the two will meet, you know. And then you get somebody else who would report with just as much fervor that in fact there was a close working relationship between Saddam Hussein and al Qaeda: two totally contradictory views out of the same agency, depending [on] which part of the portfolio they were involved with.

I want to do a little on foreign affairs and a little on current events, and then I actually want to liberate you from that chair [chuckles], if you'd like.

Okay. All right.

We talked yesterday about how some American analysts foresaw the collapse of the Soviet Union because they understood that a system so morally bankrupt at its core and so thoroughly dishonest in its conduct of diplomacy around the world was very likely issuing wildly inflated claims for its annual GDP, for example. Do you think the same could be true for China today? Is China as a Stalinist system so rotten to the core that its collapse, like the Soviet Union's, is inevitable?

I don't think so. As I look at China, you know, still a Communist system. The first time I went was with Ford in about '74, '75. Mao was still alive, and everybody was wearing the same uniform and marching in lockstep. Their morning runs and so forth. There was only one decent hotel in Beijing, and it wasn't very good. The world [has] changed so dramatically.

But I look at China as a place that has achieved phenomenal growth, economically. They have so far been able to sort of maintain their overall political structure while dramatically advancing their ability to be an important part of the world economy. We are heavily intertwined, our economy is, with theirs. They have moved hundreds of millions of people out of abject poverty into a more prosperous lifestyle. I think that it's a, you know, strong, dynamic economy with significant military potential. And I don't see that anything like that has happened in the Soviet Union. It doesn't mean there isn't corruption in China; I think there is. But I think, you know, we're far enough into one another's economy that we've got a better feel for how we measure their progress, their levels of production and so forth. I mean, we're into their knickers a long way and vice versa. The Soviet Union was—I don't think they've ever really made that transition. I think their economy is much shakier. Much more dependent on a single resource, energy.

You're talking about Russia today.

Russia.

Okay.

And I think the level of corruption is probably higher there than in China. That's my view.

So you don't hold the view that a Stalinist system that is brutally repressive of its own people's freedoms is, *because* of that feature, foreordained—

To fail.

—to failure or to ruin, yeah.

I used to hold that view. [pauses] I'd have to say I guess I've been surprised at how well the Chinese have done, starting from that base, over a long period of time. I can't claim to be a Chinese expert, or a Russian or a Soviet expert, but it strikes me that the Chinese have done a remarkable job of preserving their political structure and prospering in spite of it.

I mean, it does take a Tiananmen Square along the way.

Sure—or Hong Kong. I mean, they're having problems in Hong Kong right now, over free elections; you're never quite sure how that's going to sort out. But I think there has been an evolution in the sense that there was almost an article of faith that the closer they get to free enterprise, [a] market-oriented economy, the more likely they are to have to make political compromises in terms of the political structure they had developed. And to some extent, they *have* made some of those kinds of changes. But they have been more successful than I would have expected they could have been, given their political structure. I can't speak for others, but [it] seems to me that's increasingly a consensus view.

Do you see a military conflict between China and one of its weaker neighbors, perhaps with one of these territorial disputes as the pretext, as highly likely in the short term?

Mmm, I can't predict that. I don't think, at least I have not thought in the *past*, that China's interested in a head-on conflict with the U.S. I don't think it's in their interest or in our interest. I think there are areas of potential friction out there. The islands off Japan obviously are a place where we have interest and clearly the Japanese are deeply concerned about it. At one point we looked at China, early on in our administration, as a potential ally in dealing with the North Korean nuclear problem. That hasn't come to pass. They've not really been an ally there, partly because I think we botched it on our side. But I—are they likely to get into a dustup of some kind? In a sense, they already are with the Vietnamese in terms of who owns—

Fishing rights and things.

Yeah. The Philippines are affected by some of that. I remember there used to be a—Shell had a major development west, several hundred miles, west of the Philippines, same general area. But I can't predict that there's going to be a head-to-head confrontation. But the Chinese, again, are increasingly, I think, able to throw their weight around. They've developed a ballistic missile capability that is probably targeted on our carriers; invested heavily, I think, in improving their own military capabilities; and are extraordinarily dangerous when you start to talk about cyberwarfare. So they're, you know, a major potential threat and at the same time an economic competitor.

Does the fact that China owns so much of our debt constrain our foreign policy and national security decision making?

I don't think so. I don't think it has.

Do you think that the window has closed for Israel to pursue military action against the Iranian nuclear program in the event that the on-running P5+1 talks eventually do fail? Do you think that the Israelis have simply talked about that for too long and that the targets in that time have been hardened or dispersed significantly?

Mmm, I'm going to take a pass on that one.

Okay.

It's a good question. I don't want to make headlines—and no matter what I say—

[laughs]

It's an extraordinarily important issue. But I am reluctant to make forecasts and predictions especially with this administration in power.

Some observers place the start of the Arab Spring not with the Tunisian fruit vendor but with the ordinary Iranians who protested in the streets of Tehran in June 2009 over the rigged presidential elections and who were brutally crushed by the IRGC [Iranian Revolutionary Guard Corps] and the militia there. At the time, some said that President Obama did nothing to help the democracy movement in Iran because he wanted to preserve the prospect of nuclear diplomacy with the regime. In your view, was there anything that the United States could have done—covertly or otherwise—to support that movement at that time and thereby maybe have helped catalyze some kind of major change in Iran?

I'm not familiar enough with what they did and didn't do to be able to judge it. You know, your one hope, sort of peaceful hope, with respect to Iran is a change in regime, and—that's generated internally. That may be the best opportunity that we ever had during that period of time when there *was* domestic unrest with respect to the regime in Iran. But I look at it and I'm very, very concerned about what's going on at this point. I am convinced the administration is primarily interested in getting out of town without having the Iranians embarrass them by demonstrating that they now have, or will soon have, nuclear capability. And—but I also, I'm— well, let's just leave it at that. I think it's one of the biggest problems we face. I think if Iran acquires that capability, they won't be the only ones in the region that have it, that there will be a nuclear arms race in the Middle East. And that strikes me as an extraordinarily dangerous proposition.

Characterizing the kind of government that exists in Iran right now is not a clear-cut proposition. You have a theocracy on one hand but it's also, with the increasing role of the IRGC throughout all aspects of Iranian life, a hybrid

of theocracy and military dictatorship. You just averred to the potential for regime change, but—since this revolution is now, well, almost forty years old—there is a regime that has managed to sort of entrench itself.

Yup.

What should we be doing that we are not?

I am not advocating a course of action. I mean, I make the statement that, in terms of sort of wishful thinking, would be that the problem of Iranian nukes would go away because of internal developments inside Iran. I don't think that is going to happen, and I don't think there is a lot the United States can do about it at this point, anyway. Now, part of that's the way I look at the Obama administration. I think their conduct is such that in terms of trying to operate covertly inside Iran or to work with others in the neighborhood who might have a shared interest, that they don't have the trust and confidence of our friends in the region to get involved in that kind of effort. They're convinced at this stage that net-net, the Obama administration is part of the problem, not part of the solution. And people out there, I don't think, are likely to work with us because of their conviction. For example, just in the last day or two, somebody sent me an e-mail where the White House [was] responding to this petition that hundreds of thousands had signed and sent to the White House, calling on the White House to designate the Muslim Brothers [*sic*] as a terrorist organization. Just yesterday, [they] put out a statement and said no, they don't see any evidence that the Muslim Brothers [is] a terrorist organization. [With] that kind of mindset, this administration is not likely to do anything based upon the proposition that they can change, or that others are willing to sign on with us, in an effort to change the regime in Iran.

One last question on Iran. Again projecting us into an unknowable future, for the sake of discussion: Were we to assume that Iran will attain a

nuclear weapons capability and in fact nuclear weapons, should we imagine that the regime would be as susceptible to the allure of the concept of mutually assured destruction as the Soviet Union was in the Cold War? Or should we assume that this regime, by nature of its character, by virtue of its theocratic bent, would not necessarily be so susceptible to MAD thinking?

I think we make a huge mistake if we assume a policy of mutually assured destruction will assure stability where a nuclear-armed Iran is concerned. MAD won't work, I don't think. I mean, I think we make a big mistake if we think we can go from the way we operated vis-à-vis the Soviets during the Cold War, where we both had significant nuclear capability, and transpose that to Iran, a nuclear-armed Iran, and assume there will be the same kind of stability.

Why is that a mistake to assume?

Well, I look at the track record in that part of that world. I see—we have already talked about Libya's efforts to acquire a nuclear capability. Thank God when the revolution occurred in Libya, and Muammar went down, the weapons design, the centrifuges, and so forth had already been turned over to the United States, because we had gone into Iraq. Thank goodness the Israelis had taken out the Syrian reactor the North Koreans had built for them at Al Kibar before ISIS took over and created a caliphate where the nuclear reactor was. But we've still got problems out there, and Iran is likely to be a big one. I worry very much about Pakistan and about the juxtaposition on the one hand of terror-sponsoring states or even states that just have a significant Islamist population inside. And you've got to remember the Taliban in Pakistan—when was it?—last summer attacked the Karachi airport and killed forty or fifty civilians. And that there's a significant inventory of nuclear weapons in Pakistan. A. Q. Khan, who was the father of the Pakistani program, has said publicly that the North Koreans bribed the Pakistanis for the current technology they are operating to enrich uranium, in the old centrifuge design. And we know they are operating those centrifuges; and American scientists have been there and seen 'em.

[Siegfried] Hecker.

So the political situation is such, you know, you can imagine if the Syrians had been allowed to complete that nuclear reactor, and to create the capacity to field their own nuclear weapons, when ISIS moved in and took over. It's a very unstable part of the world, and it's not like dealing with the Soviet Union. I think it's a big mistake for us to assume the same kind of thing will happen here, and I think that the danger of a terrorist organization, failed states, capacity for bribery and trade in this kind of technology are sufficiently great. So I don't anticipate a situation in which you can plan on stability as a result of something equivalent to mutually assured destruction. I don't think it's possible. I think the prospect for somebody ultimately using one of these weapons in the near future will rise dramatically when Iran acquires that capability and others in the area respond by acquiring their own.

Given Iran's own history, too. All right. Let's tackle some current events and maybe be able to run through them quickly. Some of these are not in your wheelhouse, and I recognize that in advance. But nonetheless, you have been around a long time.

[chuckles] As long as you've been alive, it turns out!

Yes. And I just think your view on these things would be valuable to have. Even if you don't assert yourself as expert, necessarily, in some of these areas. Mr. Vice President, when you gaze upon the images coming out of Ferguson, Missouri, what do you see?

Well—[pauses]—what I see is disturbing in the sense—it's always a tragedy when there is a death involved and so forth. But it seems to me it's a clear-cut case that the officer did what he had to do to defend himself. He was perfectly within his authorities to take action. That if [someone] reached through the open car window and slapped an officer upside the head and reached for his gun, you know, there is going to be a response. And I think the—[pauses]—I've been disappointed, I guess, in the administration's response. I think—[pauses]—I think there should have been more people who were ready to stand up and say, "Look, the evidence is pretty overwhelming. The grand jury has reviewed it thoroughly. Here's what we know. This is what happened." And that we should not sort of throw it all over on the burden of race, or racial inequality or racial discrimination, as being responsible for this particular event. I think that would be wrong and—[pauses]—it bothers me that that kind of an incident has generated that kind of response. I don't think it is about race. I think it is about an individual who conducted himself in a manner that was almost guaranteed to provoke an officer trying to do his duty, doing what he had to do.

Is it a safe bet to say that we are going to see more Fergusons?

I don't know. I'm reluctant to generalize from it. I, uh—[pauses]—well, I'll leave it at that.

On immigration, today's Republican Party is usually apt to brand almost any attempt at comprehensive immigration reform, and just about any path to citizenship for illegal immigrants who are already here, as "amnesty." What do you think about that?

Ohh [sighs]—I, you know, you're taking me back now to 1986 and Simpson-Mazzoli.[16]

INS v. Chadha.[17]

When we went through all of that once before.

But the tone and the posture of the Republican Party may be more acute today.

Well, but I think the Republican Party is of many minds. I don't think there is sort of a bloc mentality there. We may not have a majority yet for a particular course of action. That doesn't mean we couldn't get there. I think a very important part of the problem is securing the border, and I think there is a legitimate concern on the part of a great many Republicans that this president has done anything *but* secure the border, that the way he has conducted himself and the way he has pursued matters along the border has been, you know, to welcome more and more immigrants in. I think we are a nation of immigrants, we continue to depend on immigration; but there is a right way and a wrong way to do it and we've got laws that ought to be enforced. And this administration appears to be bound and determined to try to generate some kind of political benefit or value but at the same time not enforce the laws that are on the books with respect to what's legal and what isn't, and especially how we secure the border. I think the various elements in our party respond to that and have different concerns. You know, I was part of a ticket with George Bush where we got—what?—44 percent of the Hispanic vote.[18] So I—[pauses]—I hope that we'll be able to come to some kind of a combination at some point. I know it is not impossible to do because we did it once before.

Strictly as a political matter, and given certain demographic realities—which have as much to do with [the] prevalence of female voters as different ethnic groups, but [nonetheless]—must the Republican Party begin making inroads with Hispanic voters in order to remain competitive, strictly as a political matter?

No. There's always the analysis by the political analysts. The Democrats like to spend a lot of time analyzing what's wrong with the Republican

Party, and the Republicans have to do this or that. It seems to me—I saw the numbers just the other day—that one of the most rapidly growing segments of the electorate that tends to be pro-Republican are senior citizens, those over sixty-five. There are more of them than there are the minorities that the Democrats supposedly have wrapped up in terms of their support. I have to go back and check that. [To Steen:] It would be something worth looking at, Jim. But I saw that just the other day. Somebody reported that. And that, you know, the group in the electorate that's growing more rapidly tends to be Republican in terms of when you look at senior citizens and the baby boomer generation retiring, than when you look at the, well, racial minorities. So I don't necessarily start from the assumption that the problem is all ours. I don't think it is. I think if you look at the last election, the '14 congressional election, that was a pretty remarkable performance. And if I were spending time trying to analyze, if the Democrats don't start focusing on analyzing their *own* problems and quit spending their time trying to tell us what is wrong with *our* party, you know, they are going to have trouble.

Democratic political consultant Joe Trippi and I sometimes chat on the roof of the Fox News building. And he likes to talk about how the Republican share of the electorate is shrinking two points each cycle, and he will tell you further that the high-water mark of Republican presidential candidates capturing the white male vote is a statistical tie in history—George H. W. Bush in 1988 captured 60 percent of that vote, and Mitt Romney in 2012 captured 60 percent of that vote. And he cites this as evidence that the Republican Party cannot go on trying to win elections on the basis of its traditional constituencies.

Hmm. Where was he a month ago—[laughs]—when we cleaned their clock?

Except that there was very little turnout, pretty low turnout in 2014.

You know, you can argue away. I think in the end, you've got to look at election results, and I think that the Republican Party is the party today that's—has the great advantage of not being headed up by Barack Obama. And the burden the Democrats are clearly having to bear—I think that if I were a Democrat, I'd be embarrassed about what had happened over the last several years and the flawed leadership that's been provided to the country and the disastrous effort to take over one-sixth of the economy in the healthcare system, and the train wreck that's occurring with respect to the international situation. I mean, I don't feel at this stage that we owe an accounting so much as I do that the Democrats owe an accounting. And the voters in the last election, given the opportunity, pronounced a pretty significant verdict on the failures of the Democratic Party and their leadership.

What do you think of the Tea Party?

Mmm [sighs]—it's a phrase that's come to identify a certain segment of the electorate. I find that many people who identify themselves as Tea Partiers are hard-rock conservative Republicans. They believe in limited government, they believe in fiscal restraint, low taxes, a robust military capability, a lot of the basic same fundamental positions that *I* do. When I was a congressman, I had one of the most conservative voting records in the Congress. If I were there today, I would still be pretty conservative— by anybody's standards. I am glad that they are active inside the Republican Party. I think they bring a lot to the debate. I would much rather see that debate occur inside our party rather than outside it. I'm glad they see the Republican Party as the most natural home for them and the place where they are most likely to be able to advance their cause and their interest.

We talked a little bit about this before. How important is the Keystone Pipeline itself to American energy security at this point?

Well, I think what's happening, basically—and again, you would have to go check the numbers on some of this—is that a lot of that oil is going to find its way to the Gulf Coast, anyway.

Via rail.

Via rail and even trucks. I happen to have a friend who is involved in the pipeline project from the Bakken field down, connects up with, I think it's the Burlington Northern rail system in Wyoming. No, the industry will find ways to adjust and adapt.

The thing that has concerned me about it, again, is the total inconsistency of this administration with respect to energy. One of the things I worry about on the downside—and it could still happen—is that in the end the Canadians get tired of getting jerked around. The Chinese are eager to build the pipeline to get it to Vancouver and the coast and to build the loading facilities and to build the tankers to haul all that stuff to China. And they'll happily do it, pick up the freight for it. And we will have passed up the opportunity to gain an additional access to a resource that's about as reliable as we can have, coming from Canada, our closest and most reliable trading partner.

And I don't see what the environmental objections are with respect to the pipeline. I was born in Nebraska. My great-grandfather went broke farming in Nebraska back in 1890. I know where that pipeline is going to go. There are dozens of pipelines already out there. It will be underground. It's not an environmental problem. There is really no justification for it other than somebody believes they're opposed to fossil fuels period, and they don't want to do anything to advance the cause of fossils. I just fundamentally disagree with that position. We've got great resources; we ought to use 'em. They are to our advantage as an economy. We ought to be able to use our new position in the world as a major exporter, as the leading producer of oil and gas, to our great political advantage and our national and/or geostrategic situation. And instead, you know, we've got an administration that is afraid to make a decision and to go forward with an eminently reasonable project that wouldn't cost the federal government a dime.

There has been some suggestion that the actual conversion of shale discoveries into consumable energy has lagged behind the hype. Where do you see us being right now in terms of shale development? And what realistic impacts do you see it having both here and abroad in the near and long term?

Well, I think what's happened is that basically, it's a technological advancement, development, that now allows us to recover resource from areas and formations that we previously could not tap into, economically.

Fracking.

Fracking. My old company, Halliburton, was one of the leading fracking companies in the country, one of the very first to develop that technology and use it as a way to finish wells. In those days, we didn't have directional drilling. We didn't have the ability to drill down and follow for miles, you know, a relatively narrow band of shale and so forth that we can do today.

One well pad today is equal to a much larger surface area of—

Yeah. I was down recently in Texas, and they were showing me well pads with four to six wells all coming off one pad. If anything, it reduces the footprint. It's less intrusive in the environment.

But where are we at now, in terms of overall shale development? How close are we to realizing this as a viable energy source?

Oh, I think it is *very* close. And it's the recovery, you know, depending upon the formation and so forth. If you look at the Permian Basin today, you know, the Permian Basin was a big-time boom years and years ago. It's booming all over again now. And that's primarily because we now have the capacity, whereas we maybe only got 20 percent of the resource the first time around, we can go back into it now and get another 20, 30, or 40 percent of the resource that's there because of our technology, because of our capabilities. And so the technology has made it possible for us to go harvest and develop a resource, an enormous resource that we possess as a nation, in the whole area of fossil fuels. And part of that, obviously, is the shale development.

When we first went into office in 2000, as I recall, there were forty-some applications pending to build LNG importation facilities in the U.S. These are the facilities required to bring in liquefied natural gas, LNG, in tankers and offload 'em, covert it to gas, and put it into our system. Some of those are still out there now being reengineered, and they were never built, with a couple of exceptions. They are being reengineered as export facilities. And so there's no doubt in my mind but that there's an enormous development there. It's being done without any help from the federal government. Barack Obama likes to stand up and talk about how we've had this tremendous progress in energy.

In production, yeah.

Yeah! He didn't have a damn thing to do with it! I was the [chuckles] keynoter out at the wildcatters convention in Las Vegas [the] year before last. They're the guys that did it! They are the ones that made the investments and worked hard to develop the technology and took the risk—as well as a lot of the majors involved, too. Private sector is doing it and done it. And no thanks to the federal government.

And does this have the ability, or I should say the potential, to really make us energy independent?

Absolutely.

But would that require the right regulatory climate?

Well, the regulatory climate for example, the effort to shut down the coal industry creates a situation in which the only option then would be to go for gas to run those power plants. And we won't be using our coal resource. And the gas won't be available for other purposes, won't be available for export, for example. I'm not sure why you would want to do that. The market's going to work out there. There'll be decisions made, especially going forward, about building new plants, whether you build coal-fired or gas-fired. But we ought to let the market make those decisions. And we should not come in artificially, as the government is now doing, through the Environmental Protection Agency, and doing everything we can to shut down the coal industry in my home state of Wyoming. Coal produces about 40 percent of the electricity in the country today. That's enormous. That is sort of a base power element that we need. And if you come in and shut down those plants by regulation, shut down the mines that supply them by regulation, you are going to eliminate the possibility that we can take advantage so we maintain that resource and we go develop more gas and so forth.

It's not really the all-of-the-above policy that the president maintains that he is pursuing, in other words.

Of course not!

Just a few more questions and we are done.

Okay.

There's a book out now called *The Second Machine Age*, written by a pair of guys from MIT, that assesses the effects on industrialized economies of the increasingly rapid and profound changes that are being wrought by technological innovations—among them an annual doubling of computing power. With the understanding that the digital revolution is probably still in its infancy, how do you see it transforming America in the years to come?

Oh, that's a whole new subject I'd have to go give some thought to.

Come on, it's a Newt Gingrich question, right? [laughs]

Yeah. You know, you can look at the enormous impact it's had over the last few years. I mean, we're sitting here, I've got my iPad, I've got my iPhone; my laptop's around here someplace. You know, a few years ago, I wouldn't have known how to turn one of those on! I can barely—according to my grandkids—barely turn one on today. It's just a phenomenal change in our whole society.

And it's having profound impacts on our labor force.

Mm-hmm, it is. There was a piece in the *Economist* I read recently, [that] talked about three revolutions, as I recall. And one was the, oh, the late—when steam came in—eighteenth century, late eighteenth century. Then we got into the twentieth century, and—or, am I—I need to keep my centuries straight. But then to the second industrial revolution. In both cases, those generated a significant increase in employment. That the third, the one we are in now with respect to [the] digital revolution, so far, had not produced the gains in employment that the earlier ones had. That's, you know, an interesting proposition. It's the first time I had seen it suggested, was in the *Economist* just a few weeks ago. But it starts to make sense. I mean, as we see this phenomenal growth in development, in terms of the technology and what we're able to do with it, we've still got a declining percentage of participation by our workforce, our population.

Labor participation rate is the lowest it's been since 1978.

Exactly. And headed south.

And that's not entirely attributable to Barack Obama, in your view?

Well, it's a statistic that I think has been ignored for far too long. We always worry about the unemployment rate, and we don't spend enough time—politically, that has always been the significant number, was the unemployment rate, and are we up to 12 or 14 percent or whatever it might be [when underemployment is factored in]. But now we are talking about the percentage of the workforce, the percentage of the population that is in the workforce, and that, disturbingly, is on the downward slide and has consistently been there for quite a while. And—[pauses]—you know, I suppose there are different arguments for it. I am not prepared to make any bold statements on it at this point. I am a student, I guess you would say now. You get into the whole question of the extent to which government makes it—not "profitable," but, but—

"Attractive."

"Attractive." Provides an adequate level of living for people who don't work. They can be part of that unemployed—that part of the population that doesn't participate. So you can have both of those working together. Every once in a while I run into someone who has strong views on the notion that we're rapidly approaching the point where we have got more people receiving benefits than we do paying taxes. And that's worrisome in terms of its long-range political impact on the country.

Three more to go. You were talking earlier about how it has been an article of faith for some that as a country like China moves towards free-market participation, it will inevitably bring it along in a kind of democratization sense. I think there is a kind of corresponding article of faith out there today that the Internet and all of the changes it has wrought will also prove to be a democratizing force throughout the world. And some have pointed to the Arab Spring as early evidence of this: the fact that you've got this extraordinary demographic cohort in the Middle East, for the first time in human history, one hundred million people who are under the age of thirty, in these stifled societies without much economic opportunity for them there. But not just that: the fact that they're wired, and they're plugged in and they can see, in a way they never were able to before, what they are missing out on. Do you regard the Internet as an intrinsically democratizing force?

[chuckles, then pauses] Oh, boy, you know—we're blue-skyin' it now, James—

I really told you earlier that I was going to take you out of your comfort zone. [laughs]

Yeah. No, let me think—let me think about that one. I think it clearly—[pauses]—clearly has had a significant impact. "A democratizing force." Um—[pauses]—

In the sense that, whenever you have a free flow—a *freer* flow—of information, that's going to redound to the forces of good; I guess that's the underlying assumption.

Yeah, but on the other hand, I suppose you could argue that it provides ways in which the government, an authoritarian government, can control and exert control over and monitor and keep track of what everybody is up to and what they are doing. It's not a one-way street. It's not necessarily—I need to think about that before I comment further. I'm just wandering around here now.

But I think that the world would be interested in your views on those subjects.

Okay, but let me think about them before I voice views that—

I'm not even saying that I [chuckles] should necessarily be the sole channel through which you articulate your views on these subjects—but I think were Dick Cheney to write about some of these broader, bigger, global changing things that are happening right now in the information arena, and technology, I think people would be interested in your views on it.

Mm-hmm.

Two final questions. What advice would you offer to younger public officials who are coming up through the ranks now about how to deal with the news media?

Well.

Let the record reflect that I got a chuckle out of you.

[laughs, then pauses] Well, you know, when I think about it, it has changed a lot in my forty-six years since you were born [chuckles] and I came to Washington. You know, and back to the day when we had the *Washington Post* and the *New York Times* and three networks—and that was the media. And what I am struck by now is just the enormous, enormous proliferation of sources of information. And that's obviously relevant to anybody who is involved in the political wars. But in terms of how we function as a society, I don't have room on my iPad often days, just to keep up with my e-mail. And everybody is in a similar position.

Sensory overload.

Yeah, but just pure time. I mean, I've got to trash a lot of stuff to get to the important messages that I need to pay attention to and respond to. But overwhelmed—you *can* be overwhelmed just by the sheer volume of information that is available. There's a huge variety of sources, and it is dramatically, dramatically different.

I really was just asking about interpersonal relations with reporters. You know, what advice would you give to younger public officials about dealing with the news media, dealing with reporters? Do you have any?

Well—[pauses]—I think you've really got to think about what you mean about "news media." It's no longer just a handful of reporters that cover the White House. You know, I've got friends who own websites or services or who have got their own—they're making money off the business of running the Daily Whatever.

Neil Patel [the former aide to Cheney in the White House who cofounded the Daily Caller].

Are they in the news business? Well, yeah.

They're in the content business.

Yeah. It's a—[pauses]—I am not to the point where I can sort of assess where it's all headed. I think, frankly, the news media is less important than they once were. It is much less of a monopoly than it used to be. The variety of opinions expressed and the different places you can go for information or a viewpoint is enormous and growing by leaps and bounds.

Bewildering to some extent.

Yeah. And so I know back in the day, in the Ford administration, there were a handful of people that really set the stage in terms of covering the White House. I could probably, as the chief of staff, I could talk to all of 'em every day. And that *was* what went out, you know, that was one of the centerpieces from which all the information flowed. But you know, if you had a beer with Lou Cannon of the [*Washington*] *Post* and—who was covering us then for the *New York Times*? You know, there weren't very many places you had to touch in order to sort of get out the message, whatever it was the administration was interested in peddling. And it is, as I say, I think there's much less of a monopoly as there used to be on the flow of news and the people you would have to deal with if you were trying to influence events.

Is there one reporter in your career above all others whom you hold in greatest contempt as unprincipled or dishonest?

[laughs] "Greatest contempt"! That wasn't quite what I thought you were going to ask! Uh, yeah. But I'm going to chew on that one, too, before I say it.

But you will say it?

No; I'll think about it. [laughs]

[laughs] I have a guess.

You do, huh?

One that you actually rebuked on TV, saying, "You're out of line."

Mmm. I don't remember that.

Okay. That was CNN anchor Wolf Blitzer.

Uh-huh. No, it wouldn't be Wolf. I bear him no ill will. [laughs]

[laughs] Thank you very much.

DAY THREE

JAMES ROSEN: Today is December 3, 2014, the final day of our sessions with Vice President Cheney. And we are still in your library here in your lovely home, and thank you again for your time. It's been a real honor for me as well as a learning experience. So our first subject today is 9/11. I begin simply, in the broadest sense, by asking you: Do you think that there is any aspect of 9/11 that is popularly misunderstood by the American people?

DICK CHENEY: I can't think of anything immediately offhand. I just think the extent to which it has been covered, [it's] one of those events that nearly everyone who was alive then remembers. Still extensive television coverage of it. I watched an episode of *Blue Bloods* the other night. And it's got Tom Selleck asking, you know, "Where were you on 9/11?" kind of thing, in a story of police officers and the tower. I mean, it's part of the culture. There are, in terms of things that are misunderstood, I can't think of anything right offhand.

Is there anything about the event that isn't as prominent in the public imagination about it, or understanding about it, that you think should be more prominent?

Hmm! [pauses] Well, I just had the experience of—it's been about two weeks ago now—I was in New York, and they gave me a personal tour of the new museum [the National September 11 Memorial & Museum]. I'd been on the site before and seen, you know, the pool and so forth. But this is the first time I had gone down since they finished the museum on 9/11. And it's a really remarkable facility, the kind of thing that brings back an awful lot of memories. That will be valuable in educating future generations about what happened that day. And—[pauses]—you know, paying honor and tribute to those who sacrificed, to the first responders and so forth. So it's very, very well done. Is there anything that's *not* covered? I can't think of what it would be. Or that's not—

Sufficiently emphasized, or—

Yeah. But there has been so much said about it. You could go find, I'm sure that any subject you could bring up, you could find somebody who has talked about it, made a documentary about it, written an article about it. I mean, it's exhaustively covered.

And yet despite that prevalence in the public imagination and discourse, do you feel as though, at this stage of remove from the event, Americans or large segments of Americans are in danger of forgetting why it's so important or the lessons of it? Or otherwise, not in any kind of a malicious way, but just have kind of moved on.

Well, there's a certain amount of that involved. I do think there is a danger in our forgetting what that was like when I see, you know, well, somebody adopt sort of an isolationist view of what U.S. policy ought to be in the world, that they've completely ignored the lessons of 9/11. You go back and talk about the America Firsters and the people before World War II and the problems that [Franklin] Roosevelt had to overcome, which obviously changed dramatically when the Japanese attacked Pearl Harbor. But I think about Jerry Ford, who was an America Firster before the war. After his service in the Pacific, he came home and basically defeated an incumbent congressman because he wasn't an internationalist; Ford was. His whole view of the world had changed, obviously, because of World War II.

But we've got prominent folks out there now, some in my own party, who are arguing for an isolationist approach, that we don't need to be actively involved overseas. We need to bring the troops home, minimize our involvement in what's happening around the world, especially in the Middle East. And you know, my immediate reaction when I hear that is, you know: Where the hell were *they* on 9/11, when nineteen guys armed with airline tickets and box-cutters came over here and destroyed the World Trade Center, blew a big hole in the Pentagon, would've taken out the White House or the Capitol if it hadn't been for the courage of the passengers on United 93, and killed three thousand Americans? Worse than Pearl Harbor. And—

You know that those elements—and I think we can safely say among them, perhaps most prominently, we're talking about Senator Rand Paul—bristle at that term "isolationist"—

Right.

—and prefer the term "non-interventionist." I gather you regard that—

That's why I use the term "isolationist."

It's a distinction without a difference, in other words.

In my mind, it is. And it's another element, I think, or another dimension of 9/11 that I think was very important and is still today. You can find people who don't agree with my interpretation of events. But it was the *transition* that 9/11 represented in my mind, and in the mind of the president and a lot of us, that it was not a terrorist attack in the conventional sense of the kinds of problems we'd had to deal with pre-9/11. It was an act of war that was—in terms of striking the homeland, the number of casualties, the extent of the damage—certainly as serious as Pearl Harbor. And understanding that we'd moved from a situation where we perceived something like 9/11 as a terrorist attack versus an act of war had a big impact on how we dealt with the aftermath, what we did in order to prevent future attacks. You move from the traditional approach where the FBI goes out and investigates, finds the bad guys, brings them back, put 'em on trial, and send them to supermax prison to a situation in which you have authorization for the use of military force, the ability to use your national intelligence assets, your military capabilities, etc., in terms of pursuing those who perpetrated that act as well as doing everything you can to prevent the next one. And it's a significant difference. It's just not a semantic way of talking about a particular incident.

It's a wholesale reorientation of the Executive Branch and the military's mission, right?

Exactly. And the kinds of operations that you want to undertake in order to prevent it. It also puts you in a position—it certainly did us, as we thought about what we were faced with—where all of a sudden you've got the prospects for a far greater threat to the nation, when you begin to think about the possibility of that *next* mass-casualty attack, which [could be] something far deadlier than airline tickets and box-cutters.

In tackling this subject, I saw fit to kind of divide it up into different facets of it, and it just seemed natural to begin with the pre-9/11 period. Can one believe the worst about [former White House counterterrorism advisor] Richard Clarke[1]—namely, that he was a shameless, left-of-center self-promoter with a book to sell—*Against All Enemies: Inside America's War on Terror* (2004)—while still accepting the validity of his central argument? Namely, that he spent the eight months prior to 9/11 struggling without success to get the senior officials of the Bush administration to really focus on the al Qaeda threat?

Hmm! My own personal interpretation of him is the former.

Cannot both be true?

Um—[pauses]—I didn't deal with Richard Clarke. I mean, he dealt, I think, more with Condi than anybody else in the NSC. He was *around*. And I may well have been in meetings with him, but I don't recall any interaction with him during that period and often had the feeling that his robust presentations after 9/11 were after the fact.

Ex post facto.

Ex post facto explanation of what had happened prior to that period of time. Now, we were not oblivious to the dangers of a terrorist attack, by *any* means. And in my case I gave an interview—was it *Atlantic* magazine, or *Atlantic Monthly*, or *New York*, maybe *New York* magazine? We can dig it out, I'm sure; Jim [Steen] will have a copy of it—that ran along in April [2001], several months before 9/11.

This is excerpted in your memoir.[2]

Yeah.

There's a paragraph.

Where I was asked about threats to the country, and the threat I had
highlighted was a terrorist attack by a terrorist armed with weapons of
mass destruction. We also had a situation where there had been a number
of commissions looking into this whole question of homeland security.
And one of the things the president asked me to do was to review those
various recommendations and commissions. And so we brought on board
an admiral whose name escapes me now [retired Admiral Steve Abbot].
But his basic mission was to pull all of that stuff together and to begin to
look at it and so forth and see if there were things there we needed to be
doing or recommendations that ought to be followed. A lot of that work
then fed in, directly after 9/11, into the initial steps of creating an Office
of Homeland Security in the Executive Office of the President and so forth.
So to suggest that somehow we weren't concerned about terrorist attacks
or al Qaeda, I don't think would be accurate. We'd also—another thing I
remember was in August [2001] when the president authorized for the first
time arming drones. We had a situation where, the situation we'd inherited,
you could go with a drone and spot a target but you couldn't do anything
about it. You had to bring in the C-130 or the AC-130 gunship platform
with weapons on it to take it out. And the recommendation came up—I
can't remember from who, probably the agency [CIA]—that we arm
Predators, and that's really when we began that process. And that
happened, as I recall, before 9/11. So there were things we were doing that
were motivated by concerns about the continuing terrorism threat.

In his memoir—I should point out, too—

And I've never read Clarke's book, so I'm not sure what he's talking about.

**Sure—that, in our exchanges of e-mails where you wanted an outline of our
sessions, in addition to 9/11 and Iraq, this final set of sessions was also to
include "Cheney addresses his critics." And so, in running some of this by**

you, I don't want you to get the sense, necessarily, that I am personally invested in every concept that I am presenting to you but simply giving you the opportunity to address these things. Because as you know, there is a wide literature on all of this, and not all of it is reliable. And it falls to someone like yourself, I think, to confront these things, and that's a large part of my purpose today, so—

I've never been bashful in doing that.

[laughs] In his memoir, Clarke wrote that he had actually known you for twelve years at that point or had first met you twelve years earlier.

Mm-hmm.

And he does include some anecdotes that dated back to the Gulf War period. But he presents it as that he understood that you were someone who had a very keen interest in national security issues. And he wrote about a briefing that he conducted on al Qaeda for you and other senior officials in January of '01, and he writes, "I hoped Cheney would speak up about the urgency of the problem, put it on a short list for immediate action. He didn't."

I don't remember the briefing. I don't remember meeting Dick Clarke twelve years before. What was he doing then?

I'd have to look it up myself.[3]

Mm-hmm. I'm trying to think what I was doing then. I guess this would have been back in, mmm—

That would have been '89, yeah.

—in my early days in the Defense Department. I just—I have no recollection of it.

As you know, the large thematic charge against the senior officials of the Bush administration—which I think has been forcefully pressed by Bill Clinton, among others, that time he exploded on Chris Wallace—

What was that?

Oh—

Oh, that he had had a shot at bin Laden and didn't take it?

I can't remember the question that Chris asked.

Yeah.

But what was remarkable about that encounter—and it got played endlessly, not only on our network but elsewhere—was how Bill Clinton reacted so forcefully. And sort of became somewhat vituperous toward Chris, who sat there and said, "I'm asking questions." And Clinton persisted. But he mentioned Dick Clarke and all of that.[4] As you know, the central thematic thrust of the administration's critics about this pre-9/11 period was that while there was some episodic attention to al Qaeda and the threat it posed, by and large, the senior national security principals of the Bush administration were focused on other threats that proved not as imminent, such as ballistic missile defense issues or even bioterrorism, necessarily, or different things that weren't al Qaeda. I'm sure you're familiar with that strain of criticism.

Well, I've been trying to think what the criticism is. That we did not anticipate 9/11? We did not; nor did the intelligence community. Never produced any actionable intelligence. They'd say, you know, "There's a threat out there" and so forth. But—[pauses]—I guess it's hard to respond to anything as vague as that—

Right. In other words, the criticism is—

—that somehow, somehow we should have picked up on the attack before it was launched.

We talked yesterday about how you typically digested the President's Daily Brief before he did. Do you happen to recall whether the famous PDB of August 6, [2001], titled "Bin Ladin Determined to Strike in US" [spelling as in original] struck you with any particular force, caused you to take any action, or seek more information, or anything at all?

I don't. I remember the brief primarily because of all the attention it's received since those events.

Right.

But—[pauses]—you know, I guess one of the questions would be how well the intelligence community was organized to deal with those issues. How many analysts did they have on the al Qaeda problem pre-9/11? [pauses] There was a sense that, as I look back on it, that, you know, you'd had the bombing of the USS *Cole*—what?—the previous October [October 12, 2000], and as best I could tell, there had never been any action taken by the previous administration to deal with that problem. We were aware of bin Laden. On 9/11, there wasn't much doubt, once it occurred, that al Qaeda was behind the attack.

Clarke's book is replete with these quotations from memos he was sending— perhaps, as you suggest, principally to Condi Rice—in ever more dire language.

Mm-hmm.

We both know Condi Rice well—you better than me, of course. And I think we both have great respect for her and her intellect and so forth, her patriotism and service.

Yeah.

Is it a proper conclusion to take away from Clarke's parade of memos that perhaps the national security advisor was not sufficiently attuned to what Clarke was trying to tell her?

My view of Clarke is that he spent a lot of time in "the morning after" trying to create a role for himself. I always felt he was not happy that he had not been given a major role in the administration after the transition. And frankly, I've never paid much attention to him. I haven't read his book. And in terms of his relationship with Condi and how she handled all of that—[pauses]—I'm not inclined to assign much credibility to virtually anything he says.

Was the fact that 9/11 happened *by definition* an intelligence failure?

Well, certainly you could say that, yes. On the other hand—[pauses]—there *were* some things, clearly, that we learned after the fact, if you think back on it, that the way the [intelligence] community was structured, the—sort of the wall between the FBI and CIA. The fact that we had hijackers in San Diego or Southern California in communication back to sort of a home office in Southeast Asia, in Malaysia maybe, that we missed. Didn't connect the dots. Didn't pick up on the fact that they were there. One part of the government was aware they were there, but it didn't translate into the other part.

Even two FBI agents separately feeding into the system data points about bin Laden affiliates or associates training to learn how to take off a plane but not how to land in U.S. flight training schools. One report out of Minnesota FBI and the other out of Arizona.[5]

Right.

And I think it struck a lot of Americans—who, by the year 2001, were kind of accustomed to Big Brother and to the rise of computers and big data—I think were *shocked* that the FBI infrastructure was such that those two dots wouldn't be connected *automatically*.

Well, there was a lot of history to that in terms of the background between the intelligence community on the one hand and the FBI on the other. And there clearly were decisions that had been made previously, sometimes over a period of years, about those relationships and how it would work. And that contributed to our failure to respond on 9/11. A lot of that was then, you know, a focal point, well, for the Kean [9/11] Commission,[6] for the reorganization of the intelligence community and the creation of the National Security Agency [*sic*; Department of Homeland Security] and so forth after the fact. But I—[pauses]— certainly would say that is a failure of the intelligence community.

The reason that occasions any hesitation on my part in affixing that label is because I always remember the response that Lyndon Johnson gave when he was asked why he had failed to predict the ouster of Khrushchev, and he said, "Well, Khrushchev also failed to predict the ouster of Khrushchev."

Yeah.

Okay. To move forward into the period of that day where you were, of necessity, forced into crisis response. One of the things you make clear in *In My Time* is how outmoded were the facilities, particularly for communications, that were at your disposal in the President's Emergency Operations Center (PEOC). Describe for me, if you could, what it was about the facilities that was so

primitive, exactly, and whether that was having a real-time impact on your and your colleagues' ability to discharge your duties.

Well, I guess the way I was thinking back on it—[pauses]—first of all, you've got to keep in mind what had happened, in effect. I mean, everybody was stunned. Nobody had anticipated that an airplane was going to crash into the World Trade Center, and then a second airplane, and that these would be deliberate acts aimed at taking down the World Trade Center and killing thousands of people. So there's an element of shock and awe, of surprise, for everybody in the system. The communications capabilities—let me think about that aspect of it. We were operating out of a facility that I think dated from World War II: the old PEOC that had been built under the East Wing, I think, during World War II. The communications were such that, oh, for example, the television sets. I think we had three TV sets in the PEOC, but they could only—they all had to be on the same channel. So you couldn't watch CNN over here and Fox over here. And it was—

Even Lyndon Johnson had three sets in his office in the sixties that he could watch all three networks!

He did, he did—and both wire services too, the AP and UPI.

Yeah.

I had three TV sets in my office when I took over as chief of staff. Haldeman had put 'em in there. Actually, four sets. And I used to take the kids down with me on Saturday mornings to work and they loved it because they could watch all the cartoons at once.

[laughs]

There was that problem. There was the question—there is always the fog of war, a lot of false reports coming in: car bombs gone off at the State Department, those kinds of things, airplanes headed for Camp David. So you had the normal sort of chaos, I guess, that goes [on] in that kind of crisis. We had a communications problem in the sense that phone calls would drop in the—I remember when they evacuated me from the West Wing; this is after the second plane has gone into the towers in New York. And we got a report, the Secret Service got a report that Jimmy Scott, the agent who was right outside my door had responded to, that there was a plane believed to have been hijacked headed towards Crown at a high rate of speed, "Crown" being the White House. And he came in and grabbed me, and put one hand on my belt and shoulder and sort of—I didn't have any choice but [chuckles] to do what he wanted me to do, which was move rapidly downstairs. When we got down into this tunnel, where there were doors on both ends of it, a section of the tunnel was isolated. Additional agents met us down there. Lockers were opened up, weapons were being passed out. I had no idea exactly what was happening, but when we got to that point there was a small, very old black-and-white TV, sort of on a ledge and a secure telephone. That was all—in that little section of the tunnel on the way to the PEOC.

What was on the television?

Eventually what was on the television were pictures of the Pentagon after it had been hit.

So in other words, news coverage?

There was, eventually. Now, I don't know what was—maybe it was showing soap operas when we arrived; I doubt that it was even on. But the—once we got down into the tunnel, I can remember that's where I called the president. I had them get me the president on and recommended he not return. And—that we were under attack in Washington as well and that he should not come back.

What was his response?

He didn't like that at all. In the end he agreed to do it.

How did he make clear to you he didn't like it? What did he say?

Well, he wanted to come back and he wanted to come back right away. And the Secret Service made the same recommendation, and my recommendation basically was, "Mr. President, we don't know the extent of the attack. We know New York's been hit now, we know Washington has been hit as well, too. And it's my strong recommendation you not come back to D.C. until we can figure out exactly what's happening."

And do you remember how he replied, what he said?

Just that he was, you know, he really wanted to come back as soon as possible. In the end, he accepted the recommendation.

Was there in that first call with him any statements exchanged between the two of you to the effect that, "We are at war now"? Or was it just the logistical business of whether he comes back?

No, we'd talked earlier about—from my office. There were numerous conversations, and we've never been able to nail down every conversation and when it happened and so forth. But there was a conversation I had with him while I was still in my office about, you know, "Are we going to call this an act of terror?" This was before he made his first statement to the press down in Florida. And the—in terms of the "this is an act of war," I don't recall whether that phrase was used or not. I mean—

But you had discussions about—

it was a situation that was—this was far more serious than just one attack on one building in New York. Not only have they hit New York, they're now hitting Washington. That was the significant—

So the two of you framed it—you framed it thusly together? You addressed that together?

Now don't—don't overanalyze it. But—

Well, I'm just—to try to get a sense for the content of the call.

The content of the call is as I've described it: We talked about the attack. [pauses] And I'm trying to remember if there was another call while I was down there. Anyway, there were by that time, after we'd had the conversation, I'd urged him not to return. We then moved on to the PEOC. And in the PEOC about the same time is when Norm arrived, [Transportation Secretary Norman] Mineta. And we began the process of dealing with the hijacked aircraft and so forth. But in terms of this being an act of war, I think that was pretty clear from the outset.

All of the published photographs of the policymakers inside the PEOC in those grim and scary hours—the body language, the expressions on people's faces—they all show you unmistakably as the senior figure at the table—

Mm-hmm.

—the official who was running the show, the man to whom all the others were deferring.

Right.

Without trying to trap you into something like where you are trying to arrogate unto yourself, you know, some grandeur or put you in the Al Haig box or anything like that,[7] just—I'm asking whether it was—how you saw yourself in that cloistered setting that day: that the situation cried out for leadership and—in the president's absence—and that you were the logical person to do it? How did you conceive of your role at that moment?

I didn't spend a lot of time thinking about it; I just began to operate. Everybody responded to me; everybody came to me. I didn't have to say, "I'm in charge here." I think—[pauses]—part of it had to do just with the way I'd been operating as vice president, the way the president had treated me.

Your career.

My career, my background. And a lot of the people there, some of them worked for me. So there was never any question about what my role was or what needed to be done in terms of how to respond. And if you look at the people around me, it was an evolving crowd. It started small and gradually built. At one point, the Secret Service had to actually ask some people to leave, because they were putting a strain on the oxygen in the air conditioning system down there. But yeah, that's the way it worked and—

It just sort of naturally came about that way.

Yeah, exactly. I never did say, "I'm in charge here."

No. And everyone sort of instantly understood that you were the senior figure in the room and the most experienced, in a sense.

Correct.

As you sat in the PEOC and watched the second tower fall, once you knew this was likely the work of al Qaeda, were you able in your own mind, even in those earliest moments, to look beyond the immediate exigencies that you were working on, such as grounding all the flights still in the air, to be able to see with clarity that *everything* had just changed, that the United States was now on a radically new kind of wartime footing, and that policymakers and soldiers and spies were going to need new powers, new authorities, new statutory underpinnings, all the rest? Did all of that sort of flood your mind in an instant because you're the type of guy who could, in fact, see twelve moves ahead?

That process did occur, but it was more sort of over the course of the day and on into the night, when I had time to sit down and think about it. What really kicked in at that point was, well, first of all dealing with the aircraft, because Norm had a list of six aircraft with tail numbers that had been—believed to have been hijacked. Now, it turned out there were only four; but we could only account for three of 'em. And that was the two in New York and one at the Pentagon. And the other thing, I guess, in terms of the way I sort of immediately began to respond was based on my training in the continuity-of-government program. And that was a program that I had spent a good deal of time on earlier in my career. It was highly classified; some of it's probably still classified. There were a few of us, Rumsfeld was another, who had been selected. I was still a member of Congress at the time that I'd been selected for that—to operate what we call the continuity-of-government program: how you would maintain the government, a legitimate, constitutionally based government, in the event of an all-out nuclear exchange with the

Soviet Union. And we'd thought about that, planned for it, practiced. And that training sort of automatically kicked in. The first thing you— *one* of the first things you've got to do, certainly, one of the top priorities for me, was: How do we preserve the constitutional power of the presidency? If something happens to the president, I'm next; something happens to me, Denny Hastert is next, the [House] Speaker, and so forth. And so that led me to do things such as contact the speaker. Where was he? Well, we got him out to Andrews Air Force Base and then relocated him to another secure facility. And then I would—dealt with him a couple of times during the day, just to keep him up to speed with what we were doing. It was those kinds of things that immediately kicked in. In terms of who it was, who was launching the attacks, it was pretty much an assumption from the beginning that this was al Qaeda, sort of affirmed by [George] Tenet during the course of the day. I don't think there was ever any doubt in George's mind and by that afternoon, when we're having an NSC meeting with the president, he's out at Omaha then, at Offutt [Air Force Base], and we're doing a videoconference, it was pretty clear. And I think George at that point was saying, "This is al Qaeda."

As you noted earlier, everyone was alive and sentient at that time kind of remembers where he or she was and has kind of a series of images, perhaps, in their minds that stay with them. Dick Cheney's experience on 9/11 is singular. Lots of people may have been at work and watching TV with their colleagues or what have you, but yours was a singular experience: You were the person who was, by just the set of circumstances forced upon you, compelled to direct the federal response to this event from its inception. Given that, if someone were to say to you, "9/11—that day," what are the images that flash in your mind? What stays with you?

Hmm! What stays with me? Well [chuckles], a lot. I mean, it's part of it, there was so much.

Is there an indelible actual visual image that pops to mind for you?

Hmmm. I suppose it's the towers going down. Partly again, you know, there'd been so much done and written and broadcast since 9/11, it's very, very hard to separate out and say, "Well, this is what I was thinking at this moment" and not have it be influenced by everything that I've seen and all of the replays since then. So it's, you know, the towers to some extent have become the symbol of 9/11. As I say, I was just there a couple of weeks ago to go through the museum and to see the cross that was formed out of the girders that was uncovered in the rubble, that's on display. And the names of those who were killed that day, not only there but also in the Pentagon and up at Shanksville [Pennsylvania]. You know, I spent two hours there just a couple of weeks ago going through all of that. Now, there's an awful lot there. But to say, you know, there's one thing that at that moment symbolized it for me, I think probably the most dramatic piece of it was the actual collapse of the towers.

I have two more questions about this immediate crisis period, and then we'll move on to the policy response and moving forward in the post-9/11 period. How would you assess President Bush's performance on that first day in the area of his duties specific to communications with the public? Which is obviously always an important part of the president's portfolio of duties, especially in the media age.

Well, I think he handled it very well under the circumstances. I mean, in the final analysis, he's the ultimate authority. I happened to be in the White House that morning that he happened to be in Florida. But in terms of his communication with the public, it's an interesting question. But there were a couple of things that happened. One was the very first statement he made down in Florida when he left the classroom. The second was when he got to Barksdale [Air Force Base] and put some of the press off, but also had a statement, a public statement, at that time.

I was very much aware of the importance of communicating with the public. I made a decision that I would not do it for a very explicit reason: that this was in fact something the president needed to be doing, to be the one seen as he's in command, he's in charge, he's the commander in chief. And that it would be easy for me to convene the press to do an Al Haig, but that it would undermine the authority of the president. And so we decided we needed a briefing of some kind in Washington, but that's when we got [White House counselor] Karen Hughes. Karen and [Cheney aide] Mary Matalin sat down, worked out a program, and we set it up for Karen. I think she went over to the Justice Department building and held a briefing for the press, sort of brought them up to speed on what we were doing and what was happening.[8] But no, I think the president handled it as well as it could be handled. And by nightfall, he's on nationwide television addressing the nation on the events of the day. So I think that piece of it worked pretty well.

I happen to think that as time unfolded over the first week, ten days, George W. Bush, who was not celebrated as an orator up until that point, became steadier and steadier in this business of communicating with the public and in fact, really by virtue of the rhetoric he employed and his persona, helped keep America together in a psychologically fragile time. And I happen also to think that John Kerry's approach in 2004, where he never really conceded that point, kind of sealed his own electoral fate. It's sort of like—in a rough analogy—if someone walks into a car dealership, you don't insult them and say, "You were dumb to be driving the car you drove." You say, "You know what? That worked for you for the time, but I think you're ready to step up to *this*." And I think John Kerry would have done better had he paid a little bit of tribute to George Bush's performance, rhetorical performance, in keeping the country together at that time.

Yeah.

But the consensus in the literature is that George W. Bush was shaky on that first day in his—

Yeah, that's not true.

—and that he found his voice over time.

Well, I'm sure he got *better* over time. I mean, you know, if somebody were to run in the room right now and tell you they've just blown up New York City with a nuke, it'd take you a few minutes to adjust to that. You had a set of circumstances here which were unprecedented in the history of the nation. And we can all look back on it now, and we're all familiar with it, and we know what happened and when it happened, and—everybody's got their view and their experience.

It's been internalized, in a sense.

Yeah, it's been internalized. But I thought the president responded very well under those circumstances, and [am] hard put to come up with the—I'm sure there are others, but not very many, in the history of the presidency where the president was faced with anything, you know, that resembled exactly that nature. That was the worst attack ever on the homeland; the last time Washington had been attacked since the British had been here in 1814. I mean, it was an historic, unprecedented moment, and he responded very well. He knew what needed to be done, and over the course of those next few weeks, I remember the church service that I skipped because we didn't want to double up; you know, I was evacuated to Camp David, where I spent a lot of time. But I mean, that afternoon when he's at Offutt Air Force Base and we convened the National Security Council in the PEOC and have sort of the first National Security Council meeting. I don't think everybody was there yet. I don't think Powell was—[he was] en route back from Latin America or someplace.[9]

But there was never any doubt about where the president was, that this *was* an act of war. We made it very clear to everybody that it was. He produced a good speech. But no, I think any suggestion to the contrary is somebody who wasn't there.

Is it true that you contacted Tom Kean shortly before the publication of the 9/11 Commission's final report to complain to him about the report's treatment of the shoot-down order?

Not that I recall.

There's an actual quotation attributed to you from that call in—

In the report?

—in Peter Baker's book [*Days of Fire: Bush and Cheney in the White House* (2013)].

Hmm.

That you said, "This is not fair"—

I've read Peter's book. I don't remember that part of it.

I know that President Bush backed you up on that controversy and that Condoleezza Rice, in her memoir [*No Higher Honor: A Memoir of My Years in Washington* (2011)], backed you up on that whole controversy. I would say about it only the following, sir: that this controversy places you in an exceedingly rare and awkward position for Dick Cheney because it places you in the position of asserting things for which there is no documentary evidence, which is very unlike you. And I wonder if you understand why questions have been raised about that whole set of events.

No. No, I think it's been well and exhaustively covered and discussed, and I don't think there's anything else to be added. I mean, there was confusion with respect to communications and so forth and they tried, when the president and I sat down the commission, this was one of the questions we addressed. But I thought we answered it as well as it could be answered.

What was the rationale for the two of you appearing jointly before the commissioners?

It was the president's suggestion. I thought it was a good one. That our actions together on that day were as part of a team. And that that was the best way to tell the story that needed to be told with respect to the commission.

To the formal sort of policy response to 9/11 going forward: First, I just want to ask you, broadly speaking, was Condoleezza Rice an effective national security advisor?

I think so. I often disagreed with her, but in terms of her selection for the post, the president had met her at a visit he paid, I think, out to the Hoover Institute. I think George Shultz [secretary of state under President Reagan] made the connection. I knew Condi going back several years. I had been part of the Aspen Study Group that included people like Sam Nunn, I think Scowcroft, a number of us, bipartisan, and we looked at, I think I mentioned it earlier. When I was in the House, we would at least once, sometimes twice a year get together someplace in the world. It might be—and we did Switzerland one year, the Bahamas, Bermuda. We'd come together for three or four days and have experts come in as resources, and this was in the day when the Cold War was still very much an issue and we were focused on U.S.-Soviet relations. And Condi came to one of those as a resource person. She was young, not yet the chancellor at—

Provost.

—provost [at Stanford University].

Yeah.

I'm not even sure she was a full professor. Was very knowledgeable. She was there as an expert on the Soviet military. That's the first time I ever saw her, was impressed. Later on she became—went to work for Brent on the NSC during the first Bush administration. I told her then that if she ever got tired of working for Scowcroft, I had a slot for her over at the Pentagon. When I was in private life, after I left the Defense Department, I was on the board at Procter & Gamble and at one point, on behalf of the board, tried to recruit Condi to join the board. She opted instead for Chevron; that was much closer to [chuckles] where she was located. So I knew her. Then she became sort of the president's senior advisor during the [2000] campaign on national security matters. And as I say, Shultz had originated that relationship, and she ran the group called the Vulcans that were the national security advisor, advisory group. I think she was a logical choice. She certainly had the background and the credentials, a good relationship with the president. And so if you looked at the field out there of prospective national security advisors, I think Condi was a good choice. And as I say, there were times when we had significant policy disagreements. I don't think it was ever personal. But it's a tough job, and I think, you know, sort of my ideal of a national security advisor is along the lines of a Brent Scowcroft. But I think Condi was a good choice, and I think she did the job in a manner that served the president's needs and that he was very comfortable with.

I ask because, as you surely know, by many accounts Dr. Rice strove to iron out differences amongst the principals before briefing the president, rather than present to him conflicting views of key NSC participants.

Yeah.

That's one criticism of her that recurs in the literature.

Yeah, and it's a criticism that I shared on occasion: that she operated to try to smooth over differences and say there was a consensus sometimes when there was no consensus. And—

And that's misleading to "the decider," in a sense.

Well, it's the way she chose to operate and—

Why do you suppose she, she pursued that?

She may have perceived that as being her major responsibility, was to try to manage the process in a way that—[pauses]—got agreement, to the extent possible, among the principals so she could take a decision to the president that addressed the issue. And I just think it was her style of operating. My own personal view was that he was better served when he got the raw material. You can overdo that. I mean, there is a need—to some extent, that's the national security advisor's role, to try to filter out the small stuff and take the significant items to the president. But I did think there were occasions when Condi told the president there was a consensus where there was none.

Another recurring theme of the literature where Condoleezza Rice as national security advisor is concerned is that when she took that job, she simply did not have the deep levels of experience, or the previous experience in senior official posts, that you had, that Don Rumsfeld had had, that Colin Powell had had by that time; and that therefore she was—through no fault of her own, really—ill equipped to corral this group of people the way a national security advisor needs to be able to do.

Well—[pauses]—there were others who had more experience than she did, no question about it. *But* if you were to look at background experience going in, she was pretty well equipped. Also, you know, if you look back at the people who have held that post over the years in other administrations—I look at the Reagan administration. President Reagan generally is viewed as having had a pretty sound, solid national security policy. He had, I think, seven national security advisors in eight years. Look at the Obama administration. You know, I think by comparison with most past administrations, Condi was certainly as well qualified if not better qualified than most for that post.

But what I'm referring to is not about what's on paper. I'm talking about personalities and egos, and—

I'm talking about personality. I'm talking about the relationship with the president, which is very important. And so I, you know, I think she met all of those requirements. Now, there were frictions, problems in terms of managing that national security process. You know, welcome to the NFL! [chuckles] I can remember when, oh, this was, I guess, towards the end of the Reagan administration. And I think Frank Carlucci, who was an old friend of mine, he'd been the guy that called me to come to the advisory group they were putting together at the Office of Economic Opportunity back in 1969. He was my predecessor at Defense and one of the first guys I talked to when it was time to get staffed up over there. But Frank told me the story when *he* was national security advisor, which is where he was before he went to the Pentagon, that he had daily calls with Shultz and Weinberger. I thought that's some kind of coordination thing. I thought they had a pretty good relationship, but he had to do that to sort of keep the train on the tracks, in terms of trying to manage that process, because there was a lot of tension between the sec-def and the secretary of state. That's true of most administrations. I mean the one I was part of as secretary of defense was unique, because we *didn't* have much of that, because Jim [Baker] and I and Scowcroft all were very close. We had worked together before. We had all worked with the president before. And that was probably the smoothest I have ever seen, that I have ever been a part of. And there were, no question, there were tensions and problems that developed in the national security structure during the [Bush] 43 years. But I don't find it all that surprising.

Or undue—it wasn't unduly so.

Well, it was a problem, frankly. At the end of the first term the president addressed it to some extent when he let Powell go and sent Condi over to State, put Hadley in as the NSC advisor. That improved things to some extent. Never completely removed it, but I've watched those relationships in that post. I've spent months on the Iran-Contra, where a focal point of the whole thing was the national security status and mechanism in the NSC and so forth during the Reagan years, when we were selling arms to the Iranians and providing the cash to the Contras and so forth. It's a tough job. It's a very difficult thing to put together a team to run that set of relationships. I thought—[pauses]—well, I'll leave it at that. As I say, I think Condi was a good choice, it made sense, she had a good relationship with the president, and she had a good background. As I say, I did not always agree with her and we had our differences. I write about some of them in my book.

But she proved up to the job in your view?

Um—[pauses]—I think so. You know, compared to what? Who would have been better in that position? I can't really think of anyone who would have been better in that position. Again, I didn't always agree with the direction she wanted to go in. We had significant policy differences from time to time. Again, I spent a fair amount of my time in the book towards the end, when we are doing North Korea and North Korean nukes and Syria and so forth, where we—

Israel-Palestine. There's all sort of places—

Yeah, where we differed. But in terms of there [being] something inherent, Condi being weak or ineffective, I can't say that.

Secretary Rice wrote in her memoir: "The vice president's staff was determined to act as a power center of its own. Many things were done 'in the name of the Vice President,' whether he had directed them to be done or not.... [S]ome of the bureaucratic games of the Office of the Vice President played were not characteristic of my dealings with their boss."

I guess I take that as high praise. [laughs] Yeah, I played an active role. I had a staff that I expected to be aggressive. I had my own national security staff. That was by design. And I'm sure on occasion it was frustrating for her, but I saw she was in a situation where she had somebody as vice president that she had to deal with who had been hired specifically because of my background and experience in national security matters. You know, if I had been an expert on the economy, it wouldn't have been much by way of, of—

Overlap.

overlap. There was a lot of overlap in this case, and so as I say, from my perspective, we had our differences, but I never thought it was personal.

I'm asking about Condoleezza Rice because it seems to me necessary, for a full understanding of the response to 9/11, first to have an appreciation for the individuals who were executing that response and their interplay with each other. We already discussed Don Rumsfeld in some detail. So

the next individual I would like to ask you about is Colin Powell. As I did with the intelligence piece yesterday, I want to read to you—and I hope you will hear me out—a few passages from your book. Because there is a disconnect for me in some of the things you wrote in your book and some of the evidence you array in your book. You wrote, "I believed we would be a good team," meaning you and Powell, "and for our time together at the Pentagon [during Bush 41], we were." And elsewhere in the book you say, "We had worked together well during my time in the Pentagon." But then if we actually read an account of your time at the Pentagon, it seems to me the account is replete with references to disagreements with Powell—and not just disagreements but a kind of dissatisfaction with the way he was going about his duties. To wit: "Did it matter from the standpoint of the United States if Iraq had taken Kuwait? Colin Powell indicated that he wasn't convinced that it did. But it sure seemed important to me." A few pages later: "Powell seemed more comfortable talking about poll numbers than he was recommending military options." You had to say to him, and address him formally: "General, I need some options." "Powell wasn't pleased when he learned my military aides were working their own services." "I decided that Powell would stay home [rather than brief the Saudis on Gulf War military preparations].... I wasn't sure Powell would deliver the strong message they needed to hear." And then lastly: "Powell repeatedly pressed the case for long term sanctions. I had little faith in sanctions." So again and again we see this isn't a matter of disagreement during that time; this is a matter of you fundamentally doubting that this man has his head screwed on straight.

No, that's not true. That's—

He was "more comfortable talking about poll numbers than recommending military options" as chairman of the Joint Chiefs?

Well, but he'd also been national security advisor to the president.

But you see how someone could draw the inference that—

Yeah, but I—yeah, that's—

—this is *not* two men working well together.

No, I think that's a misinterpretation on your part. I really do. You know, I made the statement in there. I went and recruited Colin Powell for the job. I had watched him operate as Reagan's last national security advisor. I actually called him towards the end of the Reagan administration. This is before I ever knew I was going to be at Defense, and congratulated him, said in effect I'd enjoyed working with him and hoped we'd have the opportunity in the future. When I became secretary, the job [of chairman of the Joint Chiefs of Staff] had already been offered to [Admiral William J.] Bill Crowe. Crowe was in the job at the time, and he'd already had a conversation, I think, with Brent about extending as chairman for another two years. I wanted to get somebody else. Crowe had been there four years, which was the norm. And so I set about specifically finding a candidate to be chairman, and I settled on Powell because of his extensive knowledge and background, not only on the military but also especially as the national security advisor and the deputy [national security advisor], before that, to Reagan. So it was a very conscious recruitment effort on my part, and I was never unhappy with the fact that I had recruited him for the DOD job.

But it sounds like you were, to read these quotes.

We obviously had differences. And I don't find that surprising at all. It's an accurate reflection. And if I wrote in there and said, "Everything was hunky-dory, we never disagreed on anything," that's not true.

But hear me out. Isn't there a difference between disagreeing, a secretary of defense and chairman of the Joint Chiefs disagreeing over how a military

issue should be approached versus a secretary of defense concluding that—I mean, here Powell didn't think [Saddam Hussein's invasion of] Kuwait was a real problem for the United States.

No, he didn't.

Okay, but that's hugely strategic.

Well, but wait a minute. Think about it, what Colin and others believed at the time. I mean, this is the first early days of the crisis. Saddam's just invaded Kuwait. The question before the house is: Is this a matter of sufficient significance from the standpoint of the United States that it warrants, you know, a major military response? And there were those who had their doubts. Sam Nunn was one of them. Sam Nunn voted against using military force, even when we got up to the end. And with respect to Colin, he was more interested [in] and had a greater interest in supporting continuation of sanctions. He believed that enough and voiced it enough that I took him over and let him present it directly to the president. You know, the president's key military advisor, uniformed advisors, the chairman of the Joint Chiefs of Staff, and I felt the president ought to hear that. Colin wasn't alone. I mean, that happened to be his view at the time. When the decision was made to go forward on a military basis and go forward as the president said, "This aggression will not stand," a decision to deploy and then use the force, he was a trooper. He did exactly what needed to be done. My saying in the book that there was a difference of opinion, as I recall in the early meetings, the president, Scowcroft, and I were all pretty much alone. On the other side of—and it wasn't a stark, deep divide, I mean we all worked together, I think, pretty effectively—I think Baker was more hesitant, more interested in pushing diplomacy. And I think Colin was over in basically that same camp. That doesn't mean I don't think he was a good chairman of the Joint Chiefs or that there was some fundamental conflict.

I'll take one last pass at this before moving on. But—

Yeah. I just—I think you're overanalyzing it to suggest that somehow, because I talk about our differences, that it wasn't a good relationship or that it didn't work.

I understand. Again, by way of a rough analogy, if two electricians differ over which cable or wire might be needed or most effective in a given situation where they are trying to fix a lighting issue, that's a disagreement; that's to be expected. When the defense secretary says of his chairman of Joint Chiefs of Staff, he "seemed more comfortable talking about poll numbers than he was recommending military options," there we have Electrician A saying of Electrician B, "You seem to think you are a plumber, not an electrician." Do you follow my point?

Yeah, no. When I say "more interested in the polls," one of the things— and Colin wasn't the only military guy who felt this way. He was concerned about public support for a major military action. An awful lot—well, most of our senior military guys at the time of Desert Storm cut their teeth on Vietnam. They'd been through a situation where there'd been a lack of support for the enterprise, where the military hadn't been supported publicly. There were a lot of questions that came up as we did Desert Storm where we civilians in the Bush administration sort of had to prove ourselves that this wasn't going to be another Vietnam exercise, that we weren't going to do it by dribs and drabs, where we gradually escalate over time, use the whole force and units, not individuals, etc., all those things we've talked about before. One of the questions as we went into the build-up and then the decision to use force in Desert Storm was: Will the country support the use of military force over there? There were statements that I can recall from people who would say, you know, nobody really likes the Kuwaitis. They've got a ton of money. Most of them spend their summers in the south of

France. What does it matter if this little tiny state, country in the Persian Gulf—

Why are we risking blood and treasure for the Founding Emirs? Yeah.

Exactly. That's a legitimate question. And it's a legitimate question for the chairman of the Joint Chiefs to raise. And I looked at Colin's posture that way. Scowcroft and I used to occasionally, in our private conversations, refer to "our reluctant generals." And there *was* some hesitation on the part of the military about going to war over Kuwait and committing force and obviously the possibility of having to take casualties. And so that's some serious, serious business, and I would not expect—and *did* not expect—that everybody in the Pentagon is going to never ask questions or raise questions about, you know, are we really prepared to do this? Is this a major national question of strategy from the standpoint of the United States? There were legitimate debates and concerns. We had to overcome some of those when we went to the Congress to get authorization from it, in order to do what we wanted to do. We only won by five votes in the Senate. So it was not an extreme or unusual view. In the final analysis, the president made the decision. I supported him. I strongly urged that same basic posture. And the military saluted smartly, including Colin Powell, and carried on and did a hell of a job. But for him to have had concerns about whether or not the public would support us going to war in Kuwait was a legitimate question.

Okay.

And I put in my book and treat it that way, that this was his view. Mine was different. Mine tracked with the president's, and that's ultimately what we did. So, there's not an element of disloyalty there or hostility.

Or not having your head screwed on right.

Or not having your head screwed on right. That's total misrepresentation of what it's all about.

Okay. Moving forward, and assessing why the relationship between you and him was not as effective or congenial, or even, from a policy point of view, optimal in the Bush 43 period—

Right.

—it seems to me, and again I suspect you might accuse me of overanalyzing things—

[chuckles] I'll let you know.

—you're not the only one—my wife, as well. It seems to me that the frictions that developed, and that I think you would agree were more acute between you and him in the first Bush term, for Bush 43, seem to play out along some similar lines. Where Powell in [the] Gulf War had favored sanctions, and you had little faith in sanctions, Powell in 2002 wants to take things to the UN Security Council, and you don't have much faith in the UN as an arbitrating body for this sort of thing.

Well, we have to come back to that point. Because that's not quite accurate.

Okay. Powell again seems overly concerned with public opinion or—and his image in the press. These were the complaints that you were lodging in your book about him. Without necessarily dwelling too much on whether there was a similarity of the problems from one administration to the next with him and you, perhaps I should simply ask you why you think the relationship wasn't as effective, wasn't as good, wasn't as congenial, wasn't optimal the second time around?

I'm not sure. I've thought about it a lot over the years.

Was it because he was in a different role as secretary of state?

That's a possibility. I mean, you can think of lots of reasons. I mean, the bottom line was I thought he would make a good secretary of state. It was the president's choice, and he'd made it early on that that's what he wanted to do. There was never any doubt. We didn't do a search for secretary of state. He was—we'd talked about Powell as a prospective VP candidate, and there were two guys written off from the very beginning of the search. One was Powell, the other was [Senator John] McCain because both of them had made it very clear publicly that they didn't want to—neither one of them had any interest in being vice president. But no, I thought the choice the president made in Powell under the circumstances made sense, and I supported it. It didn't work out. And you know, you can spend a lot of time thinking about why it didn't work out. But it was strained from the beginning, to some extent. It was—I'm just trying to think. You know, there would be reports coming back, I would hear from friends around town, that we were being trashed by Colin in his comments to other people in Washington. It wasn't like it was a secret. Somebody asked him at one point, some reporter or something, about how much time he got to spend with the president, and how long his meetings lasted. He said something [like], "Well, you know, not all that long," that once you got beyond fifteen minutes he didn't have that much to say—sort of implying criticism of Bush.[10] And I don't have, you know, a carefully thought-out rationale for why it didn't work. I just know in the end it didn't work. It seemed like a good idea at the time, but in the final analysis I think the president was much more comfortable with Condi as secretary of state than he ever was with Colin.

Did the fact that it didn't work out have any significant impact on the ability of the administration to execute its policies and plans?

[pauses] Mmmm, I don't—you'd have to look at specific, I think instances, of it. Um—

In other words, when you have such a critical player on the NSC and amongst the principals not working out, we almost have to assume, almost by the laws of physics, that there is going to be some deleterious impact on the process.

I suppose you could compare it to, you go back and look at the Nixon administration, Kissinger as NSC advisor and Bill Rogers at State.

Big-time. [laughs]

Yeah! I think both the president and I, as I say, believed in the appointment. We thought it was the right thing to do, that this was the best candidate. I had the feeling lots of times that with respect to Powell—that he became a captive of the State Department rather than the other way around. Jim Baker was a great secretary of state because he was the president's man at State, and if nothing else, he could close off the elevators down at the lower floors, below the seventh floor [of the State Department building], and run the operation. There was never any doubt about who he spoke for or who he was concerned about, and he dominated the department accordingly. And he had a president, you know, who would have been a hell of a secretary of state all by himself in George [H. W.] Bush. With Powell, I felt, as I think about it and thought about it then, it was his style of operation with respect to the military and trying to build support for the troops and being the chairman of the Joint Chiefs and so forth, that what was required by way of being a successful military leader in that setting, which I think he was, can get you in trouble over at State, in the sense that if you become captured by that bureaucracy and the ideology and the—

The *weltanschauung* [chuckles].

Yeah, yeah, exactly. That, you know, one of the things you've got to do at State—it was believed at the time and probably still is, but certainly was a major point of focus—is solve the Israeli-Palestinian problem, okay? That's just something they're all gonna do—and it virtually never happens. And Powell found himself in a position where, you know, that's part of the agenda he inherits by virtue of the position he has, and sort of that's always one of the main agenda items in the State Department. But we've just been attacked, you know, on 9/11 and face the threat of further attacks and three thousand of our people killed, and that, in and of itself, changed the whole environment in terms of being able to go forward and say, "Well, if we just solve the Israeli-Palestinian problem, everything's gonna be okay." We've got a whole new *set* of problems, a whole new set of threats to the homeland. And it is no longer just, you know, how do we get [Palestinian Authority president Yasser] Arafat to meet with the Israeli prime minister to solve the—

New paradigm.

Yeah. And I felt to some extent that State never made that transition—it was hard for them—and that Powell found himself in the position where, if he sort of followed the traditional agenda of a secretary of state, he was going to be an outlier when compared to what the rest of us were focused on and how we were spending our time. It was a point at which he made a public statement early on to the effect that the policy towards North Korea would be a continuation of the one policy we'd inherited from the Clinton administration.[11] The president didn't like that. That wasn't the direction he wanted to go in. He had a different concept that we ultimately pursued: the Six-Party Talks, getting China involved and so forth. I always sensed he was to some extent frustrated, but he was out of step with what the president was focused on and where we were trying to go. And then you ran into problems, oh, in the aftermath of Afghanistan, for example, where there was a feeling in—not in the military action itself but in the aftermath of trying to set up governments and so forth, sort of the civilian side of the business of building viable governments—that State wasn't very effective, that the Pentagon ended up having to pick up some of the slack. So there was always a conflict there.

It wasn't a smooth set of relationships. Last time I saw Colin, I guess, was up at [retired General] Norm Schwarzkopf's funeral up at West Point a couple of years ago.[12] But I haven't talked to him since then, and we're obviously not close. There was a book written by, I think a woman at the [*Washington*] *Post* called—is it *Soldier*?

Mm-hmm. Karen DeYoung [*Washington Post* reporter and author of *Soldier: The Life of Colin Powell* (2011)].

Karen DeYoung. And as I recall, [in] the closing paragraph of the book, she asks him if he would agree to go back to serve again as secretary of state in the administration. And he said no. And she said, "Why?" And he had a one-word answer: "Cheney." Go look at the paragraph. It's obviously a very different kind of relationship than what we had at the Pentagon.

Enough on personalities.

Okay.

Maybe a little more on personalities.

[laughs] Can't pass that up.

Moving forward after 9/11, just two months later, you played a significant role—your office played a significant role—in the development of the policy regarding military commissions and other related aspects. Do you recall this

confrontation that is alleged to have occurred between you and Attorney General Ashcroft in the Roosevelt Room in November of 2001 over the proposal that David Addington had developed, with the cooperation of John Yoo at OLC [the Department of Justice's Office of Legal Counsel], for the establishment of military commissions? Various accounts of this session have Ashcroft really blowing his stack. Do you recall this event?

I recall the meeting. I don't recall him blowing his stack. He wasn't happy, obviously. But I don't recall that he—I think he probably expressed himself more vociferously after the meeting was over with [chuckles] than he did in the meeting. But—

Even Barton Gellman quotes someone [in *Angler: The Cheney Vice Presidency* (2008)] as saying how remarkably "rude" Ashcroft was to you in that session.

That's not my recollection of it. He disagreed with what we were doing, obviously. What he wanted was a system that gave a prominent role for our Article Three courts, and for the Justice Department. And if you went the military commissions route, obviously that's Defense, that's the Pentagon. We had looked at how we ought to proceed and looked at history. World War II, Roosevelt with the military commission to try the German saboteurs who had landed on Long Island. The commissions that were used, oh, for example to try the Japanese war criminals. The commission that was used to try the group that assassinated President Lincoln. I mean, it was a well-established pattern there, when you were dealing not with prisoners of war in the Geneva sense but rather [with] unlawful combatants, terrorists, that we thought there was ample precedent for, to go with the commissions.

Apparently, according to these accounts, what he reacted so strongly to in the meeting was where, after he registered his objections on the, on a legal

basis, you supposedly took the occasion to inform him that you already had in hand an opinion from his own deputy at OLC, John Yoo. And that's what set him off, supposedly.

I—I don't remember that, but [it] is entirely possible. We did work with Yoo a lot.

The literature further records that three days after that showdown with Ashcroft, you arrived for your regular lunch with President Bush carrying a four-page order for the military commissions, drafted by Addington, which the president signed on that occasion, and that neither the secretary of state nor the national security advisor—who would have legitimate interests in this kind of development of policy—had been apprised of the existence of that document, nor of the fact that it was being signed by the president that day. Is that true?

Mmm, it may be true. I do remember discussing it with the president.

And this is cited as another of those occasions where you, as you put it to me yesterday, "short-circuited" the system.

Yeah, it was one of those things that I felt strongly about and pushed aggressively to get through the system and get it done. And—

But why not go through the typical interagency process for something of this sensitivity?

I don't remember the exact reasons why we decided to do it that way. In the aftermath especially of 9/11, we needed to get things done, and on occasion I would use the position I had, and the relationship with the president I had, to short-circuit the system. No question about it. This sounds like one of them.

To the enhanced interrogation techniques: To your knowledge was President Bush briefed about the actual methods that were to be employed in the EITs?

I believe he was.

I ask because in *Decision Points*, the president recalled having been briefed on the EITs. Yet [former CIA general counsel] John Rizzo in his memoir, *Company Man* [(2014)] disputes that and says that he contacted George Tenet about it, after reading the president's book, and that Tenet backs him up in the belief that Bush was *not* briefed.

No, I'm certain Bush *was* briefed. I also recall a session where the entire National Security Council was briefed. The meeting took place in Condi's office—I don't think Powell was there, but I think he was briefed separately—and where we went down through the specific techniques that were being authorized.

Why do you say you're "certain" that Bush *was* briefed?

Well, partly because he *said* he was. I don't have any doubt about that. I mean, he was included in the process. I mean, that's not the kind of thing that we would have done without his approval.

To that point, James Risen, who is not the same person as me—

It's not James Rosen, okay. Got it.

—despite a lot of confusion.

Very important point.

[laughs] James Risen wrote in *State of War: The Secret History of the CIA and the Bush Administration*, published in 2006: "Cheney protected the president from personal involvement in debates over handling the prisoners. It's not clear whether Tenet was told by Cheney or other White House officials not to brief Bush" or if Tenet just didn't do it. "Cheney and other officials knew" that Bush was not being briefed. Bush was insulated to give him deniability.[13]

I don't have much confidence in Risen.

That's not the question I'm putting to you. Is what he alleges here true or false?

Uh, that we tried to have deniability for the president?

Yeah.

I can't think of a time when we ever operated that way. We just *didn't*. The president needed to know what we were doing and sign off on the thing. It's like the Terrorist Surveillance Program. You know, one of the main things I did there was to take Tenet and Hayden in hand and get the president's approval for what we were doing, and there's a classic example why I don't believe something like this. The president wanted *personal* knowledge of what was going on, and he wanted to *personally* sign off on the program every thirty to forty-five days. To suggest that somehow we ran a system that protected the president from knowledge about the enhanced interrogation, I just, I don't think it's true. I don't believe.

But can you say as a fact, "I *know* that's not true"? Rather than having to surmise?

I can remember sitting in the Oval Office with [Steve] Hadley and others—I think others were in there—where we talked about the techniques. And you know, one of the things that was emphasized was the fact that the techniques were drawn from that set of practices we used in training our own people. I mean, it was not—we were not trying to hide it from the president.

Okay.

With all due respect, I don't give any credence to what Risen says there. Now I've never read his book; I've never met the gentleman. It's just not the way we did business.

I've only got a couple of more questions on 9/11 and then if you'd like we can take a break and then continue with Iraq.

Okay.

Do you know who David Rothkopf is?

David Rothkopf? No, doesn't ring a bell.

He is a former managing director of Kissinger Associates. He went on to write a book called *Running the World: The Inside Story of the National Security Council and the Architects of American Power* (2005), which is regarded, generally, as the finest study of the NSC and its inner workings. He is now the publisher of *Foreign Policy* magazine and ForeignPolicy.com. And some people actually posit that were Hillary Clinton to seek and win the presidency, Rothkopf might actually be tapped to be national security advisor.

I've never heard of the guy.

Okay, that's fine.

[chuckles] World renowned, but okay.

[laughs] So as a kind of sequel to _Running the World_, which is this well-regarded history of the NSC, he published another book recently, sort of extending his look at the inner workings of the NSC from the Bush-Cheney period into the Obama administration. And I interviewed him in connection with the release of the book for a little show I have about books and authors called _The Foxhole_. And he told me as follows: "9/11 was something that required a response from the United States, a strong response, against the perpetrators. But we fell into the terrorists' trap. The terrorist trap is to actually get us to over-respond. We reordered our entire national security apparatus to make terrorism our principal concern. It should have been _a_ concern. We let it claim all the bandwidth and all the budget and it was extremely damaging to us." Your thoughts?

Yeah, I don't buy it. You certainly would have to say that we had not allocated sufficient resources _before_ 9/11 to protect us, and 9/11, I think, as an act of war really brought home the need for us to focus on the likelihood of further mass-casualty attacks on the U.S. with far deadlier consequences than what happened on 9/11. That sounds like a guy who wasn't in the PEOC on 9/11. I don't know where he was on 9/11. Maybe he was off writing a book someplace, but—

You know, however, there is a school of thought out there that 9/11 has been allowed to assume an outsized role in national security policymaking over the years.

I just disagree with it. I don't think it's right. I think it sounds a little bit like Obama going to Cairo in '09, his first year in office, sort of the center of the Muslim world, and apologizing, saying the U.S. overreacted to

9/11. I don't buy it. I think we did what we felt was necessary and needed to be done, that a key priority for us after 9/11 was to make sure it never happened again, and we devoted a lot of time and energy and resources to exactly that effort—I might add *successfully*. For the time we were in office, we did not get another mass casualty attack against the United States. There were arguments about Guantanamo, and periodically after we set up Guantanamo there would be a burning desire on the part of the State Department to close Guantanamo. And I can't count the hours we spent in what I considered to be—obviously, others [chuckles] had a different view—considered to be totally wasted exercise arguing about "Let's close Guantanamo." It's still open today. It's still there for a reason. You've still got a couple of hundred really bad guys, terrorists, that you need to have someplace you can keep them. You don't want to bring them to the United States and give them the rights and prerogatives they would have as an American citizen in a legal proceeding. If anything, we've let too many of them go, in terms of those that have returned to the battlefield. But our European friends would be—and lots of times I wasn't convinced it was so much our European friends, it was people inside the State Department—who said, "Oh, gee, we can't have a prison for terrorists," a Guantanamo kind of situation.

I think we did what needed to be done. And I *don't* think we overreacted. And I think there's maybe after-the-fact analysis. I think there were people who were supportive of what we were doing at the time, when the crisis was upon us, who now went back saying, "Well, they shouldn't have done this or they shouldn't have done that." It's, you know, you got Richard Clarke, on the other hand, [arguing], "They didn't do enough when I told them they should have done more" kind of thing. I think we did a good job. I think we did the right thing. And I don't have any problem defending it. I think it was—and I never heard of your friend Rothkopf, or whatever his name is [chuckles], so I can't, can't credit his concerns. But I think the next time there is an attack, and I think there *will* be, a lot of that would go by the boards.

Where Guantanamo is concerned, did you have *any* concerns that the way it was set up and the various statutes that were applied and policies enacted with respect to it did create a situation in which truly an innocent man could languish in that place for, like, a decade?

Mm-hmm. [pauses] Frankly, I didn't worry a lot about that. I wanted to make certain that we had a place where we could take, in fact, take guilty individuals.

How did you *know* they were guilty if they weren't put on trial?

Well, most of 'em weren't exactly bashful about admitting what they'd done. Khalid Sheikh Mohammed, you know, the worst of the worst, the mastermind of 9/11, a guy who among other things cut [*Wall Street Journal* reporter Daniel] Pearl's throat and was *proud* of it! The— [pauses]—in terms of "innocent," I think there has been a fair amount of work done, because there *have* been a number of people who have been released back to their home countries during the course of the Bush administration, repatriated, if you will—

Something like five hundred.

Yeah, so, you know, there *has* been a review process that I think has been a good one. But I didn't sit around wringing my hands at night worrying about an innocent terrorist down in Guantanamo. I mean, these were people we captured on the battlefield or caught in the act, and they were well cared for, treated far better than they would have been in their own country, in terms of the facilities, the services that were provided for them, and the things we did to meet the highest standards—I mean, they're probably better than some of the municipal jails here in the United States. So I thought we handled it very well and—

Especially given the fact that all of you were in a sense undertaking all of this in a way that was unprecedented.

Yeah.

There was no manual for how to respond to 9/11.

That's correct. There was no manual. And an awful lot of this ended up in the courts. The Supreme Court ruled on more than one occasion. We went back to the Congress for authorization at certain points. And I always remember the meeting I held, and I've talked about it publicly— this is when there was some controversy maybe generated by your friend [James] Risen, your brother, fellow traveler—[chuckles]—

[laughs]

because he wrote, I think—

Talk about guilt by association!

[laughs] Yeah! He was the guy that got the leak on the terrorist surveillance program.

Right, I was just about to ask about this.

And we—this was along in '04—and there was, you know, growing controversy about the program. So there'd been a period of time there, with respect to unrest in the Justice Department, when Ashcroft refused to sign the renewal and so forth. And we had a situation there where, when we set the program up, a decision had been made that we would brief only the chairman and ranking member of the Intel Committee in the House and Senate, only four members of Congress. And we did that; we did it in my office. Hayden would come in, who was running the program, and Tenet. And we would brief the members and tell them what we were doing and how we were doing it. Then we got down to spring, early summer of '04, and we decided we needed to broaden the congressional people in the know, and so we got a meeting in the Sit Room with the speaker, majority and minority leader in the House, majority and minority leader in the Senate, chairman and ranking member of the Intel Committees. Nancy Pelosi was one of those present.

Despite her later protestations.

Yeah. This was about terror surveillance, and I had Hayden brief. Tenet was there as well. And then I went around the room and [asked] two questions. Number one: Do you think we ought to continue this program, or should we shut it down? And it was unanimous: Continue the program. It's producing vital information. We told them what we were doing with it. And then secondly I went around and I said, "Do you think we need to come back to the Congress and get additional authorization to continue the program?" And they said absolutely not. If you do that, it will be disclosed, you'll blow the cover. Tell the bad guys how we are reading their mail. And it was unanimous—*both* parties.

So I think we did those things we needed to do to make certain that we were operating within the statutes and the laws. We worked hard, for example, when we got into enhanced interrogation techniques. We're about to have—I heard a rumor yesterday, that sometime next week they may finally kick out this report that the Senate Democrat Intel Committee members are trying to produce. The [Central Intelligence] Agency was very cautious and insistent upon not going forward until they had sign-off. And that meant an opinion from the Justice Department that what we were going to do was legal and consistent with our international obligations and it had been authorized by the president of the United

States and the senior NSC people. Which is exactly the right way to go. I had watched through Iran-Contra when the agency to some extent was hung out to dry. Good guys sent on missions they thought had been authorized and then when the stuff hit the fan, you know, the politicians have all headed for the hills, they're not anywhere around. I felt very strongly that that shouldn't happen again, but the agency did, too—[CIA officer] Jose Rodriguez and the others who actively worked the program. And we bent over backwards to adhere to the law, to not do something that was "torture," etc., etc. So I feel very good about it. I don't spend a lot of time worrying what the critics have to say about it, or Rothkopf or others who said we overreacted to 9/11. I just don't buy it. I think that that's Monday morning quarterbacking.

You know the criticism that is lodged is that, far from taking pains to ensure that these kinds of programs were conducted according to the law, what was done was the law was reshaped purposefully to allow you to do what you wanted to do.

Okay. Fair enough. FDR ever do that? [chuckles] I mean, I point out the facts on the meeting of the Terrorist Surveillance Program. When you get in the congressional leadership, bipartisan, both houses, and say, "Here's what we are doing; do we need to come back and get additional authorization from you guys?" and the answer was uniformly, "No."

Three final questions here, all on the NSA Terrorist Surveillance Program. You alluded just now to this confrontation with DOJ over the reauthorization in March of '04. We talked a little bit about that already. Is it accurate to say of Vice President Cheney's role in that and his approach to it that you felt that the president should stand firm despite the threats of resignation from then–deputy attorney general James Comey and then–FBI director Robert Mueller and perhaps as many as a dozen lawyers in the Department of Justice? All of which, to most observers, would have, had it happened,

triggered a kind of Saturday Night Massacre on steroids and a lot of political heat to come with it. That it was your view that the president should stand firm and *take* those hits for the sake of the program and the larger war on terror.

My recollection is we never discussed it.

You and the president?

Yes. That, you know, it came up hurriedly; he dealt with it; there wasn't any big meeting where we considered what to do. He made the decision pretty much on the spot, that morning, when he and Comey had talked and he also heard that Bob Mueller at the FBI had the same concerns.

What did you *think* he should do?

Well, I was—I can't say that he made the wrong decision. I think he was concerned and had legitimate concerns that he didn't want to have a blowup. And as I say, it was his call to make. I was aggravated, I guess, by virtue of the fact that we had been to Justice *every* single time we had renewed the program—*every* single time, gotten the same answer. And now all of a sudden the new—well, all of a sudden Ashcroft bailed, turned it over to Comey, and Comey no longer was going to be part of the program, so.

And the irony of that whole situation is that for all the tumult internally, a few words were sort of amended here and there, and the program largely continued as it was, right?

Right.

When the *New York Times* published the famous James Risen story about the NSA's Terrorist Surveillance Program, I believe you were overseas, and I believe I was with you when that hit, in December of 2005. You write in *In My Time* that you regarded it as a violation of Section 798 of Title 18 of the U.S. Code, which prohibits the publication of classified information about America's communications intelligence.

Right.

Did you or anyone else at that time that you know of advocate for the criminal prosecution of Risen or the *Times*?

Mmm, I don't think it was ever, you know, seriously considered. I think there was—that *was* my view. Either that statute means what it says or it doesn't. It's never really been tested.

But you took no steps to translate that view of yours into action.

No, the Justice Department would have to make the decision to proceed. You know, we had—

But you didn't recommend it to anyone.

No. We had a lot of other things on our mind to worry about, and I didn't think they would *do* anything. I can remember, it was Tenet [who] told me at one point—this had to do with leaks out of the intelligence community and he would have—he told me there was something like four hundred issues pending where he had referred or issues of unauthorized disclosures of classified information.

Three hundred seventy-five of them to Bob Woodward.

[chuckles] Maybe. But they were all pending over at Justice. And Justice never wanted to take on the press.

That changed.

I guess you might be an exception.[14]

That changed over time!

I didn't have anything to do with it! [chuckles]

[laughs] Final question for this session: You wrote of the Terrorist Surveillance Program in your book, "I know it saved lives and prevented attacks."

Mm-hmm.

To your knowledge, have the attacks that were thwarted by this program ever been publicly disclosed?

The president gave a speech, I think, over at the [Naval] War College. I can't remember the exact timing of it. Probably along in about '04, maybe '05.

Maybe after the program came under attack?

Yeah, where he specifically cited some examples that we had gotten cleared as examples he could cite. So you can go back and find it in the presidential speech.[15]

———

And our subject now is the Iraq War. And once again, we've already discussed quite a bit about the—

The second Iraq War.

That's right.

Okay.

I think people tend to call the first one "the Gulf War" and the second one "the Iraq War." And once again, as I explained before we approached 9/11 just now, yes, we've covered a lot of this in certain detail, so I am not going to rehash it. And again, my aim is twofold: one, to sort of address what I think of as gaps or places that could use a little further exposition; and secondly, to acquaint you with that which you are probably already well acquainted, namely, your critics, and to give you a chance to respond to some things. That is what we are doing here. It is not a systematic review of all the phases of the Iraq War. But again, we will proceed roughly chronologically, and we'll start with the run-up to the Iraq War. You recall in *In My Time* that you and President Bush privately discussed Iraq in the weeks immediately following 9/11 and that in those discussions, you urged the president to have Don Rumsfeld revisit and update the Pentagon's plans for military action against Saddam Hussein. Was there in those very early discussions between you and the president a shared belief that this new era into which we had been plunged meant that a reckoning with Saddam—while perhaps not appropriate at the moment—was nonetheless inevitable and not far off?

Well, first of all, that's not the beginning with respect to Iraq and our concern about Iraq. The beginning goes back ten years. You've got to remember the situation *we* inherited when we took over: that there were no-fly zones established north and south. Saddam Hussein was firing on our aircraft north and south. Two years prior to the time we arrived, the Congress of the United States had passed legislation, appropriated funds, for the Iraq Liberation Act to support regime change in Iraq.

Which, by the way, one can imagine that Dick Cheney would regard as an unwelcome intrusion on the prerogatives of the executive.

Not necessarily. I don't know, I was running Halliburton then.

[laughs] In theoretical terms, but—

Yeah, no. There had been, if you go back—and I talk about it in my book. I won't read you all of the pages but it's very important when we talk about Iraq and what we did in Iraq to remember the circumstances at the time. And there is a tendency for the critics lots of times to sort of operate on the basis of "Uhhh, Bush and Cheney are sittin' around the Oval Office on a Saturday morning and saying, 'Well, let's go do Iraq.'" Not true. Didn't happen that way. And that since the end of the Gulf War, there had been a series of UN Security Council resolutions passed. There had been various and sundry intelligence reports done on Iraq and WMD. There had been the '98 situation where Clinton had actually launched air strikes into Iraq, aimed at about four days' worth of strikes, as I recall.[16]

One of my favorite quotes is December of '98, when he launched Operation Desert Fox: "If Saddam defies the world and we fail to respond, we will face a far greater threat in the future. Mark my words, he will develop weapons of mass destruction, he will deploy them and he will use them." Bill Clinton, December 1998. Bipartisan support for the operation when they went after—launched those attacks. One of the Democratic spokesmen was Nancy Pelosi, then a member of the [House] Intelligence Committee. Quote: "Saddam Hussein has been engaged in the development of weapons of mass destruction technology, which is a threat to the countries of the region. He has made a mockery of the weapons inspection process," etc. John Kerry, [Senator] Carl Levin, [Senate Minority Leader] Tom Daschle, letter to President Clinton urging him to take necessary action, including air and missile strikes on suspect

Iraqi sites, to respond effectively to the threat posed by Iraq's refusal to end its weapons of mass destruction program.

It goes on and on and on, throughout the nineties, of evidence of the threat that Iraq represented to the United States, a lot of it centered around weapons of mass destruction. One of my favorites, in 2000, this is before we had been sworn in, National Intelligence Estimate on worldwide biological weapons threats. A "key judgment": "Despite a decade-long international effort to disarm Iraq, new information suggests that Baghdad has continued and expanded its offensive B[iological] W[eapons] program by establishing a large scale, redundant, concealed BW agent production capability. We judge that Iraq maintains the capability to produce previously declared agents, probably is pursuing development of additional bacteria and toxic agents. Moreover, we judge Iraq has BW delivery systems available that could be used to threaten U.S. and allied forces in the Gulf region."[17] [Here Cheney reads from his own text in *In My Time*, omitting words here and there.] "Also continuing consistent reporting Saddam had in place the personnel and the infrastructure for a nuclear weapons program and that he was continuing to acquire technologies that had the potential for either nuclear or non-nuclear use," etc., etc., etc. We had, I think it was the first intelligence report we got after the election, when we're starting to get regular intelligence reports. It was on, the title—I think the report, when I wrote the book, was still classified, but the title is "Iraq Steadily Pursuing WMD Capabilities." The very first reports we got. So there's a lot of background there about Saddam, about weapons of mass destruction, about violations.

And which was very current at the time you took office.

Absolutely very current and continued for the twenty-seven months between when we got this first report and when we finally went into Iraq in '03. So it's not as though this is something we thought up and that there was no background or justification for it at all. I mean, these are some of the most prominent Democratic leaders reading the intelligence that they received before we even arrived.

Understood.

And it's important for that to be part of the record.

So I—with that background and not challenging any of it—I still pose the same question, which is: As you describe in your book, you had these early conversations in the weeks after 9/11 about Iraq and the one thing you tell us about those conversations is that you urged the president to instruct Rumsfeld to update the military planning.

Right.

I'm just wondering what else was in those conversations and whether they contained some shared understanding between the two of you [to the effect] that: "We are in a new era, and while our immediate task is al Qaeda and the guys who did this, and rooting out that safe haven in Afghanistan, we both sort of understand that there is going to be a reckoning with Saddam and it is not long off."

Well, I don't know that it would have been stated in those terms. There certainly was a concern on our part about Iraq. A lot of it predated 9/11. But I think 9/11 helped focus the concerns, especially the link between Iraq and WMD. There was a period of time there after 9/11 where there was a question about whether or not Iraq had *been* involved in 9/11. We had CIA—Tenet came in at one point with this photograph of [9/11 hijacker] Mohamed Atta, reputed to be Mohamed Atta, taken in Czechoslovakia, in Prague, where he was reputed to have met with Iraqi—[I think] it was Iraqi intelligence. So it was a, it was an ongoing problem and concern. I believe there—[pauses]—I think I'm correct. Before 9/11, this is very early in the administration, when the president was on a trip to Mexico [in February 2001], when there was an incident where our commander on the scene [in Iraq] had actually launched an attack against some anti-air capabilities that the Iraqis possessed, and which had fired upon, or [we] were concerned they had fired upon, our planes enforcing the no-fly zone. So there had already been that kind of an exchange.[18]

So there was, yes, a general concern about Iraq. The focus on planning, you know, based on my background at Defense, that's partly what you do, especially the Joint Staff and the CINCs [combatant commanders in chief], are always going through and revising and updating plans.

When Saddam invaded Kuwait, we reached up for the plan that was then on the shelf, and that one hadn't been updated. It provided for us to go into the Zagreb mountains and defend the Persian Gulf against an assault by Soviet forces coming down from the north; I mean, it was, you know, totally out of whack. But Rumsfeld had put in place a position, which is—a posture, which is fairly standard, of revising all of the war plans. And my suggestion to the president was, "I know Don's doing this. We ought to ask him to put front and center the plans with respect to Iraq as he goes forward with his effort."

I am going to speak in broad terms, but if it was the new paradigm that you and the president shared—that the old way of looking at terrorism no longer applies as a law enforcement matter, this is now a matter of war, we have to be on a war footing—I think it was also part of that paradigm for you both that as part of that new footing, yes, we had to deal with the people who committed 9/11 but that's, that's kind of playing defense; that at some point, once we have achieved that, we're gonna go on offense.

Mm-hmm.

And I don't think anyone would fault you for feeling that way and regarding that as the appropriate policy course to follow. I just wonder whether—how early on in the process this understanding between you and the president [was reached] that we're going to have to go on offense, [and] it was recognized by you both that Iraq was going to be that theater.

Well, I can't say that it was recognized that Iraq was going to be that theater at that point. What I'm thinking about is the first time I recall considering the notion that we had to not only go after the terrorists but with those who supported terror, with the people who financed terror, with especially those who provided sanctuary and safe harbor for terrorists, that that was a departure from the past. But I recall thinking those thoughts, and I probably have some notes on it, on the night of 9/11, sitting up at Aspen [Lodge at Camp David], watching the replay of the day's events. And that this *was* a terrorist attack, but we could no longer limit ourselves when those kinds of attacks are being launched against the homeland; we could no longer limit ourselves only to going after the terrorists. We had to go after those who supported terror and made it possible. So that was part of our thinking. I think the president shared that view. We didn't talk about it that night, but that was certainly part of our thinking going forward after 9/11.

And that feature of your thinking mandated that Iraq would have to be dealt with.

Well, I don't say "mandated." Looking at Iraq as a potential target was consistent with that position that had been brought home by the events of 9/11. We couldn't wait for the next attack and then respond; we had to preempt. We had to be prepared to go after the terrorists and those who supported terrorists before they ever got that next attack off.

Because you know the line of criticism here, which is to the effect that even as of September 2001, if we are going to be looking at state sponsors of terror and enablers of terror, that Iran would have made equal if not more sense, if not for military invasion at least as a kind of prime locus of our efforts, because of its support for Hamas and Hezbollah. And prior to al Qaeda, prior to 9/11, Hezbollah was the terrorist entity that had the most American blood on its hands, from the Marine barracks bombing in Beirut in October 1983. And so you know that some people have suggested that we went after Iraq more or less because we *could*, and because it was a target that was a little easier for us than Iran, even though Iran was the more urgent focus of our attention if we are looking at "the nexus."

I just read to you a whole series of propositions that I wrote about in my book that are based upon what the relationship was like between the United States and Iraq when we arrived in office. It was different than the relationship with respect to Iran at that point, clearly. But it wasn't as if we sat down and said, "Gee, should we hit Iran or should we hit Iraq?" We inherited a situation where the Congress of the United States had voted for regime change in Iraq and appropriated money to support it, and where there was extensive intelligence—going back at least ten years—on Iraq and weapons of mass destruction. And one of the things we're concerned about after 9/11 is that the next attack will be with something far deadlier than airline tickets and box-cutters, that the worst scenario you can imagine is an attack on Washington or New York City with a nuke or a biological agent of some kind. And that—if you ever look at the lay of the land out there, you can find all kinds of reasons why, "Well, why didn't you do this or that?" Bottom line was, we were having real-world, day-by-day experiences with respect to Iraq. They had a traditional relationship, a historic relationship with terror, with al Qaeda—which we haven't talked about but is also an important consideration here—that according to George Tenet went back at least a decade. That's what he said in testimony before the Congress. So, I don't think you can fault us for not striking Iran. We went after Iraq because of the reasons I have cited.

Because you have brought this up, this photograph of Mohamed Atta, I bring to your attention what Secretary Rice wrote in her memoir: "Given to personally sifting through raw intelligence data (not assessments that have been analyzed, checked for credibility and integrated with other intelligence, but undigested information coming straight from the field), the Vice President latched onto every report of a meeting between Iraqi agents and al-Qaeda affiliates. Many of the reports were of highly questionable origin and reliability—so much so that the CIA felt strongly that there had been no complicity between Saddam and al-Qaeda in the 9/11 attacks and said so. But the Vice President's office remained convinced that there had been." Your response?

Well, Condi's just wrong in the sense that this wasn't stuff that we went out and dug up. This was stuff that had been brought to me by George Tenet, specifically the photograph of Mohamed Atta and the report that he had been in Prague. And Tenet had a source in Prague who had provided this, as well as the information of an alleged meeting between Atta and a senior Iraqi intelligence official. It wasn't something that, you know, we dredged up in the wastebaskets coming out of the CIA. George Tenet brought this to me and presented it to me and, as I recall, said there was a 70 or 80 percent probability that this had in fact happened. Now, they could never validate it. But—well, if you look at the *Meet the Press* interview I did with Tim Russert the Sunday after 9/11, a shot we did from up at Camp David. The Camp David—

The "dark side" interview.[19]

Yeah. It was a good show. Russert and I both enjoyed it, and he always talked about it as one of the best that had ever been done with respect to his time at *Meet the Press*. He asked me in that interview, did we have any evidence linking Iraq and Saddam to 9/11? And I said no. Within a week after that is when Tenet came to me and presented me for the first time with the suggestion that there *had* been a connection. So again, it's not something we dredged up. It was in fact something that the agency brought forward and presented to us.

Is Secretary Rice—just as a matter of fact—wrong, then, when she writes in this passage, "CIA felt strongly that there had been no complicity between Saddam and al-Qaeda in the 9/11 attacks"?

In the end, I think it would be fair to say—and I think the statement I make in my book—you've got to distinguish between Saddam and the attacks and a relationship with al Qaeda on one hand and relationship between al Qaeda and Iraq. Tenet himself testified to a relationship between Iraq and al Qaeda. There never was confirmation of the report that linked Mohamed Atta to a session with the Iraqi intelligence official; and they pursued that over the months, even years afterwards, and there was never any confirmation of it. What triggered our interest—well, and this—I can think of another set of circumstances where you would get conflicting reports out of the agency. The agency was oftentimes not in agreement with itself.

And that's true of intelligence reporting in general.

It is. But in this particular case, as I recall, it had to do with the question of whether or not al Qaeda, sort of a religiously motivated entity, would do business with a guy like Saddam Hussein, who's anything but a devout Moslem.[20] And you had one section of the agency that said there can't be any link because they would never deal with a nonbeliever like Saddam Hussein. And yet another section of the agency said, you know, they shared enemies, they had both felt the same about the United States, and of course they cooperated. We would get—I can remember one issue [chuckles] that got debated, and we did go back and press on the agency and try to get answers. This was on the issue of—well, it centered initially on Abu Musab al-Zarqawi. [A] Jordanian operating a terrorist camp in Afghanistan before 9/11; fled after we launched into Afghanistan and ends up back in Baghdad, supposedly—according to some reporting— being treated for injuries he'd received in Afghanistan; becomes the leader of al Qaeda in Iraq.

Links don't get much more established than that, right?

Well, pretty well established, I would think. But the other part of it was there was always this question of whether or not Saddam had a relationship with al Qaeda. And one of the pieces of information that was never in dispute—which was that safe houses were being established in Baghdad by Zarqawi or his organization. And the report came through at one point that eight or ten safe houses had been established in Baghdad, before we launched in, by Egyptian Islamic Jihad. And when that report came through I said, "Now, wait a minute, head of Egyptian Islamic Jihad is [Ayman al-]Zawahiri. Zawahiri is now al Qaeda's number two. And the organizations had been merged. So the question I sent back is: "Would it be accurate to say that al Qaeda has established safe houses in Baghdad?" It took 'em *months* to get that sorted out! Finally, they came back and said yes: same-same. But initially, you know, it wasn't an easy answer for the agency to come up with. You've got one group that's obviously gone on at great length that there's been a merger of Egyptian Islamic Jihad and al Qaeda. Zawahiri's, well, he's running al Qaeda today. But they treated him separate. I think it happened to come out of that—you know now I am speculating, at this point—came out of that unit that didn't believe there was a link, and they didn't want to say al Qaeda has been establishing safe haven in Baghdad.

That would be an example of the politicization of intelligence, correct?

Yeah. And we would push aggressively on those matters.

And you're aware that that aggressive approach by you and Scooter Libby in your visits over to the agency has been characterized by some, even in testimony, as having been, whether intentionally or not, intimidating to the mid-level and lower-level analysts, who just were—even just as a function of your presence and the way you carry yourself—felt that way.[21] You say what to that?

Go read Silberman-Robb, the commission. I think they state as much in there that the people of the agency welcomed our interest and our willingness to come out and talk and ask questions and really dig into what they were doing, that there was nothing better for an analyst than to have the feeling that the policymakers are paying attention to what he is doing. And there was never any evidence that Robb-Silberman uncovered where they could find *anybody* who felt the way you have just suggested, the critics suggest, we were trying to "intimidate" the agency.[22]

Yeah, you know, we relied heavily on the intelligence community. They were absolutely crucial in a lot of what we did. But I also had past experience that led me to ask questions—and we did. But I think what Condi's got there is just wrong. So that's maybe her interpretation but the—well, we'll have an opportunity, maybe, for me to respond in kind [chuckles] in terms of how both of us treated intelligence.

Well, go. This is that time.

Well, we had a situation, for example with respect to North Korea, where the issue was whether or not we would move forward and reward North

Korea by lifting their status that had been imposed on them as a terrorist-sponsoring state—sanctions. That's what we were giving in return for them coming clean with respect to their nuclear program. And one of the things that I'd had a hand in getting into the bickering back-and-forth was asking a question of whether or not they had highly enriched uranium [HEU]. Because their program is based on the old plutonium model, 1950s-era British technology.

And which they had at one point fairly explicitly *admitted* they did, to [Assistant Secretary of State] Jim Kelly and company—

At one point—and then backed off, yeah.

—and then kind of—then rescinded it, yeah.

And so we insisted that they give us a full and complete accounting on what they had. We knew they had their plutonium-based system; they'd already tested that system. And they sent a document back to us with the answers and the responses to the questions we'd asked, in which they denied that they had any uranium-enrichment capability. There were traces of highly enriched uranium on the paper they used to respond to us. That was pretty conclusive [chuckles] evidence that they were lying through their teeth! Condi, rather than believe that or operate based on that, went ahead anyway and pushed and ultimately persuaded the president to go ahead and lift the sanctions in spite of the fact that they were deliberately lying to us in the process of the exchanges we had with them with respect to their nuclear program.[23]

I reported on this pretty intensively at that time.

Yeah.

And if you read that piece I sent along, about "The Madness of [Assistant Secretary of State] Chris Hill," he had sent me these truly vituperative and lengthy and profane e-mails when I contacted him for comment on a story that I was breaking at the time, to the effect that the administration was going to carve out of the declaration process with North Korea the thorniest problems, one of which was an HEU program, and I think the other of which was proliferation.

Mm-hmm. Syria.

And he *exploded* in these e-mails. I happened to be in the White House, and I remember reading them on my computer where he was like, "I don't know what you're smoking! Okay? Why on earth would I agree to do that? I don't believe in carve-outs. Some of the—whoever your sources are not real conservatives," assuming that I am a conservative or you know, just not a real reporter. It went on and on. They were not off the record; because he didn't say they were off the record, but just as a sort of genteel measure, I replied to the effect that I was going to distill all of this down into a suitable reply that I could quote in a story. And that triggered e-mail number two, which was even nastier. "I don't know what you're smoking" and all this sort of thing. And then it turned out to be the case that we in fact *did* carve out those exact areas from our approach to the declaration. And Hill had been all over Asia, in sessions with reporters, saying, "An incomplete declaration is no declaration at all."

Right.

"We can't accept 90 percent."

Right.

And that turned out to be exactly what we did, and poor Steve Hadley was forced to face the press and say, "We obviously have further areas we need to work on." [chuckles] I decided, you know, effectively, that I had been lied to flat-out—and not only that, berated.

Yeah.

And so I decided that I would go ahead and publish the contents of [Hill's e-mails] and I did that in 2008.[24] Shortly thereafter, by the way, I was in an eyeglass store up in Tenleytown [in Northwest Washington, D.C.] and who is there but Chris Hill? And I was dressed informally—I was wearing a Who T-shirt—and I just decided, "You know what? I'm not going to catalyze a showdown here. I'll just hold up a *TIME* magazine in front of my face and sort of try and escape this without a confrontation." And some young lady in a lab coat emerges from one of the screening rooms and says, "James Rosen? Is James Rosen here?"

And I stand up and I—and there he is, and he's lookin' at me and he just says to me as I pass by—I don't know why he addressed me this way. The only people who call me "Jamie" are my parents at this point, where it used to be my name for the first ten years of my life. And he just looks at me and he says, "Jamie, I hope they put you on the sports desk!"

[laughter] Well, now he was a bad guy, Chris Hill was.

A bad guy in what sense?

Ah, deceitful. I think perfectly prepared to lie to the president. And I think he—I think Condi totally misjudged what she wanted in somebody who would handle what was an extraordinarily sensitive project. I mean, she herself had said at one point that an incomplete declaration is a deal-breaker. There isn't going to be any deal if in fact they don't come clean on the program. They didn't come clean. She went forward, anyway.

And your assessment of all of that is Rice herself, in some sense, must have become a captive to a State Department mindset—

Mm-hmm.

—whereby negotiations take on a life of their own, and a logic of their own, and must be extended at all costs.

Yeah. The importance is the deal, you know. Whether it advances the cause or not, you've got to get some kind of an agreement.

And the question that persists is why President Bush was susceptible to *enabling* all of that? And what's your conclusion about that?

Well, when we are all through with this, you and I will have a private conversation today.

Okay.

And I will give you, off the record, an interesting insight.[25]

Okay. Back to the period of the run-up to the Iraq War and the questions about WMD: In *In My Time* you suggest that before the war, George Tenet argued strenuously, complete with props, that Iraq was acquiring aluminum tubes for use in a covert uranium-enrichment program.

Mm-hmm.

But then later on, Tenet drew attention to a dissenting conclusion in the intelligence community's product that suggested that these tubes were

intended solely for use in the production of artillery rockets. To what do you attribute Tenet's change of position on this question?

Well, I don't remember when he changed his position.

Well, in the book you seem to imply that the change of position very much was a function of timing, in that he adopted it after it became clear there were no WMD to be found in Iraq. And—

That's possible, yeah. I don't remember the change of position. But what I *do* remember, and I'm sure—

This is on page 392 on the paperback, if you'd like to check it out.

Yeah. Um—all right, let's see where we are, 392 [consults his copy of his memoir]. Yeah, aluminum tubes. This talks about a minority view in the NIE [National Intelligence Estimate] which Tenet later emphasized, okay, that the tubes are for another purpose.

It sounds there like you're kind of accusing him [Tenet] of changing his tune when it became inconvenient—

Yeah, I think that's [accurate]—

—to remember how he *had* been advocating.

Well, what stands out in my mind is that that was a prop that was featured prominently in briefings, and I sat in a couple of those briefings with him. I think one of them was in the Sit Room in the West Wing, maybe on the Hill. He'd carry this briefcase. In the middle of talking about the North Korean nuclear problem, he'd whip out one of these aluminum tubes. And it was, you know, a nice-sized aluminum tube that we had acquired, that was used—we believed, and that was what all the reporting was saying—was being used to enrich uranium as part of the centrifuge system. And you know, he was—well, we did a number of briefings in the run-up—this was, I think, in the run-up to the vote following the NIE in the fall of, would've been '02, I guess. And—[pauses]—you know, George was, well, he was very sort of *direct* at making the case for Iraq WMD.

Were you there for the famous "slam dunk" comment?

Absolutely. I was. I was closer to him than the president was. [laughs]

Is that comment distorted in the popular imagination about Iraq? Because it occupies a really central role in all narratives about it.

Yeah.

Is it—what are we to make of that comment from Tenet?

Well, it was a Saturday morning, as I recall, and we had more time for a meeting in the Oval Office in the morning, Saturday morning. And Tenet and [then–deputy CIA director John E.] McLaughlin, the number two, showed up, basically to do the brief. And it was—Hadley was there. And I think Condi must have been there.[26] And they gave us a lay down on, basically on Iraq and weapons of mass destruction, WMD. And McLaughlin did the brief, and it was kind of fuzzy. I mean, it wasn't—McLaughlin's that kind of a guy, he is not—

A hedger.

A hedger, yeah. But he got all through, and the president turned to George—and again, he and I are sitting at the fireplace like this [gestures].

I am on that side, the president's on this side. Couch here. Couch there. And that couch was where the agency briefers always sat. And that's where George is. And the president asked, he said, "George, how good is the intel on Iraq and WMD?" And he said, "It's a slam dunk, Mr. President. It's a slam dunk." Those were his exact words. Very certain, very positive. The president asked the right question and that's the answer he got.[27] And George has spent a lot of time over the years, I think, trying to find a way [chuckles] to explain why "slam dunk" doesn't mean slam dunk—but that's what he said.

What kind of impact do you think that comment had on the president at that time?

Well, I think he was very reassuring, that, you know, all the intelligence he'd been seeing over the months—'cause we'd seen a lot of it—that in fact [there was a] high degree of confidence with respect to the reporting we had seen about Iraq and weapons of mass destruction.

To the extent that the failure to find WMDs has, over time, been cemented as perhaps the greatest-ever example of an intelligence failure—right?—was George Tenet part of the problem?

Well, he was in charge of the agency. The NIEs went through a process that he basically headed up as the director of Central Intelligence.

But is he to be held as blameless in the process as the consumers of the intelligence?

[sighs] No, I think he bears some responsibility for the reporting that came in that turned out, a lot of it, to be false. But in fairness to George, you know, this wasn't just something we saw from the agency. It was a general view.

And foreign agencies, as well.

Including foreign agencies, as well. Some of this stuff we had had been provided to us: the Germans, for example, on the mobile [biological weapons] labs, that kind of thing. There was material coming through that was incorporated or included in the reporting that came from those other sources, so—but it was—it's interesting, I think, if you go back and you look at what we were finding. We just had this most recent dust-up in the last short period of time that, my gosh, they *did* find chemical weapons in Iraq. Turned out to be a fair amount of old stuff and so forth,[28] but I think if you look carefully and objectively at the reporting, especially [what] the survey group came back to us with afterwards, it wasn't really black and white so much. You didn't find stockpiles; that's true. But it's also true—and I think David Kay [chief weapons inspector for the Iraq Survey Group following the 2003 invasion] said this much when he finished—that Saddam Hussein had the capability, had the technology, the people, the feedstock, and so forth, the raw materials to resume his WMD program, and he had every intention of doing so as soon as he could get away with it. And I think David Kay even said he was more worried *after* what he found, even though it didn't sort of validate that basic proposition, than he was before he ever went in.[29] So in the political debate, in the heat of the argument, it's much more convenient for the critics and our opponents to say that, you know, there wasn't anything there that was justified. They leave you with the impression that Saddam was innocent.

Or that the refrigerator was entirely empty when you got there.

Right. Yeah.

As we sit here today, do you regard it as a possibility that the intelligence about Saddam and his stockpiles wasn't wrong per se but rather that Saddam

somehow managed to dispose of his weapons—sent them off to Syria by train or what have you—before the inspectors could find them?

Well—[pauses]—you know, never seen any hard evidence of that. We have reporting. I don't think there are any trains in that part of the world that I am familiar with—a lot of trucks. We had to bring in East German trucks to haul our tanks when we did Desert Storm, but there were reports of trucks hauling material into Syria. But—

Nothing was ever confirmed in that regard.

Yeah, I don't know, you may want to repeat your question again so I—

I think you understood it correctly: whether you regard it as a possibility that the intel wasn't wrong, that he did indeed at that time possess stockpiles, but that he managed somehow to evacuate them before the inspectors could find them.

Yeah. I think it's partly a problem of trying to describe in black and white terms a subject that is inherently fuzzy.

Sure.

And gray. And that there's no question Saddam did represent a threat. There's no question he had been involved with WMD. He did previously have two nuclear programs. The Israelis hit him in '81, we hit him in '91. But, you know, in the heat of the moment and partly because we ended up emphasizing WMD in our indictment of Saddam, he had other transgressions. His support for terror, his violation of UN Security Council resolutions, but I think it was—

Also his brutality to his own people, his use of chemical weapons.

Exactly. But at the time it looked as though the easiest thing to prove would be with respect to WMD. I mean, we had all this reporting on WMD, and obviously he is in violation of these resolutions on WMD. But that set up a situation in which, if you didn't quite reach the threshold of stockpiles, then you end up with the charges being made that there was nothing there.

The reason I asked that last question about whether you regard it as a possibility that he somehow evacuated his stockpiles is because in the book *State of Denial: Bush at War, Part III* by Bob Woodward (published in 2006), Woodward quotes you—after David Kay briefed you and the president and others on the failure to find WMD—as having taken Kay aside and asking him, "Could the weapons have gone to Syria?" Do you remember posing that question?

Mmm, I don't directly, but I can see where I would have done that, yeah.

During the march on Baghdad, coalition forces captured whole archives of Saddam's papers, as well as thousands of hours of tape recordings that he made. To your knowledge, was all of that material properly examined by the U.S. government, or did the sheer size of the archive, along with the usual budget and manpower issues, prevent that?

I assume there were vast quantities of intelligence and information of various kinds acquired. [Saddam's was] a huge bureaucratic government, and they had to generate a heck of a lot of paper. But I don't have any special knowledge. That hasn't been brought to my attention. It's been years now, anyway.

About that speech you gave to the Veterans of Foreign Wars in Nashville in August of 2002,[30] is it true, as Secretary Rice reports in her memoir, that after you finished that speech President Bush asked Rice to call you to remind

you that no decision about military action had yet been made, and you replied to her by saying you hadn't intended to limit the president's options?

I don't remember her phone call. I know she's made that statement. John [McConnell] wrote the speech. [To McConnell:] Did you write that speech? Yeah, he did. [laughs] I don't think it had anything to do with limiting his options.

Is it true, as President Bush himself recalled in *Decision Points*, that at one of your weekly luncheons together, closer to the start of the war, you actually said to him, "Are you going to take care of this guy or not?"

[laughs] I can't—well, I suppose it is possible I would have said that. I'm not sure I would have used that exact language. If he says I said it, I am not going to quarrel with him. We had a problem in the spring of '03. We'd got a resolution passed through the UN Security Council, as I recall—this would have been late '02—that we believed was sufficient justification for us to act militarily. As we got closer and closer, [British Prime Minister] Tony Blair came to us and made a request that we go get *another* UN Security Council resolution. We didn't believe we needed it; he believed he had to have it for political reasons at home. And so the president agreed to try to get another resolution through the UN Security Council. We were unsuccessful; France, as I recall, blocked it.

Not just blocked it but *lobbied* against it.

Mm-hmm. I'm trying to remember the question you asked me now.

Well, about you saying to the president [chuckles], "Are you going to take care of this guy or not?"

All right. That we ran into problems because of the delay. There was uncertainty, growing uncertainty about whether or not we were going to follow through.

Amongst the allies?

Allies, the public here at home. And I can remember hearing from, well, a couple of former senior government officials who expressed their concern that it looked like we were waffling and uncertain about whether we were going to proceed, and that was a direct result of delaying and hoping we could get something through the UN Security Council. And it would have been within that context, about [whether] I said, you know, "Are we gonna get this done or not?" But it would not have been disrespectful. It would have been—well, let's just leave it at that. [laughs]

[laughs] All right. Moving on to the issues associated with the postwar period, after the invasion had more or less succeeded in toppling his government. I want to talk about the planning for reconstruction, occupation. You, in your book *In My Time*, stated, "We underestimated the difficulty of rebuilding."

Mm-hmm.

How large a failing was that? How central to the very problematic experience that America had in Iraq was that failure, that difficulty, the underestimation of the difficulty of rebuilding?

Mmm, well, it was important, obviously. I think that the—[pauses]—before we went in, we dealt a lot with expatriates, former Iraqi officials. Others, the expatriate community was very enthusiastic about taking down Saddam. And I think there was the belief that if we took off that top layer of government, of Saddam and his cohort, that underneath that was a government, or the makings of a government, bureaucracy, people in place, procedures and so forth—

Technocrats.

—technocrats. Put different leadership over the top and you'd be able to have a functioning government. That's one of the main places where I think we ran into difficulty, that it turned out, for example, that the entire ministry, Interior Ministry, was a snake pit. It didn't, no matter how deep you dug down, it simply wasn't a credible, viable institution. That it was a place where—[it had been] nominally in charge of internal security, but it had been so corrupted by Saddam Hussein and so forth that it was not anything you were going to be able to rely on. Partly contributed to the looting, partly contributed to the need to maintain a more robust presence there just to provide safety and security for the population. I think there were things like that that entered into it. I think the Shia-Sunni conflict hadn't been fully appreciated in terms of the degree to which that conflict came to a head. And it was there, it had been there for a long time, but Saddam had ruled with an iron fist.

Don Rumsfeld had composed, prior to the invasion, a list of—I forget the term that is used in connection with this—nineteen contingencies of how things could go very, very wrong, I guess just as an intellectual exercise. And he included among those nineteen points the prospect that there could be intense sectarian tensions in the aftermath.[31]

Yeah. Well, there were a lot of things that we anticipated that *didn't* happen. We anticipated the possibility of the use of chemical weapons by Saddam, which he was believed to have, which he'd used on his own people and on the Iranians. And it was estimated that the closer we got to Baghdad, the more likely it was that we would be hit with chemical weapons. And we spent an enormous amount of time and money making sure our guys had all the protective gear, repeating drills and exercises as they went through that process, and putting that on the air in part to persuade Saddam, which probably was successful, that we were better prepared to operate in that kind of an environment than he was. He never launched any chemical weapons against us. We were concerned about, say, oil field fires, the kind of thing we had run into after Kuwait, when he torched the Kuwaiti oil fields. So there were contingencies that we planned for that never occurred. But there were others that occurred that we hadn't planned for, obviously hadn't anticipated.

Stuart Bowen, who had previously served as deputy staff secretary at the White House in the first term, later the special inspector general for Iraq reconstruction. And in his final report,[32] he concluded that the sixty-billion-dollar reconstruction effort financed by the American taxpayer was hampered of course by security challenges, but also by what he called "blinkered and disjointed pre-war planning for postwar Iraq."

I haven't seen his report.

Is that a fair charge?

You know, would want to look at the report before I said that, but it wouldn't be right to judge it without knowing more of what he's talking about.

Well, he goes on to say—

There was no question but what there were things that were unanticipated that we had to deal with once we got there. I'm not surprised by that.

He said coalition forces "found the country in much worse condition than prewar planners anticipated" and that while planners "identified areas that would need postwar relief and reconstruction," those managing the

reconstruction "did not define specific goals, objectives, measures, and metrics until very late in the planning process."

Altogether it sounds, from a credible source like Bowen, that Colin Powell, whatever his faults, was right when he warned, "If you break it, you've bought it."

Mm-hmm. Well, I think part of the problem was the State Department, frankly. I mean, there was a general feeling that you really needed—I can remember occasions and this was even after Condi was at State—where there were concerns voiced because you couldn't get enough State Department personnel on site to be able to fill out the Provincial Reconstruction Teams and so forth. That State wasn't up to the task of managing everything that needed to be managed. I'm sure it's changed today, but there was a period of time there where the embassy in Baghdad was the biggest embassy in the world that the U.S. had. And there was conflict between, well, between the Pentagon on the one hand and State Department on the other, where the Pentagon would wind up having to pick up the slack because there was no civilian capability to move in and perform a lot of those essential functions.

And where State's typical response would be: "How can we send civilians to do this when you guys in the Pentagon haven't established the security necessary for them to operate?"

Mm-hmm. Yeah.

Kind of a Catch-22.

Well, a Catch-22, and there were debates over whether to put together the Iraqi government, the interim government afterwards. I can remember State arguing that you can't have anybody in the government who hasn't been in-country in recent months. If they had fled the country, they were suspect, they wouldn't be accepted by the Iraqi people as a legitimate government. That turned out to be bad advice, because virtually everybody that we did get into the transition government and so forth had fled the country at one time or another. But there is no question there were significant problems in terms of the aftermath once we had achieved the objective of toppling Saddam Hussein as you tried to put the country back together again.

Later on, towards the surge period, in November 2006—after the midterms but again in the midst of the deliberations about the surge— [deputy White House national security advisor] J. D. Crouch led a presentation in the White House solarium on the status of the Iraq War. For this purpose he compiled what the NSC regarded as sets of unfounded assumptions that the White House had made. Among them was the belief that "political"—

The White House would have been the NSC. These are not different entities.

Right. No, [Crouch] wasn't exempting the NSC, I don't think.

Yeah.

But—in other words, Crouch was just trying to look at where are we, why are we in the situation we are in, in November of 2006? How did we get here? And the actual slides that he used included quotes saying that one of the unfounded assumptions was that "political progress will help defuse the insurgency," which Crouch said should be replaced by the assumption that "political and economic progress are unlikely absent a basic level of security." Was that a false assumption that top policymakers, even the president, had shared in—that we can rely on the political process to defuse the insurgency?

Hmm. [pauses] Well, there was always—[pauses again]—I think there was always the expectation that one of our objectives had to be to get a legitimate government in place, and that that was going to be crucial in terms of our ultimately being able to get our own people out and turn things over to a legitimate Iraqi government. As I think about it, in terms of the "insurgency," we went through an evolution over time of what kind of problem we were dealing with. Once the government's down, Saddam's captured, he is on trial.

Is it former Iraqi army guys attacking U.S. forces, is it Shiite militias?

Is it Shia-Sunni? And in particular individuals who were seeking, you know, power for their own right.

[Shiite leader] Muqtada al-Sadr.

Yeah, Muqtada al-Sadr and so forth. How much of it was al Qaeda? You know, we had the famous letter we intercepted [in January 2004] between Zarqawi and bin Laden about what his strategy was, which was to start a civil war between Sunni and Shia. And to that end, he was doing everything he could to kill Shia. That was especially a problem along in the '06 timeframe, and the bombing of the Golden Mosque at Samarra[33] and so forth. There were a lot of cross-cutting—

—elements to this.

Elements, yeah. It wasn't just a simple insurgency. There were a lot of reasons why there was a significant level of violence, I guess, in the society, and all of these different elements played a role in that. Some of it was the deliberate effort by al Qaeda and the head of al Qaeda in Iraq. Some of it was historic conflicts between Shia and Sunni. Yadda, yadda, yadda, I mean, there were a lot of—

The "dead-enders." There's a lot of forces at play there.

Mm-hmm.

Just for the record, Crouch also listed three unfounded assumptions that had been made. Number one, the idea that dialogue with insurgent groups could reduce the violence.

Dialogue between insurgent groups?

I think between the coalition and the insurgent groups is what is referenced there.

Mm-hmm.

Second, that other countries in the region were committed to Iraqi stability. And lastly that Iraqi security forces were in fact improving. Those are some of the unfounded assumptions he says the administration made along the way, that proved problematic.

Yeah. I think—and I assume J. D. probably did this—you'd want to get an element of the time factor involved here, too. I think things did change over time. We did make progress when we killed Zarqawi—you know, a major step. When was this presentation by J. D. in the solarium?

November of 2006.

Okay. Yeah, I don't remember being there, but it was during that period of time when we were looking at all the various possibilities. We had the congressionally mandated study group. We had the Kagan-Keane operation. We had the Hadley operation and the Colonels. We talked about some of this yesterday, I think. And it was a period of ferment as we looked at and wrestled with the question as to where our strategy ought to be and where we had problems we needed to address, how to fix it.

And again, this kind of massive initiative, there really is no modern-day field manual for this sort of thing.

No, it's not—I mean, the United States had to some extent been there before in the aftermath of World War II, when you look at what we had done in Germany and Japan and Korea.

But you didn't have the non-state actors.

Exactly. We didn't have the non-state actors, we didn't have the kind of religious conflicts between Shia and Sunni. And it was just a very different time, a different place and so forth. Hard to find parallels. But there had been a time in our history when we had been able to go in and destroy our adversaries and then set up long-term governments that have turned into great friends and allies of the United States and major players on the world stage. But that was very different from the kind of situation that we were dealing with here, and nobody was still alive who had been involved back in 1945.

You just alluded to the internal debates over what kind of interim Iraqi government should be stood up after the invasion. And that calls to mind the Iraqi expatriate and advocate for U.S. military intervention Ahmed Chalabi. And I wonder as you sit here today what your thoughts are about him: the role he played in all of this, the degree of confidence that U.S. policymakers like yourself may have invested in him, whether that was wise, and so on.

I don't think we invested that much in him. He was *around*. I'm trying to remember who the big advocates of Chalabi were. He was an opportunist. It seems to me he had been living in Jordan, had been indicted, actually, in Jordan at one point, in terms of bank fraud. I'd want to check that before you say that in print.[34] But he was, you know, he was one of those people who was hostile to Saddam Hussein, potentially useful as we addressed the question of Saddam. I'm trying to remember the sequence of this again, too. I can remember a session where I brought in people from the agency to have a session to talk about past efforts at covert action inside Iraq to take down the government. It seems to me there had been a time—obviously would have been before we launched in '03—when there had been a covert action in Iraq that had been authorized, whose cover was blown, and Saddam Hussein got word of it and killed hundreds of people who were involved in the plot against him. The timeframe there would have been, I suppose, back in maybe the late nineties. So there was a search of sorts to find potential sources of opposition to Saddam Hussein and—

Who were still breathing—

—who were still breathing, and some of them were expatriates. Some of them were living in the United States. People like Kanan Makiya, the noted academic, people who were strong supporters of the U.S. intervention. Some of them for good and proper purposes, probably some of them more motivated by their self-interests. Chalabi was part of, I think, of a desire to find people who could be helpful. I'm trying to remember where he came from, in terms of—I met him once or twice.

One of the phrases that echoes today from that time was President Bush's repeatedly saying that the generals will get what they need and in essence that "I listen to my commanders in the field. And if they want more troops they will get more troops," and what have you. He repeatedly made clear that he wanted to defer to the expertise of the uniformed officers. And the question has subsequently been raised as to whether George W. Bush was a bit *too* deferential to his military generals in the Iraq War, and whether

he and the effort could have benefited from a bit more of a direct hand by him.

I think that's an inaccurate assessment. I would cite as evidence for its inaccuracy the fact that he *did* directly take hand, he did directly override what I think was a consensus view of the chiefs with the surge.

But I am talking about in those first three years, before we got to that point.

Well, you know, I think in terms of the initial mission when you've got to go in and take down Saddam Hussein, which was the mission, I thought he handled it about right. That's essentially a military mission. He worked closely with the people that were involved, he worked closely with Rumsfeld, obviously, but also with [CENTCOM commander and U.S. Army General] Tommy Franks, the man on the scene. So no, I thought the relationship was a good one. But I also think the president gets credit for then, in the course of '06, for ultimately making the decision that he wanted to take a different course, when he made significant changes in policy and personnel and basic fundamental strategy. Did it in the face of considerable opposition, publicly. Overrode, I think, what was the consensus view inside the Pentagon, or at least among most of the chiefs, and took a very courageous decision and executed it very well. When we finished in late '08, Iraq was in pretty good shape. We had in fact pretty well defeated al Qaeda, run most of them out. Sunni and Shia were working together. We had a Shia president and a Sunni vice president.

The Sunni awakening.

The Sunni awakening, and the folks out in Anbar province and so forth that signed on, partly because I think because they believed in the United States and what we were doing, and we'd demonstrated our commitment to get it right. Unfortunately—

They'd also had a firsthand taste of al Qaeda.

Sure, yeah. No, I think we were in pretty good shape when we left. And unfortunately, you know, it all came apart because there was no follow-through, etc.

By the succeeding administration?

As a result of Barack Obama's policies.

You mentioned how public support had turned against the war, certainly by the time of the surge. The president's poll numbers were very low. Was that judgment on the part of the American people that was recorded in the polls—and assuming that we can concede the scientific integrity of the polls—

[chuckles] That's a big assumption. If that was true, the Democrats would have won the last election.

[laughs] DEWEY DEFEATS TRUMAN—I get it.

Yeah.

But polling over time, such as we saw in the case of the Iraq War, can't readily be dismissed. Right? There are times where, generally speaking, we can get a pretty good read on public sentiment in this country. And I think Iraq was one of those times where the country had turned against the war effort. Significant numbers, if not majorities, were saying that the war wasn't worth it, that we shouldn't have done it and so on. And this was the environment in which, as you say, the president demonstrated this great courage by forging ahead with the surge.

Right.

**Okay? Was that judgment on the part of the American people at the time—
and which wasn't a snapshot but which was fairly consistent over time—in
your view a logical response to the actual events that were unfolding on the
ground? Or was it a reflection of a failure on the part of the top officials,
starting with the president himself, to communicate more effectively with the
people?**

Hmm! I won't challenge the notion that there was a rising opposition to
the war and, you know, to the cost of it, both in terms of lives and treasure.
One of the problems that we faced, and that we still face today, is that the
nature of the threat to the United States and the kind of problem we were
trying to deal with in Iraq and Afghanistan is pretty dramatically different
than anything we'd seen before. Right now I am reading a biography of
George Marshall by Ed Cray [*General of the Army: George C. Marshall,
Soldier and Statesman* (1990)]. I don't know if you've ever read Cray's
books. It's a great biography on Marshall—one of the best. And still, you'll
hear this in the press all the time—"My God, this is the longest war in
history," you know. "It's taken twice as long as it did for us to win World
War II." And what we've had to adjust to as a nation, I think—and the
adjustment may not be complete yet—is the fact that the kind of conflict
we are dealing with now, and the kind of threat we are trying to defeat, is
likely to occasion, you know, sustained effort, oftentimes military, certainly
from an intelligence standpoint, over *years*. There's not a day when it ends
and "peace is at hand" and we have solved the problem.

**And at a time when American attention span in general is shrinking, due to
the way we consume media and everything else.**

Shrinking, moving so rapidly from point to point. As I say, I can't get
the World War II analogy out of my head, partly because I've been
reading about what Marshall did, especially in the period from when

he became chairman [*sic*; army chief of staff] in September of '39 up until about '42 and so forth and we finally get into the war. But in a relatively short order, by current standards, he created this massive mobilization of what, sixteen million men? Over a hundred divisions in the United States Army, you know, massive turnout and production of aircraft and aircraft carriers and ships and tanks and, you know, all of the materials of warfare, and then went off and defeated the Japanese and the Germans. The degree of effort required was enormous—but it also came to an end. And we look back on it now: From a historical standpoint, it obviously had long-term ramifications and so forth; but there was the end. There was the VE Day and VJ Day. My dad came home from the navy and we moved back home to Lincoln. It was a whole different set of circumstances, I think, in terms of our historical experience with war and conflict. And now when we fast-forward to 9/11 and the post-9/11 era and the twenty-first century, we are looking at a very different kind of circumstance in terms of the threats we face and how we will have to deal with them. And I think sort of the first example of that is what happened to us both with respect to Iraq and Afghanistan. We still have troops in Afghanistan today and we started there in 2001.

And the impact on public opinion?

And the impact on public opinion. I think, you know, part of the task is to remind people why we are there and what we are doing.

Could Bush have been more effective at that?

I don't know; possibly. We did an awful lot of it, anyway. The main thing that obviously you hoped for is that you could get it wrapped up and resolved in some acceptable fashion. And that has turned out to take longer and be more difficult. Part of the difficulty was I don't think there was a national consensus between Republicans and Democrats on what we were trying to do. There may have been at the outset, but when you end up with fundamental kind of differences that existed between our outgoing administration in '08 and the incoming Obama administration in '09, when this whole campaign has been built around reversing the policies that we'd put in place over the course of our time in office and responding to the so-called war on terror. And with, I think, a fundamentally different worldview that Obama represents, that is very different than ours. I'm not sure there was any speech that could have been given [that] would have solved that problem.

The question remains: Was this persistent dissatisfaction with the war on the part of the American people at that time a logical response to the facts on the ground or did it reflect some less-than-effective communications effort?

No. [pauses] I don't know; it probably was some of both, but nobody had ever had to make that kind of communications commitment over that period of time before. I mean, it's just a different world. It's a different era. It's a different threat. And the kind of response that's going to be required going forward for the United States is going to be a lot more like what we've experienced since 9/11 than we did before, that period before 9/11. And how do you deal with it? Well, you're going to have to. A lot of it is going to be leadership and—

Persuasion.

—persuasion, bringing people along. But it may also—depends in part on circumstance. One of the things I have been struck by in the last few months is the extent to which there has been a dramatic shift in public opinion about U.S. involvement overseas with the rise of ISIS. You know, that really turned on a dime in a relatively short period of time, where public attitude towards the use of military force has been suddenly far more acceptable in recent months than it was during the period of time we are talking about here.

A few televised beheadings will have that effect, I guess.

Exactly.

Does it bother you that even in the period prior to 9/11, the American capacity to absorb casualties, or the American willingness to absorb casualties, in conflicts really shrank? And what I mean by this is: You talked just now about how Americans were responding to the number of U.S. casualties in Iraq. But in historical terms, as you know as a student of military history, the number of U.S. casualties suffered in the Iraq War was fairly low for a venture of that size. Whereas were you to compare it with just the campaign to capture Guadalcanal, or—you would know better than I—Iwo Jima, the casualty figures associated with those are in the tens of thousands, right?[35]

Mm-hmm.

Part of this, probably, I suspect, has to do with a diminished respect for authority on the part of the American people, post-Vietnam and Watergate. But to what do you attribute this shrinking willingness on the part of the American people to accept casualties? Are they spoiled by Kosovo, or what is it, exactly? Or Vietnam was the issue?

I'd have to go back and spend some time on it. I'm not sure that I understand the assumptions that are built into your question.

People didn't question it when we undertook operations that cost tens of thousands of American lives just to seize some strategically valuable piece of real estate in the Pacific theater in World War II. Here, they get all—

Well, but they didn't see it that way. I mean, you had World War II, precipitated our involvement, obviously, by Pearl Harbor. But once that occurred, you'd gone from a position where there was an intense resistance to foreign involvement. There was still great frustration over the way World War I ended. A large, large body of opinion opposed to U.S. military involvement. An army that was, what, number seventeenth or eighteenth in the world in 1939? And the attack on Pearl Harbor changed all that, and overnight the nation came to understand why it was important for us to go forward. Part of that was Roosevelt's leadership. But when tasked, we clearly rose to the challenge, to the tune of more than four hundred thousand dead Americans in that enterprise. Do we still have the capacity to do that kind of thing going forward? I don't know.

And isn't that worrisome?

Well, it *is* worrisome because, you know, it's sort of a key question. It was a key question *then*. If there's no Pearl Harbor, how does Roosevelt deal with the problems of Nazi Germany and Europe and so forth? I just think the kind of conflict and threats to the nation that we face today are pretty dramatically different. Spend time on cyberwarfare. The nature of the problems and conflicts we are faced with. It's not at all clear to me how all that's going to sort out, and what kind of steps are needed that we are going to have to take going forward in order to deal with those threats. It's not even clear we *understand* the threats. So I am, you know, reluctant to make—

Sweeping judgments about Americans' capacity for this or that—

Yeah. You know, we clearly have had it in the past when it was needed. I hope we've got it now, going forward. But we've got to be able to define the threat. We've got to have good leadership. We've got to be able to develop the kind of national consensus that we've had in the past in order to be able to make the sacrifices that are required in order to succeed.

To mobilize, in short. I've only got two or three more questions. I have never forgotten the time when White House Press Secretary Ari Fleischer, doing the daily press briefing in October 2002, was asked about a prospective invasion of Iraq potentially costing nine billion dollars a month. And Fleischer answered that the cost of a single bullet would be far less. And he did that from the podium, and kind of had to walk it back.[36]

I'm not even sure what he means.

Well, in other words, it was suggested that what he was saying was, if the Iraqis would just do this themselves with a bit of regime change—

Oh.

—*sua sponte*, we wouldn't have to do that, right? It was Gerald Ford who signed the executive order banning the U.S. from engaging in assassinations of foreign leaders. And I've often wondered how things might have turned out had we pursued a single-bullet option with Saddam Hussein, if the situation would have been much worse. And I wonder if your conception of the powers of the commander in chief in wartime would permit him the use of assassinations, Executive Order 11905 notwithstanding.[37]

Mmm, what about a Predator with a five-hundred-pound bomb on top of Abu Mussab al-Zarqawi, the head of al Qaeda in Iraq?

Is it an assassination by definition if it's a non-state actor?

By definition, it was an act of war. I mean, we never addressed it or thought about it as an assassination. In a sense, you know, you're getting up to the point where with modern technology and good intelligence you can identify the individual you want to eliminate and do it. And the president has that authority. Now, nobody's raised the question: Does that violate the executive order?

Right.

As I recall, the executive order was issued at a time when we were going back, looking at the revelations of the CIA's assassination attempts on [Fidel] Castro and so forth in the Kennedy administration. I'm not sure that's all that relevant these days.

Given the American experience in Iraq, should the concept of regime change be permanently discredited as a tool of U.S. foreign policy?

No. I think what we did in Iraq was the right thing to do. I still believe that. I think there were significant gains that we made out of that. We've talked about the nuclear situation. We clearly took Saddam out of the nuclear business. You can argue about what kind of stockpile did he have. But there's no question he had been in the business before, he'd produced and used weapons of mass destruction, and he was finished when we got rid of him. No question but what that set the stage for Qaddafi to follow through and surrender all his materials, and that set the stage for us to take down A. Q. Khan. And that also, as I say, was the only time the Iranians ever hesitated on their nukes.

Would you say that the intelligence failure that was so manifest in the run-up to this particular use of regime change as a tool of foreign policy raises the bar for the use of it in the future or somehow makes it more difficult for us to employ it in the future?

Why would it make it more difficult?

Because of international opinion saying, "Well, you know, you tried regime change once before, and that was on the basis of faulty intelligence; why would anyone ever accept the United States' engaging in regime change again?" I think I know your answer, probably. [chuckles]

Yeah, I think we have to be careful about letting international opinion guide American policy. There are times when nothing is going to happen if the United States doesn't make it happen, doesn't provide the leadership. For example, I would be a strong advocate of taking out militarily the Iranian nuclear program. And probably a lot of our European allies wouldn't share that view.

What do you think the spillover effects would be—[which] you obviously are willing to countenance?

What are the effects going to be if we don't? We've got to answer that question, too. That's one that never gets discussed. I'm always hesitant when we start to talk about international opinion and what it means and that we dare not cross that line that indicates where international opinion finds it acceptable or not acceptable.

The reason I pose that specific question of whether or not the experience in this case raises the bar for it going forward, I don't mind telling you, is because I put the exact same question to Bob Gates in Iraq in August 2010 when I was on a trip with him: "Given the American experience in Iraq, should the concept of regime change be permanently discredited as a tool of U.S. foreign policy?" And he said [paraphrasing], "No. However, the way we got into this use of regime change raises the bar for us to do it again." Because regime change is always going to be based on intelligence and this experience is going to color perceptions of it. That was basically his answer. He then

went on to say [paraphrasing], "You always have to go back to Hitler in '37 and how many lives you might have been able to save if he had been dealt with earlier."[38]

Yeah.

Two final questions. The story is often told—probably apocryphal—that when President Nixon, on his first visit to China in February 1972, asked Chou en-Lai what he thought had been the impact of the French Revolution, Chou replied, "Too soon to tell."

[laughter] Well, that's a good answer!

How long should Americans, Iraqis, the world have to wait before the overall impact, value, and wisdom of the Iraq War can be properly assessed?

Oh, I think it's, partly that there is a great temptation to sort of put boundaries around it and say, you know, it begins here, it ends there. We've in effect reached this far and no farther. I don't think you can do that. I think it's part of a much larger set of trends and developments that we're going to have to deal with for a long time to come. Because it *is* the Middle East, because of the changing nature of technology that makes it possible for a handful of individuals to do enormous damage to us. Partly because it's in that part of the world that is all caught up in the problems and the challenges and so forth of the interaction between the old caliphate and the Ottoman years and the rest of the world.

In other words—

It's not, I mean, it's an event in an ongoing set of problems and concerns, but I think it will always have to be evaluated within that broader context.

After ten years, we should have a good idea of whether a marriage is working out. At what point—

It's not a marriage.

No, I understand; it's a rough analogy. But at what point will it be fair to say, "That was a good idea," "That was a bad idea"? Or "That was a success" or "It was not a success"?

Oh, as far as I'm concerned, it was the right thing to do, and I still believe that. I think my own personal view is what will be deemed a failure is our failure to follow through, the determination of the Obama administration to withdraw from that part of the world at a moment when our presence is probably more important than it's ever been. At a moment when the prospects for fundamentally negative developments that affect the United States and other parts of the world is growing. The threat is growing and our capacity to deal with the threats is being diminished. And that's a byproduct of the unwillingness or the inability of the Obama administration to follow through on what we started in Iraq.

Last question. For any public figure I think there are really three of you. In your case, there is the real Dick Cheney, right? The guy that loves to fish, the guy that loves his grandchildren: the real person. Then there's the Dick Cheney that you cultivate assiduously as a public figure. This would include your campaign literature, the speeches you give; this is where you attempt to create a persona that isn't exactly you as you are, but that you seek to project. And then lastly, there is the Dick Cheney that others project and which in your case may have come to dominate the public perception. And you know the words associated with it: Darth Vader and so on. Do you think that you, Dick Cheney, are popularly misunderstood or that you have been misrepresented in some way and that that misrepresentation has taken root with the American people?

No. I don't sit around worrying a lot about those who disagree with me or are critics. That goes with the turf. And I've often said before, if you want to be loved, you got to go be a movie actor. But you don't belong in the business I've been involved in most of my life, dealing with difficult issues and serving in positions where you have to make decisions, support policies that are sometimes painful and costly and difficult to implement.

In terms of the views of others—[pauses]—I guess the ones I care about most are the people who have been actively involved in some of these enterprises in the military or in intelligence. I frequently run into, in my travels, people who served either when I was secretary of defense or when I was vice president, who have been involved with a lot of the issues we've been talking about, who thank me for the views I have expressed and continue to express. And I guess those are the ones that count most in terms of my spending any time thinking about it at all. But I love what I have been able to do. I've been privileged to be involved in some historic events over the last forty years. I am glad I was there. I am glad I had the opportunity to contribute. And I don't feel sorry for myself or feel that I am unjustly or unduly criticized by those who disagree with me. I mean, I don't worry about it.

Mr. Vice President, thank you very much.

Thank you.

I hope you enjoyed this.

It was interesting.

ACKNOWLEDGMENTS

M any people gave graciously of their time, talents, connections, and counsel to make *Cheney One on One* a reality—but no one was more generous than Vice President Cheney himself, and his wife, Lynne, for inviting me into their home and allowing me to conduct the interviews that comprise this book. The whole idea behind the enterprise was to use the extended transcript format—which I have loved since adolescence, when I devoured books like David Sheff's *The Playboy Interviews with John Lennon and Yoko Ono* (1981)—to explore the mind of Dick Cheney, whom I had covered intensively as a reporter and always regarded as one of the most fascinating and enigmatic public figures of the last half century. At the lunch that preceded our sessions, I drew the lopsided Cheney smile when I told him I had just finished reading Jonathan Cott's *Susan Sontag: The Complete "Rolling Stone" Interviews* (2013) and wanted to give Cheney the same treatment. One need not be a Sontag fan, I said, in order to recognize that hers was an evolved mind, and that the long-form interview, free of editorializing by the writer but shaped by his questioning, gives that kind of mind the freest rein. That the former vice president still went forward, even after mention of John Lennon and Susan Sontag—two individuals from whom Cheney surely derives little inspiration—speaks, again, to his boundless generosity.

Several individuals close to the Cheneys helped facilitate the interviews. These include Mrs. Cheney, who brought messages and comfort to the injured interviewer; Liz Cheney, my friend and acquaintance from too many green-room encounters to count; Kara Ahern, who handled scheduling and kept us honest on time; Kristin Koch; and Alexandra Jajonie. Jim Steen, present throughout the sessions, was exceptionally diligent and kind in tracking down stray names, facts, and figures that eluded us during the tapings. Likewise, John McConnell, present for almost all of the sessions, recalled pertinent facts. Gus kept the lattes coming.

The individual most critical besides the vice president and me was my Fox News colleague George "Skip" McCloskey, the audio engineer who recorded the sessions and generously provided copies to the vice president and me; without Skip, there *is* no *Cheney One on One*—only yesterday. Another Fox News colleague, Nick Kalman—a highly decorated Navy combat photographer and loyal friend—took the keen-eyed photographs of Cheney that illustrated the *Playboy* interview. Still another Fox News colleague, Meghan Welsh, extracted the Cheneyana from two dozen books I'd collected about the Bush-Cheney era—not counting Cheney's memoir and a few other volumes that could not be delegated—and organized it for easy review. Meghan also prepared the first draft of the transcripts; her diligence was critical to the project. As always, I remain grateful to many others at Fox News—too many to name, but most notably our chairman and CEO, Roger Ailes—for supporting me in countless ways.

At *Playboy*, chief content officer and editorial director Jimmy Jellinek and deputy editor Steve Randall demonstrated great patience, generosity, and integrity in nurturing the magazine excerpt of *Cheney One on One* to fruition, and thereby enabled me to realize a longstanding dream of appearing in The *Playboy* Interview. *Playboy* also kindly permitted the reprinting of material that originally appeared inside the magazine. My thanks also to Gil Macias, Theresa Hennessy, and Nora O'Donnell.

I am deeply indebted to Marjory Grant Ross, president and publisher of Regnery Publishing, and to Harry Crocker, vice president and executive editor, for recognizing the potential for *Cheney One on One* as a book project and for steering it to publication at warp speed while maintaining Regnery's high standards. My editor Tom Spence, art director John Caruso, publicity director Patricia Jackson, and assistant managing editor Katharine Spence also brought their expertise to bear and have my deep gratitude. At Javelin, my literary agents Keith Urbahn and Matt Latimer, and their assistant, Vanessa Oblinger, have shown great patience and make even the publishing business fun. My thanks also to those kind souls who provided blurbs. I stand, like all reporters and non-fiction authors, on the shoulders of the many fine journalists, biographers, and historians who preceded me.

Where necessary, I inserted footnotes to supplement the discussion or correct the record in the few instances where the former vice president, or I, erred in our recollections. For the sake of clarity, certain terms with multiple spellings, such as "al Qaeda," have been standardized here. In one case, I have redacted the names of two senior U.S. intelligence officials who briefed me and other reporters on background in December 2007, as background briefings are not attributable by name and the briefers are still alive. Only a few minor words were added to, or changed in, the published transcripts, again to enhance readability.

Despite the kind assistance of all the people thanked here, I alone am responsible for any errors in the text, and my apologies to those I inadvertently omitted from my roll call of gratitude: Elliott Abrams, Neal Adams, Mike Allen, Eduardo Arteagas, Peter Baker, Marty Baron, Brad

Blakeman, Inez and Joao Cabritas, Ron Charles, Bronwyn and David Clark, Debra Lerner Cohen and Ed Cohen, Susan Coll, Mark Cunningham, Denny Drabelle, Yochi Dreazen, Lorraine and Joseph Durkin, Jennifer Barron and Ryan and Quinn Durkin, Erich Eichman, Eric Felten, Ron Fournier, Jack Fowler, Brooke Gard, Nina Barrett and Jeff Garrett, Jerry Garvey, Philip Glass, Susan Glasser, Juleanna Glover, Jonah Goldberg, Garrett Graff, Brad Hamm, Steve Hayes, Jacob Heilbrunn, John Herzberg, Laura Hillenbrand, Connie and Chris Hillman, Mikey Hoare, D.J. Hoek, Rick Hohlt, Elodie and Austin Hunt, Derek Hunter, Michelle and David Joubran, Cheryl Knudson, Tom Korologos, Nicole Lamy, Lars Larson, Kevin B. Leonard, Annette and Ted Lerner, Mike Levine, Steven Levingston, Daniel Lippman, Rich Lowry, Edward B. MacMahon Jr., Maia and Dan Magder, Marlene and Fred Malek, Tom Mallon, Jon Meacham, Dan Miller R.N., John J. Miller, Elliot Mintz, Robert L. Mitchell, Dan Moldea, Jonathan Movroydis, Graham Nash, Luke Nichter, Larry O'Connor, Rob Odle, Paul O'Donnell, Tracy and Todd Pantezzi, Ben Pauker, Kaja Perina, Susan and Michael Pillsbury, John Podhoretz, Ashley Pratte, Sarah M. Pritchard, Michelle Rice, Dr. Shilpa Rose, Dalene Quiachon and Eric, Charles, and Hannah Rosen, Regina and Mike Rosen, David Rothkopf, David and Kristin Roush, Julia Rovinsky, Dr. Saud A. Sadiq, Pete Sams, David Sanger, Cheryl Saremi, Paul Saunders, Cindy and Ryan Schwarz, H. Andrew Schwartz, Nancy Shevell, Dmitri Simes, Heather Smith, Crook Stewart, Scott Stossel, Andrea Mays and James Swanson, Beth and DJ Sworobuk, Evan Thomas, Navin Thukkaram, Kathy Lash and Joe Trippi, Gayle and Joel Trotter, Kim Caviness and Lyn and Bob Vaus, Matt Viser, Michael Von Sas, Ron Walker, Ildi and Mory Watkins, Robert Weide, Sir Peter and Lady Susie Westmacott, George Will, Brian Wilson, Ethan Wise, Sheila and Tom Wolfe, and Zoe.

Finally, no words are adequate to thank my family—my wife, Sara, to whom this book is dedicated, and our sons, Aaron and Gray—not only for how they put up with my misdirection away from their wants and needs during the research, transcription, and editing of this book, but most profoundly for the love and grace they bestow on me unconditionally, in good times and bad. Every day with them is a blessing I strive to be worthy of. I love you.

—James Rosen
Washington, D.C.
July 2015

NOTES

INTRODUCTION

1.   David Makovsky, "The Silent Strike," *New Yorker*, September 17, 2012.

DAY ONE

1.   President Bush's actual remarks at the Yale University commencement on May 21, 2001, were: "Most important, congratulations to the class of 2001. To those of you who received honors, awards, and distinctions, I say, well done. And to the C students I say, you, too, can be President of the United States. A Yale degree is worth a lot, as I often remind Dick Cheney, who studied here but left a little early. So now we know: If you graduate from Yale, you become President; if you drop out, you get to be Vice President." See "Commencement Address at Yale University in New Haven, Connecticut" (May 21, 2001) at http://www.presidency.ucsb.edu/ws/?pid=45895.

2. Dick Cheney with Liz Cheney, *In My Time: A Personal and Political Memoir*, paperback ed. (New York: Threshold Editions, 2012), 30.

3. The Battle of Stones River took place December 31, 1862–January 2, 1863, in middle Tennessee.

4. Legal counsel (2001–2005) and chief of staff (2005–2009) to Vice President Cheney.

5. During a House floor speech on April 15, 1970, when he was minority leader, during the abortive effort to impeach Supreme Court Justice William O. Douglas, Congressman Ford said, "What, then, is an impeachable offense? The only honest answer is that an impeachable offense is whatever a majority of the House of Representatives considers it to be at a given moment in history." See J. Y. Smith and Lou Cannon, "Gerald R. Ford, 93, Dies; Led in Watergate's Wake," *Washington Post*, December 27, 2006.

6. A proposed rule change at the Republican National Convention, which was narrowly defeated, would have required Ford to identify his running mate, as Reagan had already done, before the presidential balloting.

7. Cheney was correct: President Ford defeated Governor Reagan in the New Hampshire, Florida, and Wisconsin primaries, while Reagan bested Ford in North Carolina.

8. A friend of Cheney's from their days at Natrona County High School in Casper, David J. Gribbin III was chief of staff in Cheney's congressional office and later served under him at the Pentagon, as assistant secretary of defense for legislative affairs.

9. Henry S. Rowen served as assistant secretary of defense for international security affairs from 1989 to 1991. An economist almost two decades Cheney's senior, Rowen had previously served in high-level government posts, including the chairmanship of the National Intelligence Council, and the presidency of the RAND Corporation. With Charles Wolf Jr. he coedited a book entitled *The Impoverished Superpower: Perestroika and the Burden of Soviet Military Spending* (San Francisco: Institute for Contemporary Studies, 1990).

10. Cheney actually said "Nixon" here but caught his error in his own review of the transcript.

11. The Goldwater-Nichols Department of Defense Reorganization Act of 1986, signed by President Reagan, streamlined the chain of command of the U.S. military.

12.   Issued in 1985, the Inman report—known formally as the Report of
      the Secretary of State's Advisory Panel on Overseas Security and
      named informally after the panel's chair, Bobby Ray Inman—marked
      a response to the 1983 Marine barracks bombing in Beirut. It urged
      far-ranging reforms to security for U.S. personnel and facilities
      overseas, many adopted by the State Department.

DAY TWO

1.   Richard Norton Smith, *On His Own Terms: A Life of Nelson
      Rockefeller* (New York: Random House, 2014).
2.   U.S. Central Command, one of nine unified commands in the military.
      CENTCOM's area of responsibility covers the Middle East.
3.   A retired Four-Star General, John M. "Jack" Keane had risen to vice
      chief of staff of the U.S. Army and served on the Defense Policy Board
      Advisory Committee. He is generally credited as one of the architects
      of the "surge" of American forces in Iraq in 2007.
4.   Frederick Kagan, a scholar at the American Enterprise Institute and
      a former professor of military history at the U.S. Military Academy,
      was another of the early surge proponents.
5.   A fellow at the Council on Foreign Relations and critic of American
      strategy in the war on terror, Stephen Biddle was another member of
      the Defense Policy Board Advisory Committee.
6.   Eliot Cohen, a longtime professor at the Johns Hopkins University,
      also served on the Defense Policy Board Advisory Committee.
7.   In July 1995, during the Bosnian War, Serbian forces massacred more
      than eight thousand Muslim Bosniaks in the town of Srebrenica.
8.   According to Cheney's memoir, the story in question was David
      Ignatius's *Washington Post* column of May 22, 2007 ("After the Surge:
      The Administration Floats Ideas for a New Approach in Iraq"). In the
      memoir, however, Cheney also notes Sanger's stories, e.g., "White
      House Is Said to Debate '08 Cut in Iraq Combat Forces by 50%" (May
      27) and "In White House, Debate Is Rising on Iraq Pullback" (July
      9); see Dick Cheney and Liz Cheney, *In My Time: A Personal and
      Political Memoir*, paperback ed. (New York: Threshold Editions,
      2012), 456–60.
9.   Lynne Cheney, *James Madison: A Life Reconsidered* (New York:
      Viking, 2014).

10. Alan Keyes succeeded Ryan as the Republican nominee.

11. Cheney accurately cited the findings of this report, which was compiled for the office of the secretary of defense by the International Security and Defense Policy Center of the RAND National Defense Research Institute; see Seth G. Jones, *A Persistent Threat: The Evolution of al Qa'ida and Other Salafi Jihadists* (RAND Corporation, 2014), at http://www.rand.org/content/dam/rand/pubs/research_reports/RR600/RR637/RAND_RR637.pdf.

12. The President's Commission on CIA Activities within the United States, established in 1975 and chaired by Vice President Rockefeller.

13. National Intelligence Council, "National Intelligence Estimate: Iran: Nuclear Intentions and Capabilities," November 2007, unclassified version available at http://www.dni.gov/files/documents/Newsroom/Reports%20and%20Pubs/20071203_release.pdf.

14. Baier's report aired on *Special Report with Brit Hume* on December 3, 2007.

15. By executive order on February 6, 2004, President Bush established the Commission on the Intelligence Capabilities of the United States Regarding Weapons of Mass Destruction to assess "whether the Intelligence Community is sufficiently authorized, organized, equipped, trained, and resourced to identify and warn in a timely manner of, and to support United States Government efforts to respond to, the development and transfer of knowledge, expertise, technologies, materials, and resources associated with the proliferation of Weapons of Mass Destruction, related means of delivery, and other related threats of the 21st Century and their employment by foreign powers (including terrorists, terrorist organizations, and private networks)." The cochairmen of the commission were Charles Robb, a former senator, and Judge Laurence Silberman of the U.S. Court of Appeals for the D.C. Circuit. The commission issued its final report in March 2005.

16. The Immigration Control and Reform Act of 1986, cosponsored by Senator Alan Simpson and Representative Romano Mazzoli.

17. *Immigration and Naturalization Service v. Chadha* (1983).

18. Exit polling in the 2004 presidential election indicated that the Bush-Cheney ticket had captured 44 percent of the Latino vote, but subsequent, and credible, analysis suggested the true figure was closer to 40 percent, still a modern high for Republican tickets. See Roberto

Suro, Richard Fry, and Jeffrey S. Passel, "Hispanics and the 2004 Election: Population, Electorate and Voters," Hispanic Trends, Pew Research Center, June 27, 2005, http://www.pewhispanic. org/2005/06/27/hispanics-and-the-2004-election/.

DAY THREE

1. Richard Clarke was the counterterrorism coordinator for the National Security Council under President Bill Clinton. He continued in the same position for the first year of President George W. Bush's administration and later served as the special advisor to the president on cybersecurity and cyberterrorism. After his departure from the Bush administration, in 2003, Clarke was harshly critical of its handling of the threat from al Qaeda before the 9/11 attacks and of the invasion of Iraq.
2. The article Cheney was referring to—"The Quiet Man," excerpted on pp. 318–19 of *In My Time* (paperback ed.)—was originally published by Nicholas Lemann in the May 7, 2001, edition of the *New Yorker*.
3. During the George H. W. Bush administration, Clarke served as assistant secretary of state for political-military affairs.
4. The interview in question aired on *Fox News Sunday* on September 24, 2006. Noting Clinton's withdrawal of U.S. troops from Somalia after the "Blackhawk Down" incident in 1993, the bombing of U.S. embassies in Kenya and Tanzania in 1998, and the attack on the USS *Cole* in 2000, Wallace asked: "Why didn't you do more to put bin Laden and al Qaeda out of business when you were president?" Clinton responded angrily and at length, at one point telling Wallace: "All of President Bush's neo-cons thought I was too obsessed with bin Laden. They had no meetings on bin Laden for nine months after I left office.... You did Fox's bidding on this show. You did your nice little conservative hit job on me." Moments later, the former president challenged Wallace: "I want to know how many people in the Bush administration you asked, 'Why didn't you do anything about the *Cole*?' I want to know how many you asked, 'Why did you fire Dick Clarke?'" See the transcript online at "Transcript: William Jefferson Clinton on 'Fox News Sunday,'" FoxNews.com, http://www.foxnews. com/story/2006/09/26/transcript-william-jefferson-clinton-on-fox-news-sunday.html.

5.   The FBI agent in Minneapolis was Coleen Rowley; the FBI agent in Phoenix was Kenneth Williams.

6.   Created by the Congress and President Bush in November 2002, the National Commission on Terrorist Attacks Upon the United States, known informally as the 9/11 Commission, was chaired by former New Jersey Governor Thomas H. Kean and former Indiana Congressman Lee H. Hamilton and issued its final report in July 2004.

7.   This was a reference to Secretary of State Alexander Haig's memorable and ill-conceived statement to reporters shortly after the attempted assassination of President Reagan on March 30, 1981: "I am in control, here in the White House, pending return of the vice president...." See Tim Weiner, "Alexander M. Haig Jr. Dies at 85; Was Forceful Aide to 2 Presidents," *New York Times*, February 20, 2010.

8.   Hughes's briefing was actually held at FBI headquarters. See "September 11, 2001: Attack on America; Press Briefing by Karen Hughes, Counselor to the President," http://avalon.law.yale.edu/sept11/press_briefing02.asp.

9.   On September 10–11, 2001, Powell was attending the Organization of American States' General Assembly in Lima, Peru.

10. Neither I nor a team of researchers could find any record of a published statement by Powell to this effect. Nor could his biographer, Karen DeYoung of the *Washington Post*, recall such a statement when asked about it, over breakfast in Vienna, in July 2015.

11. During a news conference with Sweden's foreign minister in Washington on March 6, 2001, Powell told reporters, "We do plan to engage with North Korea to pick up where President Clinton and his administration left off. Some promising elements were left on the table, and we will be examining those elements." Senior administration officials disavowed Powell's comments in background briefings that same week.

12. General Schwarzkopf died in December 2012. The memorial service Cheney recalled having attended, at the Cadet Chapel at the United States Military Academy at West Point, was held in February 2013.

13. For the sake of brevity, my recitation of this passage from Risen's book condensed the actual text, which reads: "Cheney made certain to protect the president from personal involvement in the internal debates on the handling of prisoners.... It is not clear whether Tenet was told by Cheney or other White House officials not to brief Bush or whether

he made that decision on his own.... Certainly, Cheney and senior White House officials knew that Bush was purposely not being briefed.... It appears that there was a secret agreement among very senior administration officials to insulate Bush and to give him deniability." James Risen, *State of War: The Secret History of the CIA and the Bush Administration* (New York: Free Press, 2006), 14–15. The thrust of the passage, however, was effectively conveyed in my question.

14. In May 2013, the *Washington Post* disclosed that as part of a national security–leak investigation into my exclusive reporting for Fox News on North Korea's nuclear weapons program, the FBI—under the direction of Attorney General Holder—had secretly designated me a "co-conspirator" in an alleged violation of the Espionage Act with the State Department analyst whom authorities had concluded to be my source. Subsequent reporting determined that in addition to tracking my physical movements at the State Department, the FBI had seized my personal e-mails and phone records, additional phone records belonging to Fox News, and even the phone records of my parents on Staten Island. It marked the first time in modern U.S. history that the federal government had branded a reporter a criminal for doing his job, and the revelations sparked widespread condemnation over what was seen, almost universally, as a concerted assault on press freedoms in the Obama era. During an address on counterterrorism policy at National Defense University, the president pronounced himself "troubled" by the case and directed the attorney general to revise the Justice Department's guidelines for the treatment of reporters in such investigations. The majority staff of the House Judiciary Committee issued a report concluding that Holder had deliberately misled lawmakers on the subject, in congressional testimony delivered shortly before the *Post*'s initial report; and Holder later identified the case as the biggest regret of his tenure as America's top law enforcement official. Wishing to avoid a costly and debilitating trial, the analyst ultimately pleaded guilty to reduced charges. See Ann E. Marimow, "A Rare Peek into a Justice Department Leak Probe," *Washington Post*, May 19, 2013; Brian Stelter and Michael D. Shear, "Justice Dept. Investigated Fox Reporter over Leak," *New York Times*, May 20, 2013; Ryan Lizza, "The Justice Department and Fox News's Phone Records," *New Yorker*, May 21, 2013; "Remarks by the President at

the National Defense University," transcript of May 23, 2013, speech, available online at https://www.whitehouse.gov/the-press-office/2013/05/23/remarks-president-national-defense-university; Daniel Klaidman, "Holder's Regrets and Repairs," *Daily Beast*, May 28, 2013; Charlie Savage, "Holder Tightens Rules on Getting Reporters' Data," *New York Times*, July 12, 2013; Daniel Strauss, "House Judiciary Chairman Calls Holder's Testimony 'Deceptive and Misleading,'" *Hill*, August 1, 2013; Ann E. Marimow, "Ex-State Dept. Adviser Pleads Guilty in Leak to Fox News," *Washington Post*, February 7, 2014; Jonathan Capehart, "Regrets, Eric Holder Has a Few," *Washington Post*, October 31, 2014; and David McCabe, "Fox Reporter Dismisses Holder's Regrets," *Hill*, October 29, 2014.

15. While President Bush did address the Naval War College in June 2007, the speech Cheney was recalling—in which the president disclosed that the United States and its allies had disrupted "at least ten serious al Qaeda terrorist plots" since 9/11, three of them targeting U.S. sites—was delivered at the National Endowment for Democracy in October 2005. See "President Discusses War on Terror at National Endowment for Democracy," available at http://georgewbush-whitehouse.archives.gov/news/releases/2005/10/20051006-3.html. For details on the disrupted attacks, including one targeting the Library Tower in Los Angeles, see Peter Baker and Susan B. Glasser, "Bush Says 10 Plots by al-Qaeda Were Foiled," *Washington Post*, October 7, 2005.

16. Operation Desert Fox, conducted by U.S. and UK forces in December 1998, encompassed four days of air strikes against Iraqi targets.

17. National Intelligence Council, *Worldwide Biological Warfare Programs: Trends and Prospects, Update* (NIE 2000-12HCX, December 2000), 22.

18. See James Dao and Steven Lee Myers, "U.S. and British Jets Strike Air-Defense Centers in Iraq," *New York Times*, February 17, 2001.

19. The interview in question aired on September 14, 2001. It contained Cheney's memorable statement: "We also have to work, though, sort of the dark side, if you will. We've got to spend time in the shadows in the intelligence world.... That's the world these folks operate in, and so it's going to be vital for us to use any means at our disposal, basically, to achieve our objective."

20. This was the actual term the former vice president used, and is transcribed here accurately.

21. See, for example, Walter Pincus and Dana Priest, "Some Iraq Analysts Felt Pressure from Cheney Visits," *Washington Post*, June 5, 2003.

22. Cheney was correct. In its final report, the Silberman-Robb Commission cited testimony by a former head of the State Department's Bureau of Intelligence and Research who said "policymakers never once applied any pressure on coming up with the 'right' answer on Iraq." The panel concluded that "senior decisionmakers continually probed to assess the strength of the Intelligence Community's analysis, but did not press for changes in the Intelligence Community's analytical judgments" and had acted in "good faith." See the Commission on the Intelligence Capabilities of the United States regarding Weapons of Mass Destruction, *Report to the President of the United States* (March 31, 2005), 188–189.

23. See Glenn Kessler, "New Data Found on North Korea's Nuclear Capacity," *Washington Post*, June 21, 2008. Aluminum tubes that the North Koreans turned over as part of the declaration process were also found to contain traces of HEU, all at a time when Pyongyang was actively denying having an HEU program. On the tubes, and the North Koreans' initial admission of having an HEU program, and rescission of it a few days later, see James Rosen, "North Korean Tubes Found to Be Contaminated with Uranium Traces," FoxNews.com, December 22, 2007, http://www.foxnews.com/story/2007/12/22/north-korean-tubes-found-to-be-contaminated-with-uranium-traces.html.

24. James Rosen, "The Madness of Chris Hill," *National Review*, July 3, 2008, http://www.nationalreview.com/article/224925/madness-chris-hill-james-rosen.

25. Cheney made good on this promise, leading me to his dining room for a brief and hushed conversation shortly after the final interview session had concluded.

26. See Bob Woodward, *Plan of Attack*, paperback ed. (New York: Simon & Schuster, 2004), which placed the "slam dunk" meeting on December 21, 2002—a Saturday, as Cheney recalled—and also reported Andy Card in attendance; Scott Shane and Mark Mazzetti, "Ex-C.I.A. Chief, in Book, Assails Cheney on Iraq," *New York Times*,

April 27, 2007; and George Tenet, *At the Center of the Storm: My Years at the CIA* (New York: Harper, 2007).

27. Cheney's recollection here of the exact wording of the Bush-Tenet exchange differs slightly from the account presented in Cheney's memoir. See Dick Cheney with Liz Cheney, *In My Time: A Personal and Political Memoir*, paperback ed. (New York: Threshold Editions, 2012), 395.

28. See C.J. Chivers, "The Secret Casualties of Iraq's Abandoned Chemical Weapons," *New York Times*, October 14, 2014.

29. Cheney is correct on both counts. The Iraq Survey Group's final report, which documented the failure to find WMD stockpiles in Iraq, nonetheless concluded, "From 1999 until he was deposed in April 2003, Saddam's conventional weapons and WMD-related procurement programs steadily grew in scale, variety, and efficiency." See "Comprehensive Report of the Special Advisor to the DCI on Iraq's WMD," September 30, 2004, accessible at http://www.globalsecurity. org/wmd/library/report/2004/isg-final-report/. And in January 2004, Kay testified before the Senate Armed Services Committee: "I actually think this may be one of those cases where it was even more dangerous than we thought." Two days later, Kay said that "it was reasonable to conclude that Iraq posed an imminent threat." See the transcript "Dr. David Kay's Testimony to the Senate Armed Services Committee" (January 28, 2004) at http://www.globalresearch.ca/articles/ KAY401A.html; and Christopher Marquis, "Ex-arms Inspector Finds Himself in a New Place: The Center of a Political Maelstrom," *New York Times*, February 2, 2004.

30. One of Cheney's most memorable speeches, his address to the 103rd National Convention of the Veterans of Foreign Wars on August 26, 2002, forcefully made the case for military action against Iraq. Cheney asserted, "Simply stated, there is no doubt that Saddam Hussein now has weapons of mass destruction. There is no doubt he is amassing them to use against our friends, against our allies, and against us."

31. In fact, Rumsfeld's classified memorandum to the file, dated October 15, 2002, listed twenty-nine "problems that could result from a conflict with Iraq" and included such prescient predictions as "U.S. could fail to find WMD on the ground in Iraq and be unpersuasive to the world.... U.S. could fail to manage post-Saddam Hussein Iraq

successfully...[and] Iraq could experience ethnic strife among Sunni, Shia and Kurds." A PDF image of the memo is accessible at http://nsarchive.gwu.edu/NSAEBB/NSAEBB418/docs/7%20-%20Iraq%20 -%20An%20illustrative%20list%20of%20potential%20 problems%20-%2010-15-2002.pdf.

32. Stuart W. Bowen, *Learning from Iraq: Final Report from Special Inspector General for Iraq Reconstruction* (March 2013), accessible at http://www.cfr.org/iraq/learning-iraq-final-report-special-inspector-general-iraq-reconstruction-march-2013/p30167.

33. The February 22, 2006, bombing of the golden-domed al-Askari Mosque in Samarra, one of the holiest sites to Shiite Muslims, is widely credited with having inflamed existing sectarian tensions in Iraq following the U.S.-led invasion and with having contributed materially to the worsening of security conditions there.

34. In April 1992, a Jordanian military tribunal convicted Chalabi of thirty-one counts of embezzlement, theft, forgery, currency speculation, making false statements, and other charges, stemming from Chalabi's role in the founding of Petra Bank. While Chalabi has always denied the charges, he was sentenced, in absentia, to serve twenty-two years at hard labor. See Jane Mayer, "The Manipulator," *New Yorker*, June 7, 2004. Cheney, in his remarks here on Chalabi—"I met him once or twice"—appears to dispute Mayer's assertion that Chalabi "forged a close bond with" the vice president in the prewar period.

35. A 1949 study by the U.S. Marine Corps estimated that the six-month campaign for Guadalcanal in World War II incurred some 1,200 American casualties. (Later studies, such as Bryan Perrett's *The Battle Book: Crucial Conflicts in History from 1469 BC to the Present* [1992], place the figure as high as 1,600.) In the thirty-five-day battle of Iwo Jima, most accounts estimate, U.S forces sustained over 7,700 casualties. For further comparative purposes, restricting ourselves to the modern era—thus excluding the carnage of the Civil War—we may consider the Battle of Okinawa, in which the estimated U.S. death toll was roughly 12,500. According to the website icasualties.org, in Operation Iraqi Freedom—a campaign that spanned more than a decade, from 2003 to 2011—the United States sustained 4,485 casualties.

36.   See the transcript "Press Briefing by Ari Fleischer" (October 1, 2002) at http://georgewbush-whitehouse.archives.gov/news/releases/2002/10/20021001-4.html. For Fleischer's explanation, in an interview with CNN, that he was making a "rhetorical point" and not "a statement of policy," see Kelly Wallace, "Fleischer Clarifies 'One Bullet' Line," CNN.com, October 2, 2002, http://edition.cnn.com/2002/ALLPOLITICS/10/01/wh.saddam/.

37.   Amid ongoing revelations about Watergate, Vietnam, and the Kennedy administration's efforts to assassinate Fidel Castro, President Ford on February 18, 1976, signed Executive Order 11905, which implemented various reforms of the intelligence community and explicitly banned the U.S. government from engaging in, or conspiring to engage in, "political assassination."

38.   See the transcript of my interview with Gates (September 2, 2010) at http://www.foxnews.com/politics/2010/09/02/transcript-fox-news-interview-defense-secretary-robert-gates-james-rosen/.

BIBLIOGRAPHY

Abrams, Elliott. *Tested by Zion: The Bush Administration and the Israeli-Palestinian Conflict*. New York: Cambridge University Press, 2012.

Allen, Michael. *Blinking Red: Crisis and Compromise in American Intelligence after 9/11*. Dulles, VA: Potomac, 2013.

Ashcroft, John. *Never Again: Securing America and Restoring Justice*, paperback ed. New York: Center Street: 2007.

Baker, Peter. *Days of Fire: Bush and Cheney in the White House*, paperback ed. New York: Anchor, 2014.

Bamford, James. *A Pretext for War: 9/11, Iraq, and the Abuse of America's Intelligence Agencies*, paperback ed. New York: Anchor, 2005.

Benjamin, Daniel, and Steven Simon. *The Age of Sacred Terror: Radical Islam's War against America*, paperback ed. New York: Random House, 2003.

Bowen, Stuart W. *Hard Lessons: The Iraq Reconstruction Experience*, paperback ed. Washington, DC: U.S. Government Printing Office, 2009.

Bremer, L. Paul, III, and Malcolm McConnell. *My Year in Iraq: The Struggle to Build a Future of Hope*, paperback ed. New York: Threshold, 2006.

Brynjolfsson, Erik, and Andrew McAfee. *The Second Machine Age: Work, Progress, and Prosperity in a Time of Brilliant Technologies.* New York: W. W. Norton, 2014.

Bush, George W. *Decision Points.* New York: Crown, 2010.

Cheney, Dick. "Congressional Overreaching in Foreign Policy." In *Foreign Policy and the Constitution*, edited by Robert A. Golwin and Robert A. Licht. Washington, DC: AEI Press, 1990.

———. *Heart: An American Medical Odyssey.* New York: Scribner, 2013.

Cheney, Dick, and Liz Cheney. *In My Time: A Personal and Political Memoir.* New York: Threshold Editions, 2011.

Christie, Ron. *Black in the White House: Life inside George W. Bush's West Wing*, paperback ed. New York: Thomas Nelson, 2009.

Clarke, Richard A. *Against All Enemies: Inside America's War on Terror*, paperback ed. New York: Free Press, 2004.

Clinton, Bill. *My Life.* New York: Knopf, 2004.

Coll, Steve. *Ghost Wars: The Secret History of the CIA, Afghanistan, and Bin Laden, from the Soviet Invasion to September 10, 2001*, paperback ed. New York: Penguin, 2004.

Cott, Jonathan. *Susan Sontag: The Complete "Rolling Stone" Interview.* New Haven: Yale University Press, 2013.

DeFrank, Thomas M. *Write It When I'm Gone: Remarkable Off-the-Record Conversations with Gerald R. Ford*, paperback ed. New York: Berkley, 2008.

DeYoung, Karen. *Soldier: The Life of Colin Powell*, paperback ed. New York: Vintage, 2007.

Franks, Tommy. *American Soldier*, paperback ed. New York: Regan-Books, 2004.

Gates, Robert M. *Duty: Memoirs of a Secretary at War*. New York: Knopf, 2014.

Gellman, Barton. *Angler: The Cheney Vice Presidency*, paperback ed. New York: Penguin, 2009.

Goldsmith, Jack. *The Terror Presidency: Law and Judgment inside the Bush Administration*, paperback ed. New York: W. W. Norton, 2009.

Goldstein, Gordon M. *Lessons in Disaster: McGeorge Bundy and the Path to War in Vietnam*, paperback ed. New York: Holt, 2009.

Gordon, Michael R., and Bernard E. Trainor. *Cobra II: The Inside Story of the Invasion and Occupation of Iraq*, paperback ed. New York: Vintage, 2007.

———. *The Endgame: The Inside Story of the Struggle for Iraq, from George W. Bush to Barack Obama*, paperback ed. New York: Vintage, 2013.

Hartmann, Robert T. *Palace Politics: An Inside Account of the Ford Years*. New York: McGraw-Hill, 1980.

Hayes, Stephen F. *Cheney: The Untold Story of America's Most Powerful and Controversial Vice President*. New York: HarperCollins, 2007.

Heilbrunn, Jacob. *They Knew They Were Right: The Rise of the Neocons*, paperback ed. New York: Anchor, 2009.

Hersh, Seymour M. *Chain of Command: The Road from 9/11 to Abu Ghraib*, paperback ed. New York: Harper Perennial, 2005.

Hill, Christopher R. *Outpost: Life on the Frontlines of American Diplomacy*. New York: Simon & Schuster, 2014.

Isikoff, Michael, and David Corn. *Hubris: The Inside Story of Spin, Scandal, and the Selling of the Iraq War*, paperback ed. New York: Three Rivers Press, 2007.

Kean, Thomas H., and Lee H. Hamilton. *The 9/11 Commission Report: Final Report of the National Commission on Terrorist Attacks upon the United States*, paperback ed. New York: W. W. Norton, 2004.

Kessler, Glenn. *The Confidante: Condoleezza Rice and the Creation of the Bush Legacy*. New York: St. Martin's Press, 2007.

Makovsky, David. "The Silent Strike." *New Yorker*, September 17, 2012.

Mann, James. *Rise of the Vulcans: The History of Bush's War Cabinet*, paperback ed. New York: Penguin, 2004.

Mayer, Jane. *The Dark Side: The Inside Story of How the War on Terror Turned into a War on American Ideals*, paperback ed. New York: Anchor, 2009.

Packer, George. *The Assassins' Gate: America in Iraq*, paperback ed. New York: Farrar, Straus and Giroux, 2006.

Panetta, Leon, and Jim Newton. *Worthy Fights: A Memoir of Leadership in War and Peace*. New York: Penguin, 2014.

Rice, Condoleezza. *No Higher Honor: A Memoir of My Years in Washington*, paperback ed. New York: Broadway, 2011.

Ricks, Thomas E. *Fiasco: The American Military Adventure in Iraq*, paperback ed. New York: Penguin, 2007.

Ridge, Tom, and Larry Bloom. *The Test of Our Times: America under Siege…and How We Can Be Safe Again*, paperback ed. New York: St. Martin's Griffin, 2010.

Risen, James. *State of War: The Secret History of the CIA in the Bush Administration*, paperback ed. New York: Free Press, 2007.

Rizzo, John. *Company Man: Thirty Years of Controversy and Crisis in the CIA*, paperback ed. New York: Scribner, 2014.

Robb, Charles S., and Laurence H. Silberman. *The Commission on the Intelligence Capabilities of the United States regarding Weapons of Mass Destruction: Report to the President of the United States*, PDF ed. 2005.

Robinson, Linda. *Tell Me How This Ends: General David Petraeus and the Search for a Way out of Iraq*. New York: PublicAffairs, 2008.

Rodriguez, Jose A., and Bill Harlow. *Hard Measures: How Aggressive CIA Actions after 9/11 Saved American Lives*, paperback ed. New York: Threshold, 2013.

Rose, Gideon, and James F. Hoge, eds. *How Did This Happen? Terrorism and the New War*, paperback ed. New York: PublicAffairs, 2001.

Rosen, James. "Cheney's Rise: The Most Powerful Vice President Ever," *TALK*, May 2001.

———. "The *Playboy* Interview with Dick Cheney," *Playboy*, April 2015.

———. *The Strong Man: John Mitchell and the Secrets of Watergate.* New York: Doubleday, 2008.

———. "To Baghdad and Back with Dick Cheney," *Playboy*, May 2006.

Rothkopf, David. *National Insecurity: American Leadership in an Age of Fear.* New York: PublicAffairs, 2014.

———. *Running the World: The Inside Story of the National Security Council and the Architects of American Power*, paperback ed. New York: PublicAffairs, 2006.

Rumsfeld, Donald. *Known and Unknown: A Memoir.* New York: Sentinel, 2011.

Sanger, David. *The Inheritance: The World Obama Confronts and the Challenges to American Power*, paperback ed. New York: Three Rivers Press, 2009.

Sheff, David, and G. Barry Golson, editor. *The "Playboy" Interviews with John Lennon and Yoko Ono.* New York: Putnam, 1981.

Suskind, Ron. *The One Percent Doctrine: Deep Inside America's Pursuit of Its Enemies Since 9/11*, paperback ed. New York: Simon & Schuster, 2007.

Tenet, George. *At the Center of the Storm: My Years at the CIA.* New York: Harper, 2007.

Waltz, Michael G. *Warrior Diplomat: A Green Beret's Battles from Washington to Afghanistan.* Washington, DC: Potomac, 2014.

Wenner, Jann. *Lennon Remembers: The "Rolling Stone" Interviews.* San Francisco: Straight Arrow Books, 1971.

West, Bing. *The Strongest Tribe: War, Politics, and the Endgame in Iraq.* New York: Random House, 2008.

Woodward, Bob. *Bush at War,* paperback ed. New York: Simon & Schuster, 2003.

———. *Plan of Attack,* paperback ed. New York: Simon & Schuster, 2004.

———. *State of Denial: Bush at War, Part III,* paperback ed. New York: Simon & Schuster, 2007.

———. *The War Within: A Secret White House History, 2006–2008,* paperback ed. New York: Simon & Schuster, 2009.

Wright, Lawrence. *The Looming Tower: Al-Qaeda and the Road to 9/11,* paperback ed. New York: Vintage, 2007.

Yoo, John. *War by Other Means: An Insider's Account of the War on Terror.* New York: Atlantic Monthly Press, 2006.

INDEX OF MAJOR
PEOPLE AND TOPICS

A

Abbot, Steve, 200
Abizaid, John P., 133
Addington, David, 80, 106, 118, 120, 132, 163, 233–34
Afghanistan, Afghans, 13, 148–49, 280
  al Qaeda in, 147, 250, 256
  relationship with Pakistan, 150–51
  Taliban in, 148
  war in, 5, 23, 148, 231, 250, 256, 281
Against All Enemies (Clarke), 199
Air Force One, 13
Al Kibar, 2, 4–8, 21, 125, 178
al Qaeda, 83, 199
  and Iraq, 133, 136, 253–57, 274, 278–79, 285
  9/11 and, 11, 100, 161–62, 203, 211–12, 250
  possible cooperation with Saddam Hussein, 172, 255–56

  pre-9/11 intelligence 199–203
  spread of similar organizations, 147
American Enterprise Institute, 134
American Political Science Association, 73
American Political Science Review, 50, 52, 73
Andrews Air Force Base, 212
Angler (Gellman), 233
Angleton, James Jesus, 89, 162–63
Annapolis, MD, 6–7, 127
Ann Arbor, MI, 110–11
Arab Spring, 176, 190
Arafat, Yasser, 231
Arens, Moshe, 165
Ashcroft, John, 131–32, 233–34, 241, 244
Asia, 204, 259
Assad, Bashar al-, 4, 6
Atta, Mohamed, 250, 254–55

authorization for the use of military
    force (AUMF), 83, 198

B

Baghdad, 8, 152–53, 249, 256–57, 267,
    270, 272
Baier, Bret, 168
Baker, James "Jim," 97, 102–3, 134,
    155, 221, 225, 230
Baker, Peter, 8, 130, 139, 216, 293
Baltics, the, 92, 145, 158–59
Barak, Ehud, 165
Barksdale Air Force Base, 213
Bash, Dana, 13–15
Beirut, 100, 253
Benghazi, Libya, 167
Berlin Wall, 164
Biddle, Stephen, 134
Biden, Joseph, 143, 167
bin Laden, Osama, 11, 202–4, 274
Bolton, John, 168
Bowen, Stuart, 271–72
Bremer, Paul, 136
Brown, Tina, 14
Buckley, William F., Jr., 38, 54, 63–64,
    92–93
Bush, George H. W., 102–3, 157, 182.
    See also Bush 41
    administration of, 218, 223, 230
    Cheney's role in administration, 2, 10,
        32
    as CIA director, 160
    Desert Storm and, 83–85, 103, 153, 226
    presidential library of, 111
Bush, George W., 26, 102–3, 157, 170,
    181, 229. See also Bush 43
    administration of, 2, 12, 19, 161, 199,
        202, 221, 228
    Cheney's role in administration, 2–3, 6,
        8–11, 89, 104–5, 112–32, 216
    immediate response to 9/11, 213–15
    Iraq War and, 74, 85, 132–42, 169, 247–
        48, 267–68, 277–78, 281
    John Kerry and, 60
    North Korea and, 4, 7–8, 123–28, 261
    personal relationship with Cheney, 8,
        131–32, 142
    post-presidency of, 19–20
    presidential library of, 112, 143–44
    same-sex marriage and, 61
    surveillance programs and, 13, 234–36,
        240
    Tea Party and, 20
    Vladimir Putin and, 154
Bush-Cheney era, 8, 12, 19, 109, 238,
    292
Bush Doctrine, 110
Bush 41, 83, 111, 223. See also Bush,
    George H. W.
Bush 43, 109, 112, 221, 228. See also
    Bush, George W.

C

Cahill, Mary Beth, 60
Cairo, 144, 238
Camp David, 95, 110, 207, 215, 252,
    254
Canada, Canadians, 184
Cannon, Lou, 193
Card, Andrew "Andy," 118–19, 132
Carlucci, Frank, 220
Carter, James "Jimmy," 118, 147, 156
Casper, WY, 26, 34, 42–44
Central Intelligence Agency (CIA), 3,
    71, 89, 103, 105, 112–14, 120, 160,
    163–64, 167, 172, 200, 204, 242,
    250, 254–55, 263–64, 266
    enhanced interrogation and, 20, 235
Chalabi, Ahmed, 276–77
Cheney, Lynne, 14, 17, 26–29, 33,
    42–44, 49, 60, 68–69, 73, 142, 150
Cheney, Mary, 58–62

Cheney, Samuel Fletcher, 18, 62
China, Chinese, 172–74, 184
    economy of, 172, 190
    Nixon and, 76, 288
    North Korea and, 123, 231
    Pakistan and, 151
    South China Sea and, 156
    U.S. debt and, 175
Church, Frank, 160
Church Committee, 160–61
Clarke, Richard "Dick," 199–204, 239
Clausen, Aage, 50
Cleveland Clinic, 36
Clinton, Hillary, 237
Clinton, William "Bill," 13, 116, 202,
    231, 248
CNN, 13, 194, 206
Cohen, Eliot, 134
Cold War, the, 49, 92, 99, 158, 161,
    164, 171, 178, 217
Comey, James, 131–32, 243–44
conservatives, conservatism, 19–20,
    90–92, 100, 161, 183, 259
continuity-of-government program,
    69–70, 211
Council of Colonels, the, 134–35, 275
Cray, Ed, 21, 280
Crimea, 155
Crocker, Ryan, 14–15, 149, 151, 153
Crouch, J. D., 273–75
Crowe, William J. "Bill," 224

D

Dagan, Meir, 1, 4, 125
Dallas, TX, 67–68, 112, 142
Damascus, Syria, 3–4, 124–25
Daschle, Tom, 248
Days of Fire (Baker), 8, 130, 216
Decision Points (Bush), 132, 235, 268
Defense Intelligence Agency (DIA), 105,
    164

DeFrank, Tom, 89
Democratic Party, Democrats, 20, 73,
    97, 143, 156–57, 161–62, 181–83,
    242, 248, 250, 279, 282
Desert Storm, 30–31, 82–83, 102–3,
    164, 226, 266. See also Gulf War
DeYoung, Karen, 232
Duelfer, Charles, 170

E

Economist, the, 188
Egypt, Egyptians, 110, 146–47, 256
Eisenhower, Dwight D., 18, 157
enhanced interrogation techniques
    (EITs), 20, 235–36, 242
Environmental Protection Agency
    (EPA), 121, 145, 187
Episcopal Church, 33
Europe, Europeans, 14, 145–46, 155–
    56, 158–60, 239, 284, 287
Evans, Rowland, 155
Executive Order 11905, 285

F

Faga, Marty, 163
Falkland Islands, Falklands, 153–54
Federal Bureau of Investigation (FBI),
    16, 32, 71, 131, 198, 204–5, 243–44
Ferguson, MO, 179–80
Fleischer, Ari, 285
Florida, 92, 209, 213
Ford, Gerald "Jerry," 14, 16, 48, 57, 82,
    91–93, 96, 106, 118, 120, 197, 285
    caricatures of, 85–87, 95
    Cheney as chief of staff under, 4, 70, 85,
        117, 160, 172, 193
    comments on Cheney's vice presidency,
        88–89
    Nixon pardon and, 87–88

presidential library, 110–11
Fox News, 12–13, 15–16, 182, 292
fracking, 185
Franks, Tommy, 278
Frist, Bill, 137

G

Gates, Robert, 21, 128, 134–35, 139,
   156, 287
Gellman, Barton, 233
General of the Army (Cray), 21, 280
Gerald R. Ford nuclear submarines, 16,
   48–49
Goldwater-Nichols Act, 101, 136
Gonzales, Alberto, 118, 132
Gorbachev, Mikhail, 92, 100, 155
Guantanamo, 12, 23, 239–40
Gulf War, 103, 129, 153, 164–65, 201,
   223, 228, 247–48. *See also* Desert
   Storm

H

Hadley, Stephen "Steve," 1, 3, 5, 109,
   114, 124–26, 134, 139, 148, 221,
   237, 259, 263, 275
Halliburton, 185, 248
Hamas, 253
Hamilton, Lee, 162
Hastert, Dennis "Denny," 212
Hayden, Michael "Mike," 119–20, 236,
   242
Hayes, Stephen "Steve," 13
Heart (Cheney), 15, 59
Hecker, Siegfried, 179
Helms, Jesse, 90, 92
Helms, Richard, 167
Hezbollah, 100, 253
highly enriched uranium (HEU), 7,
   258–59

Hill, Chris, 259–60
Holder, Eric, 10, 16, 147
Hughes, Karen, 214
Hurricane Katrina, 116, 141
Hussein, Saddam, 152, 247, 267, 270,
   277
   invasion of Kuwait, 164–65, 225, 251
   papers and tapes belonging to, 267
   possible cooperation with al Qaeda,
      172, 254–56
   U.S. takedown of, 129–30, 247, 250, 269,
      273–75, 278, 285
   weapons of, 153, 164, 166–70, 248–49,
      261–67, 270–71, 286
Hyde, Henry, 98, 163

I

*Immigration and Naturalization Ser-
   vice v. Chadha*, 180
In My Time (Cheney), 15, 58, 154, 164,
   205, 245, 247, 249, 261, 269
intelligence, 120, 261
   Bush 43's interest in, 114–16
   Cheney's experience with, 3–4, 17, 21,
      79, 99, 105–6, 113–14, 160, 160–67,
      254
   Iraq and, 8, 12, 21, 85, 128–29, 167, 248–
      50, 253–54, 264–67, 286–87
   9/11 and, 202–5
   politicization of, 167–71, 255–57
International Atomic Energy Agency,
   165
Iran, Iranians, 4, 15, 152, 176, 253–54,
   270
   nuclear program, 130, 167–69, 175–79,
      286–87
Iran-Contra, 80, 95, 101–2, 221, 243
Iranian Revolutionary Guard Corps
   (IRGC), 176

Iraq. *See also* Desert Storm; Gulf War;
    Iraq War; Kuwait
  ISIS and, 147
  ~~Osirak air strikes, 129~~
  rebuilding of, 132–33, 151–53, 271–73
  weapons of. *See under* Hussein, Sad-
    dam
Iraq Liberation Act, 247
Iraq Study Group, 134
Iraq Survey Group, 265
Iraq War, 5–6, 8, 11–12, 14, 17, 19,
    22–23, 128, 273–78, 286–88
  casualties, 283–85
  discussion about strategy change in,
    130–40
  emotional toll of, 74–75, 280–82
  9/11 and the lead-up to, 247–57, 261
  surge and, 8, 12, 128, 130, 132, 134–40,
    151–52, 273, 278–79
Iron Curtain, 92
ISI, 149–50
Islamic Jihad, 256
Islamic State of Iraq and Syria (ISIS), 8,
    127, 147, 152, 159, 178–79, 283
isolationists, isolationism, 197
Israel, Israelis, 129, 157, 164–66, 175,
    266
  Al Kibar and, 1–5, 21, 125–27, 130, 178
  conflict with Palestine, 6–7, 14, 222, 231

J

Japan, Japanese, 21, 55, 129, 174, 197,
    233, 276, 281
Jerusalem, 4
Johnson, Lyndon B., 71–72, 86, 104,
    140–41, 157, 205–6
Joint Chiefs of Staff, 12, 89, 103, 133–
    34, 223–27, 230
Joint Special Operations, 134
Jordan, Jordanians, 256, 276–77

K

Kagan, Fred, 134, 275
Karzai, Hamid, 148–49, 151
Kay, David, 265, 267
Keane, Jack, 134, 137–38, 275
Kelly, Jim, 258
Kennedy, John F. "Jack," 18, 56, 67–70,
    72, 157, 286
Kerry, John, 60, 214, 248
Keystone Pipeline, 145, 183
KGB, 154–55
Khalilzad, Zalmay "Zal," 149
Khan, A. Q., 129, 178, 286
Kim Jong Il, 7
King, Tom, 153
Kings of the Hill (Cheney and Cheney),
    51
Kissinger, Henry, 76, 89–92, 120, 139,
    230
Knowles, Warren P., 51–52
Kuwait, 83, 102, 153, 164–65, 223,
    225–27, 251, 271
Kyoto Protocol, 121

L

labor participation rate, 189
Left, the, 19
Levin, Carl, 248
Libby, Scooter, 8, 14, 106, 115, 130–31,
    257
Libya, Libyans, 101, 129, 178
Lott, Trent, 97, 140

M

Makiya, Kanan, 277
Makovsky, David, 6
Maliki, Nouri al-, 151–53
Marsh, Jack, 160–61
Matalin, Mary, 106, 214

Mayaguez, 88

Mazzetti, Mark, 168

McCain, John, 229

McConnell, John, 19, 39, 43, 55, 106, 118, 268

McConnell, Mitch, 139–40

McLaughlin, John E., 263

McLean, VA, 17, 25, 149

McMaster, H. R., 135

media, the, 191–92

Meet the Press, 254–55

Methodist Church, 33–34

Michel, Bob, 162

Middle East, 6–7, 14, 127, 146–47, 156–57, 176, 190, 197, 288

Mineta, Norman, 209

Mohammed, Khalid Sheikh, 240

Moscow, Russia, 76, 146, 153

Mossad, 1, 125

Mubarak, Hosni, 110

Mueller, Robert, 131, 243–44

Mullen, Michael "Mike," 138

Musharraf, Pervez, 148–51

Muslim Brotherhood, 177

mutually assured destruction (MAD), 178–79

N

National Intelligence Estimate (NIE), 167, 249, 262

National Security Agency (NSA), 13, 105, 205

National Security Council (NSC), 5, 126, 215, 235, 237

National September 11 Memorial & Museum, 196, 213

natural gas, 145, 159, 184, 186–87

Nebraska, 41–42, 184

New Orleans, LA, 116

New York Times, 8, 12, 139, 168, 191, 193, 245

9/11, 11, 17–19, 23, 147, 195–97. *See also* September 11
  as an act of war, 55, 84–85, 100, 116, 208
  changes in the aftermath of, 114, 119, 250–52, 256, 281–82
  Cheney's memories of, 69–70, 110, 208–13
  Cheney's shoot-down order, 11, 216
  President Bush's handling of, 9, 123, 207–8, 213–16
  role in American foreign policy, 12, 144, 197–98, 217–21, 231–32, 234, 237–40, 243, 250–56
  warnings leading up to, 11, 199–205

9/11 Commission, the, 205, 216

Nixon, Richard, 16, 19, 74–78, 87–89, 91–92, 118, 230, 288

No Higher Honor (Rice), 216

non-interventionist, non-intervention-ism, 197

North Atlantic Treaty Organization (NATO), 146, 157, 159–60

North Korea
  nuclear program of, 2–9, 123–27, 174, 178–79, 222, 231, 257–59, 262
  Syria and, 2–9, 123, 127, 178, 222

Novak, Robert, 155

Nunn, Sam, 33, 217, 225

O

Obama, Barack, 10–11, 17–20, 116, 142–44, 147, 152, 155–56, 159, 176–77, 186, 189, 220, 238, 279, 282, 289

Office of Economic Opportunity, 220

Offutt Air Force Base, 212, 215

Olmert, Ehud, 5, 127

O'Neill, Paul, 131

O'Neill, Thomas "Tip," 96

On Watch (Zumwalt), 89

Operation Desert Fox, 248

Operation Desert Storm. *See* Desert Storm

Operation Orchard, 5

P

Pace, Pete, 134, 138–39
Pakistan, Pakistanis, 13–16, 148–51, 178–79
Panama Canal Treaty, 92
Patel, Neil, 111, 192
Paul, Rand, 197
Pearl Harbor attack, 21, 55, 129, 197–98, 284
Pelosi, Nancy, 242, 248
Pennsylvania, 11, 213
Pentagon, the, 138, 218, 220, 233
   Cheney's career at, 135, 149, 161, 164, 171, 223, 227, 232
   Iraq War and, 136, 232, 247, 272, 278
   9/11 attack on, 11, 55, 197, 207, 211, 213
Permian Basin, 185–86
Persian Gulf, 110, 227, 249, 251.
Petraeus, David, 137, 140, 151, 153
Philippines, the, 175
Pike, Otis, 160
Pike Committee, 160–61
Plame, Valerie, 170
Playboy interview, 10–11, 20
Poland, Polish, 158
Portman, Rob, 61
Predator drones, 200, 285
President's Daily Brief (PDB), 2–3, 112–15, 160–61, 203
President's Emergency Operations Center (PEOC), 205–7, 209, 211, 215, 238
Putin, Vladimir, 145–46, 154–59

Q

Qaddafi, Muammar, 101, 129, 286

R

Reagan, Ronald, 157, 217, 221, 224
   Cheney's opinions on, 95–102, 220
   1976 presidential primary and, 90, 92, 95
   Panama Canal and 92–93
   Soviet Union and, 91–92, 99
Republican Party, Republicans, 15, 52, 73, 92, 97–100, 140, 156–57, 180–83, 282
Rice, Condoleezza "Condi," 216
   Al Kibar and, 6, 8, 21, 124, 127–28
   criticism of Cheney, 12
   as national security advisor, 113–14, 120, 199, 203–4, 217–22, 235, 254, 257, 263, 267–68
   as secretary of state, 138, 221, 229, 258, 260–61, 272
Risen, James, 12–13, 235–37, 241, 245
Robb-Silberman Commission, 170, 257
Rockefeller, Nelson, 90, 92, 106, 117–18, 160
Rodriguez, Jose, 243
Rogers, Bill, 230
Romney, Mitt, 182
Roosevelt, Franklin D., 73, 75, 134, 197, 233, 284
Rothkopf, David, 237, 239, 243
Rumsfeld, Donald "Don," 57, 88, 93, 211
   Bush 43 administration, 12, 109, 120, 130–38, 219, 247, 250–51, 270, 278
   Nixon administration, 74–75, 77–78
Running the World (Rothkopf), 237–38
Russert, Tim, 254–55
Russia, Russians, 76, 89, 145–46, 153, 155–56, 158–61, 173–74
Ryan, Paul, 167

S

Sadr, Muqtada al-, 274
same-sex marriage, 20, 61–62
Sammon, Bill, 13
San Diego, CA, 204
Sanger, David, 139
Scowcroft, Brent, 103, 217–18, 221,
    225, 227
Scully, Matt, 57
Second Machine Age, The, 188
September 11, 2001, attacks, 4. *See also*
    9/11
shale gas, 146, 185–86
Shanksville, PA, 213
Shia, Shiites, 152, 270, 274, 276, 278
Shultz, George, 217–18, 220
Simpson-Mazzoli Act, 180
Six-Party Talks, 6–7, 123, 125, 128,
    231
Soldier (DeYoung), 232
South China Sea, 156
Southern California, 204
Soviet Union, 70, 73, 91, 99–100, 155,
    158, 161, 164, 171–74, 178–79, 212,
    217–18, 251
Spencer, Stuart "Stu," 90
State of Denial (Woodward), 267
State of War (Risen), 236
status of forces agreement, 144, 155
Steen, Jim, 19, 38–39, 43, 68, 94, 106,
    111, 163, 182, 199
Stokes, Louis, 71
Stokes Committee, 71
Sunnis, 151–52, 270, 274, 276, 278
surge, the, 8, 12, 128, 130, 132, 134–
    40, 151–52, 273, 278–79
Syracuse, NE, 41–42
Syria, Syrians, 6–7, 127–28, 146–47,
    152, 159, 265–67. *See also* Al Kibar

T

Taliban, the, 148, 150–51, 178
TALK magazine, 13–14
Tea Party, the, 17, 20, 183
Tenet, George, 114, 120, 160, 166, 212,
    235–36, 242, 245, 250, 254–55,
    261–64
Terrorist Surveillance Program, 13, 119,
    236, 241, 243, 245–46
Texas, 15, 111, 114, 185
Thatcher, Margaret, 153–54
Tiananmen Square, 174
TIME magazine, 70, 160
Trippi, Joe, 182
Truman, Harry, 66–67, 87, 156–57
Turbowicz, Yoram, 1
Turgeman, Shalom, 1
Tydings, Joe, 72–74

U

Ukraine, 155, 159
unitary executive, 80–81
United Nations (UN), 5, 103, 126–27,
    157
United Nations Security Council, 228,
    248, 266, 268–69
United 93, 197
University of Wisconsin, 50–51, 72–73
University of Wyoming, 23, 27, 31, 49,
    67, 111
U.S. Department of Defense (DOD),
    103, 133, 136, 156, 201, 218, 224
U.S. Department of Homeland Security,
    114, 200, 205
U.S. Department of Justice (DOJ), 131,
    214, 233, 241–46
U.S. Department of State, 87, 135–36,
    152, 155, 207, 221, 239, 258–59
    Al Kibar and, 5, 7, 123–24, 126, 230–32
    Iraq War and, 272

Middle East peace process and, 7, 127
Six-Party Talks and. *See* Six-Party Talks
U.S. House of Representatives, 50–51,
   71, 74, 82, 86, 95, 97–98, 103, 111,
   162, 217, 242
   Appropriations Committee, 87
   Intelligence Committee, 105, 160, 162–
      63, 241–42, 248
   Republican Policy Committee, 95
U.S. Senate, 15, 20, 32, 50, 77, 82–83,
   96–97, 137, 139, 140, 143, 227, 242,
   248
U.S. Supreme Court, the, 241

V

Vietnam War, 13, 72, 74, 80, 88, 103–
   4, 175, 283

W

Wallace, Chris, 202
War Powers Act, 80
Washington Post, 12, 191, 193, 232
Washington Times, 13
Watergate, 10, 13, 75–76, 78–80, 82,
   86, 88, 110, 167, 283
weapons of mass destruction (WMDs),
   4, 6, 12, 21, 55, 128–29, 166–67,
   169–70, 200, 248–50, 253, 261–67,
   286
Webster, Bill, 163
Weekly Standard, 13
Weinberger, Caspar, 171, 220
West Point, 18, 54, 134, 232
White House Correspondents' Associa-
   tion Dinner, 11
World Trade Center, 19, 55, 197, 206
World War II, 18, 22, 103, 156, 197,
   206, 233, 276, 280, 284
Write It When I'm Gone (DeFrank), 89

Wyoming, 19, 23, 26–28, 33, 43–44,
   56, 65, 115, 139, 184, 187

Y

Yale University, 17, 26–31, 45, 49,
   63–65
Yongbyon, North Korea, 2
Yoo, John, 233–34

Z

Zarqawi, Abu Musab al- (AMZ), 133,
   256, 274, 285
Zawahiri, Ayman al-, 256

ABOUT THE AUTHOR

James Rosen is the chief Washington correspondent for Fox News. An award-winning journalist, Rosen has covered the White House and State Department beats, and reported from Capitol Hill, the Pentagon, the Supreme Court, nearly all fifty states, and forty countries across five continents.

In May 2013, the *Washington Post* disclosed that the Obama administration, while investigating the sources for Rosen's reporting on national security subjects, termed him a criminal co-conspirator of the Espionage Act. The secret FBI documents, submitted to a federal court, marked the first time in modern U.S. history a reporter had been designated a criminal by the federal government for doing his job. The case sparked a nationwide debate over press freedoms in the Obama era and, after the enactment of federal reforms, Attorney General Eric Holder identified his handling of the matter as the biggest regret of his tenure at the Department of Justice.

Rosen's first book, *The Strong Man: John Mitchell and the Secrets of Watergate* (2008), drew wide critical acclaim. The author's articles and essays have appeared in the *New York Times*, the *Wall Street Journal*, the *Washington Post*, *Harper's*, the *Atlantic*, *National Review* and *Playboy*; and he is the host of the FoxNews.com program *The Foxhole*.

Born in Brooklyn and raised on Staten Island, Rosen holds degrees from the Johns Hopkins University and Northwestern University's Medill School of Journalism. He lives in Washington with his wife and two sons.